Mathematics and Beauty

AESTHETIC APPROACHES
TO TEACHING CHILDREN

Mathematics and Beauty

AESTHETIC APPROACHES TO TEACHING CHILDREN

Nathalie Sinclair

Foreword by William Higginson

Teachers College, Columbia University
New York and London

Published by Teachers College Press, 1234 Amsterdam Avenue, New York, NY 10027

The section in Chapter 4 entitled "The Mathematical Aesthetic in Action" first appeared as an article of the same name by Nathalie Sinclair in the *International Journal of Computers for Mathematical Learning*, 7(1), 45–63 (2002). Reprinted with kind permission of Kluwer Academic Publishers.

Library of Congress Cataloging-in-Publication Data

Sinclair, Nathalie.
    Mathematics and beauty : aesthetic approaches to teaching children / Nathalie Sinclair ; foreword by William Higginson.
      p. cm.
    Includes bibliographical references and index.
    ISBN-13: 978-0-8077-4722-3 (pbk. : alk. paper)
    ISBN-10: 0-8077-4722-X (pbk. : alk. paper)
    1. Mathematics—Study and teaching—Research. I. Title.
    QA11.2.S55 2006
    372.7—dc22
                                                     2006018105

ISBN-13: 978-0-8077-4722-3 (paper)   ISBN-10: 0-8077-4722-X (paper)

Printed on acid-free paper
Manufactured in the United States of America

13 12 11 10 09 08 07 06   8 7 6 5 4 3 2 1

Contents

Foreword *by William Higginson*   vii

Acknowledgments   xi

1. **Introduction**   1
    Where Beautiful Mathematics Comes From   1
    The Aesthetic as a Vital Lens on Learning   4
    Plan for the Book   9
    A Background Note   12

PART I: BEAUTY AND PLEASURE IN HUMAN EXPERIENCE

2. **Reclaiming the Aesthetic from the Arts**   17
    The Fluidity of Human Faculties   17
    The Aesthetic Nature of Inquiry   21
    Connecting the Aesthetic to Learning: First Steps   26
    Fitting the Pieces Together   28

3. **"Wired" for Beauty and Pleasure**   29
    Homo Aestheticus   29
    A "Sense of Order"   33

PART II: BEAUTY AND PLEASURE IN MATHEMATICS

4. **Developing a Mathematical Aesthetic Lens**   39
    The Aesthetic   39
    The Mathematical Aesthetic   42
    The Mathematical Aesthetic in Action   43
    The Aesthetics of Detachment   56

5. **Aesthetics and the Development of Mathematics**   59
    Debriefing the Kissing Triangles   59
    The Importance of the Mathematical Aesthetic   61
    Fitting the Pieces Together   65

PART III: FOCUSING THE AESTHETIC LENS ON STUDENTS

6. The Motivational Role of the Aesthetic   **69**

The Aesthetic Dimension of Problem Selection   71

The Aesthetic Dimension of Problem Posing   74

Coloring with Numbers   83

Fitting the Pieces Together   97

7. The Generative Role of the Aesthetic   **99**

Three Examples of the Generative Role   100

Mindful Mathematics   108

Fitting the Pieces Together   109

8. The Evaluative Role of the Aesthetic   **113**

Which Solution Is Better?   117

Wonder and the Aesthetic   129

Valuing the Aesthetic   131

Fitting the Pieces Together: Aesthetics and Inquiry   133

PART IV: AESTHETIC ENCULTURATION

9. Peering Inside the Mathematics Culture   **139**

From Outside to Inside the Culture   139

What Do Mathematicians Value?   140

The Aesthetic Dimension of Mathematical Values   144

10. Mathematical Values in Teaching   **153**

Revealing Values in Topics, Tasks, and Tools   154

Communicating Values in the Classroom   162

Some Closing Words   175

Notes   **177**

References   **183**

Index   **191**

About the Author   **196**

Foreword

Nathalie Sinclair is a gifted teacher, comfortable with learners of all ages and able to relate easily and well to students and teachers in the classroom. At the same time, as someone who has studied mathematics at the graduate level herself, she is both able to understand the world-view of the research mathematician and able to fit easily into discussions in the research institute's common room. Nathalie's book is a contribution to mathematics education, a field long at the forefront of vigorous discussions about the nature, purpose, and means of academic instruction. From "new" to "applied" to "problem-based" to "constructivist/standards/fuzzy," almost every decade of the last half-century seems to have had its version of ambitious curriculum reforms for school mathematics. The final phases of these initiatives have had several constants. On the human front, these have often included: embattled proponents and angry opponents of the reform, confused parents, frustrated teachers, and low-achieving learners.

Mathematics is almost universally seen as an essential component in any well-balanced and comprehensive school curriculum for both elementary and secondary school learners. This position is usually rationalized by pointing to the foundational role that the discipline plays in many fundamental aspects of contemporary society. While the real depth and sophistication of this argument is infrequently heard in curriculum discussions, it seems unlikely that this view will be seriously challenged in the near future as the characteristics and implications of an "information society" become ever more evident.

A small group (relative to the population as a whole) that has played a key role in many reform initiatives is that of research mathematicians. Sometimes initiating the reforms—as was the case in the "new math" venture of the 1960s—but more often taking the part of opponents, their involvement is frequently very passionate. This reflects and is influenced by their deep emotional feeling for their craft. They speak of the nature of mathematics and of the satisfaction in creating mathematics in almost exactly the same ways as devotees of the arts: Beauty is all.

A second group of individuals is much larger: disenchanted and often unsuccessful learners of mathematics. The mathematics learning experience of many children has been, on the whole, quite negative. There are at least two versions of this phenomenon. One is the observable class of very low- to non-achievers, a distressingly large group in many jurisdictions. A second, less visible group—which overlaps with the former but is still distinct—is that of the emotionally stressed learner.

The classroom experience of mathematics, even for those who "succeed" as judged by external paper-based criteria, can be unpleasant and psychologically damaging. Of all the subjects in the school curriculum, mathematics has the unique and dubious distinction as being the most closely linked in the public mind to the experience of "anxiety." Recent research shows these feelings to be widespread. A British study found that contemporary lower-secondary students find their mathematics classes to be "TIRED," that is, characterized by Tedium, Isolation, Rote Learning, Elitism, and Depersonalization. An international study of school children's images of mathematicians generated a very large number of unattractive individuals and unpleasant behavior, including a surprisingly high correlation with acts of violence. Finally, we have the harsh reality that the standards for "success" in school mathematics are in many ways set at an excessively low level. Many "good" mathematics students, for reasons not of their own making, have had only a stunted exposure to the more mechanical aspects of a deep, powerful, and historically rich human creation. All in all, this is a depressing picture. Many very bright, highly motivated individuals with substantial resources have labored long and hard to address these concerns, with very little success. What else might be tried?

This is a question that Nathalie's book addresses, and her response is quite simple. The prevailing view about mathematical ability in general, and sensitivity to mathematical beauty in particular, is an elitist one. It takes as a given that only a few individuals have the capacity to be moved by the aesthetic dimensions of the discipline. From this tiny pool of individuals come our group of passionate researchers in mathematics, and a few kindred spirits in fields such as physics and computer science. For the rest, it is assumed that "utility" will have to suffice.

In a move similar to the shifting of the Darwinian perspective on evolution from "survival of the fittest" to "survival of the fit," Nathalie decided to investigate the potential of bringing "beauty" into the matrix of curriculum considerations. What might classroom experience in mathematics look like if it was assumed that sensitivity to beauty is not the sole preserve of only a few (who are often portrayed in quite unattractive social terms), but rather was open to all?

Once this door was opened, a large and fascinating number of questions quickly emerged, many of which came out of the world of mathematics. Although terms like *beauty*, *harmony*, *elegance*, and *balance* can be frequently found in mathematics textbooks, relatively little research had been done to make their meaning more precise. Similarly, relatively little was known of children's ideas about beauty, particularly with respect to school subjects. And so Nathalie's research began, in settings as varied as school classrooms and offices in research institutes.

In the end, this book brings together new insights and affirmations of existing realities into an extensive and thought-provoking whole. To accomplish this, Nathalie has woven together ideas and theories from a wide range of academic fields. The work, on one level, is intimately involved with students learning mathematics in school. On a second level, the work is also fundamentally philosophical. It deals with classic questions from aesthetics (What does it mean to be beautiful?) and from epistemology (What does it mean to "know" a piece of mathematics?). It gives rich insights into the different ways in which aesthetic factors surface in the disciplinary functioning of some world-class mathematicians. Its insights into the processes of mathematical thought, particularly around motivation, bring it close to classic questions in psychology and to more recent studies in cognitive science. It addresses some long-standing questions in the philosophy of education articulated many years ago by scholars like John Dewey. Its ingenious use of specially created, sophisticated, and flexible computer-based activities gives interesting glimpses into the cognitive and aesthetic perspectives of learners. Overall, this work contains a provocative set of philosophical, psychological, mathematical, technological, and educational insights that makes a compelling case for the inclusion of aesthetic considerations in the materials and approaches we bring to mathematics students at all levels.

The result is something that will be of interest to scholars in many fields. In addition, it has important messages for parents concerned about their child's reaction to school mathematics, for teachers who may see glimpses of a different way of thinking about a key subject, and for curriculum writers who need to think about how these findings may enter the educational experience of a generation of learners.

Ours is an age of hyperbole. Most often fuelled by self-interest, exaggerated claims flow easily from the word-processors and microphones of ideologues, scam artists, and salesmen of various sorts. One hesitates in this general "market" to make statements that might lead readers to conclude that they are being subjected to views from such perspectives. But sometimes risks are necessary, and having passed a moderately rigorous examination of conscience, I make here a strongly positive statement and recommendation. This is an exceptionally important book. Should it be received in the way one might hope for—widely read and constructively criticized, with insights and recommendations taken to heart—it could be the starting point for many cognitive, social, and educational benefits. This potential exists because this work addresses a critically important educational area in an innovative and exciting way.

—William Higginson

Acknowledgments

The seeds of this book were planted by Bill Higginson, who helped me see beauty in the ways children do mathematics, and who guided me toward the ideas and the scholars that have shaped my work. I am very grateful for the encouragement, patience, and precision of my two most critical readers, David Pimm and Nicholas Jackiw, and for the guiding conviction of Peter Taylor and the late Martin Schiralli. I am indebted to Jonathan Borwein, who gave me new ways of imagining what mathematics with a computer could be like, and to the many students who trusted my ideas (when my ideas were good) and who trusted me (when my ideas were bad). I am fortunate to count among my most supportive readers and collaborators my closest friends and family: Lovisa, Papa, Maman, Stéfan, *et mon chéri.*

CHAPTER 1

Introduction

Children frequently and enthusiastically engage in the arts—they paint, sing, dance, and play all kinds of musical instruments. Despite these activities, few people speak of children's aesthetic sophistication, and even fewer think of these words in the context of mathematics learning. Yet when we listen to actual students, we find signs—hints, traces, and possibilities—of the impact that beauty and pleasure can have in directing their actions. The two brief stories that follow locate some of these signs and will, I hope, temper any disbelief readers may have about combining the three words: *children, beauty,* and *mathematics.* The first story recounts the mathematical experience of a young child and hints at the ways in which mathematical beauty and pleasure can be evoked at an early age. If the first story makes obvious that, despite their mathematical naïveté, the aesthetic properly belongs to the mathematical experiences of children, the second story goes on to relate how attending to students' aesthetic responses in mathematical situations can help us—teachers, researchers, learners—understand their actions and beliefs.

WHERE BEAUTIFUL MATHEMATICS COMES FROM

When I was 9, I remember riding in the pick-up truck, squeezed between my parents in the front seat. I asked my mother how far we were from our destination and she read off the distance from the map, in miles. Canada had recently converted from the imperial to the metric system, but our maps were old ones. When I asked for the kilometer equivalent, she responded with what seemed to me lightning speed. How had she done it so quickly? I knew the conversion involved multiplying by some complicated number—not a whole one—my teachers had drilled us for years prior to the changeover with equivalence charts and rules and rhythms. So I knew this was not something one did in one's head; shouldn't she have needed at least pencil and paper?

She soon explained. There was no need to bother with the actual conversion factor, something like 1.609. Instead, one just rounded it to 1.6, which was just the same thing as 1 + 0.5 + 0.1. And that made the conversion more like a walk in the park. Take the number of miles, say 40, then add half that number (anyone can do that) and then one tenth of it (just take off the last zero!) to get 40 + 20 + 4. So 40 miles was near enough to 64 kilometers, an answer my father confirmed with the odometer. I was so impressed: It was as if the numbers had magically rearranged themselves just to show us the answer. We tried her method with a few more imaginary destinations.

My mother's mathematics was familiar: she used the same operations I was learning in school. But she used them as tools to suit her own purposes. She had not only rounded the troublesome conversion factor—with a brash gusto I'd not encountered in school, but very much admired—but she also turned the 1.6 into a new number that subtly revealed its roots, its basic ingredients. Had I been asked, I could have *done* the sum 1 + 0.5 + 0.1, but I would never have *undone* it the way she had. That this clever trick could be explained to me—with neither equivalence charts nor nursery rhymes—without losing its magic, seemed all the better. This was, for me, a new way of seeing decimals, and, not long thereafter, a whole new way of approaching multiplication.

Certainly not every mother has such tricks up her sleeve; and not every 9-year-old would have the same reaction. I know I am not alone, though. Adults who can multiply large numbers in their heads frequently impress young children. Very young children are also fascinated by large numbers that are verbally conjured, as if the very act of stating a number's name attested to one's authority to wield a previously unfathomed immensity with precision. Even adults can experience feelings of wonder and awe when confronted with the very big or the very small.

Are these reactions those of aesthetics? As an adult, I can think of mathematical ideas that are similarly magical, clever, or revealing and call them "beautiful." However, at the age of 9, I had not learned how to use the adjective "beautiful" to describe mathematics—that was a term reserved for sunsets and dresses. Instead, I think I was pleased by the idea that my mother could take both liberties with and control of mathematics. Perhaps arithmetic did not just order you to operate with its terse imperatives; perhaps it could be made to follow your command. What I wanted was to make things simpler, to reduce the perilous complexity of multiplying by 1.609 to a procedure I could not only reproduce but even, perhaps, recreate. This reduction of surprise and complexity to predictability and simplicity was very important to me—both as a motivation and as a reward. According to psychologist Jerome Bruner (1969), these

sorts of mental transformations are "the most fundamental form of pleasure in man's intellectual life" (p. 618).

Having learned much later in my mathematical career that "beautiful" can indeed be an appropriate adjective to use in mathematics, I now
call "beautiful" those mathematical ideas that successfully, *for me*, achieve
Bruner's "fundamental form of pleasure." Over the course of this book,
I will have much more to say about the subjective nature of the aesthetic
implied by those italicized words. For now, I want simply to draw attention to the fact that even for a young, mathematically naïve child, aesthetic
sensibilities and values (a penchant for simplicity, for finding the building
blocks of more complex ideas, and a preference for shortcuts and "liberating" tricks rather than cumbersome recipes) animates mathematical
experience.

For many, the term *aesthetics* applies to specific products and practices:
the products of "high art," as defined by museum masterpieces, and the
practices of art critics, who operate on the finished products of artists. Two
moves are needed to begin thinking about how the term *aesthetics* applies
to children doing mathematics: first, the move from the arts to mathematics, and second, the move from art critics to children. Mathematics also
has its products and practices. The museum masterpieces can be thought
of as being the theorems, proofs, and solutions of mathematics, while its
practitioners (or critics) are the professional mathematicians themselves,
who decide which products deserve to belong in the museum (which theorems are published in journals, studied by others, included in textbooks,
etc.). Clearly, no children participate in this product/practice relationship,
neither in the arts nor in mathematics. Yet consider the aesthetic domain
of production that we find in the arts, that which belongs to the artists
who engage in their own practices of producing, doing, or creating artistic
artifacts. This domain is akin to that of mathematical production, which
belongs to professionals and to children, both of whom are engaged in
producing, doing, and creating mathematics.

The reader may object at this point, noting that children will never be
able to appreciate the beauty or elegance of museum mathematics, nor
able to produce those artifacts of mathematics. After all, these mathematical artifacts, according to professional mathematicians, must possess aesthetic qualities such as economy, inevitability, and unexpectedness. However, my mother's conversion trick would seem to meet at least some of
these criteria. It was certainly economic and unexpected *to me*, but perhaps not so economic to my younger brother, who would not have been
able to multiply by 0.5 or by 0.1, and probably not very unexpected for
my math teacher. To make matters more complicated, some professional
mathematicians might also insist that mathematical beauty depends on

significance, generality, and depth. Are children capable of judging mathematical significance or appreciating the depth of a theorem? Are mathematicians themselves even able to tell us what such criteria mean?

While not all of these criteria are equally accessible to school students, my story illustrates how a young child can find pleasure in mathematics and even appreciate the simplicity and transparency of a mathematical solution. The particular solution lacks significance and depth, at least from my current more knowledgeable standpoint, and certainly would not make it into the mathematical museum. But as a producer of mathematics, my 9-year-old child self may have found both a depth and generality that eclipsed the rules and rhymes of her previous experience.

A major theme in this book relates to the contextual nature of the aesthetic, and to the notion that learners can engage their aesthetic sensibilities in productive ways, without necessarily being able to appreciate the theorems, solutions, or proofs that belong to "museum" mathematics. In the coming chapters, I attempt to unravel exactly what these aesthetic sensibilities are, how they develop, and how they interact with more cognitive and affective abilities usually associated with mathematics learning.

THE AESTHETIC AS A VITAL LENS ON LEARNING

Why would educators want children to have the kind of pleasurable, memorable, or magical experience I recounted above? The National Council of Teachers of Mathematics (NCTM) plays a major role in defining and shaping the goals of mathematics education in the United States (and beyond). The authors of their document *Principles and Standards for School Mathematics* (2000) suggest that students should develop an aesthetic appreciation for mathematics, simply because "mathematics is one of the greatest cultural and intellectual achievements of humankind" (Ch. 1, p. 4). This sort of a cultural argument is often paralleled in curriculum debates about teaching literature: children should read the "great books" in order to be able to appreciate the literary achievements of humankind. While such arguments appeal to some, others find them outdated, or at least insufficient for the more utilitarian task of preparing children for the current and future demands of society. By shifting points of view, however, a focus on *how* children learn can serve both conceptions of what and why society wants them to learn. Thus, the following story has to do more with understanding and improving how students learn than with making sure they appreciate past achievements (the cultural argument) or making sure they can meet society's economic and technological needs (the utilitarian argument).

Zoe, a grade 8 student working in math class, examines the collection of colored polygons that appear on her computer screen. She starts moving the polygons around with the mouse, pausing and bending her head to the side every now and then. Slowly, she starts forming two different groups of polygons, one on each side of the screen. When she has finished classifying them, she types "Symmetry shapes" under one group and "No symmetry shapes" under the other. With a smile on her face, she announces, "There, that's better now."

Her teacher approaches and points out a tilted isosceles triangle Zoe has placed in the "No symmetry" group. She shows Zoe how to rotate the triangle into a more upright form and asks her whether she still thinks the triangle has no symmetry. With just a moment's hesitation, another of surprise and then with conviction, Zoe announces, "it's up and down." She ponders a bit, and then sums up the situation by stating that the tilted triangle "is not symmetric if we are looking at it, but if it's just on its own, then it's symmetric." She moves it into the "Symmetry shapes" group. Then, Zoe turns around and notices that the two boys behind her have classified the polygons according to their number of sides, with group names "triangle," "quadrilateral," "pentagon," "hexagon," and "more than six sides." Her teacher asks Zoe which classification rule she thinks is better. With a great sense of fairness, Zoe tells her teacher, "You can't really say that one is better than the other; they are just different." One of the boys, Luke, adds, "You can only tell which is better if you are really smart."

The teacher pushes Zoe a little more and Zoe finally admits, "Well, mine is simpler, because everything falls into just two groups instead of all the ones they [the boys] have." Alex, who is Luke's partner, retorts, "But ours is simpler to see; you just have to count the sides." She nods tentatively but appears unconvinced. Later, when the boys have gone, she secretly but proudly tells her teacher, "I think that the symmetry thing is more interesting than the number of sides because it's more, well, not really obvious, but really about the shape itself."

This episode lasted less than 10 minutes. Moreover, for a group of three grade 8 students, it does not overwhelm with mathematical sophistication. Yet most would likely agree that important mathematical things happened, especially for Zoe. A researcher analyzing the episode with the usual cognitive lens would perhaps note that Zoe does not really understand symmetry, or that her understanding of symmetry is somewhat dominated by vertical reflective symmetry. She had trouble with the skew reflective symmetry and did not even mention rotational symmetry at all. To zoom back a bit, if the previous class has focused on the names of polygons based on their number of sides (triangle, quadrilateral, pentagon, etc.), a researcher might also conclude that the boys were more successful in using mathematical vocabulary than Zoe was. A strictly cognitive lens tells us about the extent to which Zoe understands symmetry and how the boys can apply yesterday's lesson. But it does not capture all of the mathematically important things that have happened to the students.

A researcher analyzing the episode with a more affective lens might remark that Zoe was intensely engaged during her initial categorization, and that she showed feelings of pleasure and satisfaction upon completing the task. She seemed also somewhat intimidated by the boys, reserving her final comment until she was alone with me. In addition, this affect-oriented researcher might infer that Luke believes that mathematics is for smart people, and that he cannot contribute to decisions about which mathematical rules or solutions are better than others. Zoe, on the other hand, may believe she can contribute to such decisions, but hasn't quite gained enough confidence to do so in front of the boys. An affective lens tells us about the wide set of beliefs and emotions that students bring into the classroom. However, it cannot explain why Zoe experiences pleasure, what makes her want to classify the polygons, or what animates the students' negotiations about the value of their respective classification schemes.

Whether they are focused on the activities of student mathematicians or the activities of professional mathematicians, both the cognitive and affective analyses are necessary and revealing, but not sufficient. They miss the kind of interpretations that are needed to understand why humans do mathematics and even how humans create mathematical ideas. This may sound far-fetched, so let me first explain what I see in Zoe's episode through an aesthetic lens.

From the beginning, Zoe's decision to classify reveals an aesthetic sensibility, an urge to create some regularity and predictability. Of course, Zoe may have learned that in geometry class, classification is the *modus operandi*—school students spend an inordinate amount of time classifying geometric objects such as angles, triangles, and quadrilaterals. She might therefore have decided to do what she thought was expected of her. Yet her concluding smile and visible sense of satisfaction suggest that she took pleasure in arranging the polygons, that she wanted to impose some "sense of fit" on the unorganized collection. Indeed, after that episode, as her teacher, I noticed that Zoe had an uncanny knack for seeing symmetry everywhere, as if symmetry was her own personal perceptual stamp on the world. Because she could productively place this stamp on the collection of polygons, it became both epistemologically and personally relevant to her.

The aesthetic urge to classify affected Zoe's actions, leading her to formulate the problem she set herself to solve—to decide which shapes belong to each group. Zoe could have noticed many mathematical features of the polygons, including size, color, regularity (congruent angles and sides), convexity, the type of angles involved (acute, obtuse, right), and the number of sides. She could have based her classification rule on any one of them. Yet she chose symmetry as the determining feature because, judging from her last revelation to me, symmetry is intrinsically interesting to her. She even seems to think that symmetry is a powerful mathematical principle, since it better characterizes the polygon than its number of sides does. She also prefers symmetry as a classification rule because it produces a simple binary division. The boys' rule could have produced an infinite number of categories, had there been more polygons in the collection, but Zoe's rule would only ever yield two.

While Zoe expressed a preference for either/or simplicity, the boys expressed a preference for another kind of simplicity. They liked the fact that their rule was simple to apply; it just involved counting and not any head-bending or line-of-symmetry-locating. In negotiating their preferences, the students showed they cared about the value of their mathematical work. The aesthetic judgments they make contrast to the judgments they may make about whether or not their work is procedurally correct or acceptable to the teacher. In fact, with little provocation, the students were willing and able to identify criteria—simplicity and depth—that could be used to judge the better of the two rules of classification, criteria that are not so different from the ones used by professional mathematicians.

In this episode, an aesthetic lens helps explain what instigated Zoe's mathematical inquiry, what Zoe found mathematically appealing and relevant, and what Zoe valued in her mathematics. Even if hers represents a single case, it is suggestive: It reveals that it is at least possible for school-age students to respond aesthetically to mathematical situations and to use aesthetic values in appraising the significance of mathematical ideas. Perhaps more importantly, more pragmatically, Zoe's episode suggests that aesthetic sensibilities can play an important role in motivating student mathematical inquiry, both in terms of stirring interest and commitment and in terms of evoking productive mathematical actions and behaviors.

For many educators, one of the most persistent problems in mathematics education is motivating students to *want* to learn or do mathematics. Although this problem attracts much attention in the literature, such attention tends to isolate motivation from the actual doing of mathematics. To a large degree, it attempts to coax students into palatable mathematical contexts, rather than seeking to discover the conditions under which mathematical activity itself can be intrinsically motivating. Yet in my own experiences of teaching, on the occasions in which students are fully engaged in the mathematics classroom—when they are "turned on"—they are motivated by the actual doing of mathematics, rather than by preliminary enticements and subsequent verbal praise.

Unfortunately for educators, many students of mathematics never experience, or even get a glimpse of the tension, wonder, pleasure, and release that are all part of *doing* mathematics. In fact, they may easily come to believe that mathematics lacks the very human dimensions of experience that make any endeavor or discipline relevant. Could school mathematics have more to offer students? Might learners come to experience that pleasurable "sense of fit" in mathematics that engages their deepest and strongest feelings?

Consider the following quotations:

"A spin through the human condition nobody else can provide."
"You will find here a collection of delightful stories [. . .] witty,
     amusing, and instructive."
"[. . .] a rich and fascinating book. It has everything and every-
     thing that it has is delightful, curious, enlightening, engrossing,
     interesting, informative, funny, stirring, poignant."
"This book reads like a mystery; it was difficult to put down."

Most students would be hard-pressed to believe that these quotations all relate to books about mathematics. In contrast to their experiences of mathematics in the classroom, these quotations make mathematics sound as humanly rich and multidimensional as the best books they have read. The responses the quotations describe reveal that mathematics can ignite—equally and deeply—the cognitive, affective, and aesthetic dimensions of human experience and sense-making. Of course, most mathematicians know this. They know it would be commonplace to find two colleagues arguing over the "elegance" or "beauty" of a certain proof or to find themselves enthralled by a bewitching problem. They know that mathematics is not merely the cold, bloodless, unfeeling pursuit of truth, and they admit that their discoveries and inventions rely on "extralogical" ways of reasoning and knowing (Burton, 2004; Sinclair, 2004b). They talk about intuition or insight and about a special sixth sense or a gut feeling. Invariably, especially to nonmathematicians, such talk makes this side of mathematics sound inaccessible and mysterious.[1]

Indeed, many mathematically minded people doubt whether student learners are sophisticated enough to appreciate the aesthetic qualities of mathematical ideas or to have access to those aesthetic sensibilities that constitute the mathematical sixth sense. Instead, such people insist that students must first learn many, many facts and methods before they can even catch a glimpse of the aesthetically driven world of the mathematics research community. After all, most students would probably find words such as *beauty* and *elegance* oddly misplaced in a sentence about mathematical ideas or results. They could perhaps imagine two mathematicians arguing over the truth of a proof, but would probably wonder: What could be "elegant" or "beautiful" about a proof and why would it matter? For most students, beauty involves the senses—the visual, tactile, and especially auditory—and these senses find little stimulus in the typical, anaesthetic mathematical textbook. Moreover, mathematics, for these students, involves correct answers and true facts and being wrong, not the kinds of values and subjective responses that might be encountered in literature, music, or art classes. As Seymour Papert (1980) observes, "If mathematical aesthetics gets any attention in the schools, it is as an epiphenomenon, an icing on the mathematical cake, rather than as the driving force which makes mathematical thinking function" (p. 192).

Are student learners really too unsophisticated? What could happen in a mathematics classroom that invited aesthetic sensibilities and made the negotiation of aesthetic values central? Could such a classroom enrich students' learning experiences, improve or educate their mathematical powers, or help them gain greater access to the culture of mathematics? The primary goal of this book is to show that aesthetic sensibilities and values are, in fact, intimately connected to the way students both understand and do mathematics.

PLAN FOR THE BOOK

This book is divided into four parts, each focusing on different aesthetic contexts. Since aesthetic discourse is usually associated with the arts and, in pedagogical writing, with art education, the goal of Part I is to establish the plausibility, and perhaps even the inescapability, of the aesthetic in the widest possible range of contexts, including, of course, mathematics and mathematics learning. Chapter 2 aims to explain how aesthetic sensibilities and ways of knowing belong naturally, almost necessarily, to human inquiry and experience. I will be drawing on both philosophical and empirical research on the fundamental intertwining of the cognitive, affective, and aesthetic dimensions of human experience.

Chapter 3 contends that artists are not the only ones who have access to aesthetic sensibilities and that humans are more or less "wired" for aesthetic response. These two chapters provide a background for the rest of the book, in terms of articulating the reasons why an aesthetic approach is appropriate both in mathematics itself and for describing and interpreting mathematics learning.

To summon the widest aesthetic discourse, I will be broadening the concept of the aesthetic to include its many concerns, which Pimm (2006) has described as "*What* to attend to (the problems, elements, objects), *how* to attend to them (the means, principles, techniques, methods) and w*hy* they are worth attending to (in pursuit of the beautiful, the good, the right, the useful, the ideal, the perfect or, simply, the true)" (p. 160, emphasis in original). This use of the concept will likely feel foreign to those who use the term *aesthetic* exclusively in nonscientific or noneducational contexts. Part I aims to make the above conception seem less foreign and even, hopefully, quite useful in describing a wide range of other human experiences.

While the first part consists of more general claims about domains of knowledge and their practitioners, Part II aims to establish an aesthetic framework conceived specifically for mathematics. The first story of this introduction provides a sense of the mathematical aesthetic in its rawest form—through the eyes of a young child—in order to pave the way for a broader conceptualization of the aesthetic that includes both children and their nonartistic endeavors. Chapter 4 begins to refine a sense of the mathematical aesthetic by specifying the particular roles that the aesthetic plays in mathematical inquiry. The distinct roles of the mathematical aesthetic—of which there are three, namely, the motivational, generative, and evaluative—will provide an initial and primary means of formulating a mathematical "aesthetic lens" that will be used in the pedagogical contexts of Chapters 6 through 10. The aesthetic lens is brought to life by means of an illustrative example of mathematical inquiry, one that will assist in connecting the mathematical aesthetic of the research mathematician to that of the school learner.

Chapter 5 attempts to generalize the observations made in Chapter 4 by taking the roles of the aesthetic vivified in one example and showing how those roles are inherent in mathematical inquiry in general. My intent is to evaluate and dispel claims that the mathematical aesthetic should be treated as a fanciful hobby indulged in by illustrious mathematicians. In preparation for Part III, this chapter also considers how much the discipline and practices of mathematicians can or should inform mathematics education, particularly from an aesthetic point of view. I argue that the aesthetic lens developed in Part II, based primarily outside pedagogical contexts, applies productively to the activities and beliefs of learners.

The third and perhaps most ambitious part of the book takes the mathematics learner as its object of study. It focuses on middle school students, in part because of their well-known developing dislike for mathematics at that age, and in part because of my own extensive experience with 12- to 15-year-old children. I analyze many examples of student mathematical activity using the aesthetic lens developed in Part II. The lens does not strictly focus on cognitive or affective aspects of their mathematical experiences, but reveals instead the ways in which their aesthetic sensibilities can evoke, sustain, and give meaning to their mathematical activity. Of course, the aesthetic lens will also illustrate the extent to which the aesthetic manifests itself in middle school learning. Moreover, it will help me probe for ways in which educators might support and nurture students' aesthetic sensibilities and values.

In Chapters 6, 7, and 8, respectively, I focus independently on each of the three roles of the aesthetic described in Part II. Starting with the *motivational* role, I show that some of the aesthetic qualities of a mathematical situation that attract mathematicians to certain problems (connectedness, fruitfulness, apparent simplicity, visual appeal, and surprise) can similarly compel students to begin and persist working on mathematical problems. Chapter 6 seems to me of particular importance in terms of student motivation, which I see as "holding" rather than merely "catching" student attention (a distinction discussed in Dewey, 1913). In addition to analyzing individual examples of the aesthetic's motivational role, I apply the lens collectively and comparatively to a whole class of students.

Chapter 7 explores the *generative* role of the aesthetic in the mathematical activity of students, analyzing three examples in learning environments where students are encouraged to use qualitative reasoning. These examples provide a broader sense of the kinds of aesthetic responses that students can have, as well as the different levels of sophistication, with respect to professional mathematicians, with which students are able to make use of these responses.

Chapter 8 focuses on the types of aesthetic criteria used by students in evaluating their own mathematical work and, more importantly, the purposes of these criteria: When and why do students evaluate mathematical entities using aesthetic criteria? I draw on several examples of students discussing "better" solutions to show that when students can approach mathematics with an awareness of its values and not only its truths, they can have strong aesthetic preferences, some of which are perhaps surprisingly contiguous with those of the professional mathematical community.

While Part III takes individual learners as its context of focus, Part IV considers the broader context of the mathematics classroom and focuses on the aesthetic dimension of mathematical enculturation—that is, on the aesthetic *values* produced in and perpetuated by the mathematics culture. How does the mathematics culture contribute to the aesthetic dimension of school mathematics? How does a teacher shape the development of students' aesthetic sensibilities? How might the aesthetic manifest itself at the level of whole classroom interactions?

The mathematics educator Alan Bishop (1991) has argued that educating people mathematically involves much more than just teaching mathematics: It requires developing in students a fundamental awareness of the socially negotiated values that underlie mathematics. This book is primarily concerned with aesthetic values and, like mathematical values, aesthetic ones are only implicitly and uncritically taught in contemporary classrooms. Chapter 9 will investigate the aesthetic dimension of mathematics enculturation—that is, the aesthetic values produced in and perpetuated by the mathematics culture. It takes as a given that enculturation happens over time, and depends on the particulars of different environments (whether from classroom to classroom or country to country), and can be influenced by a variety of subtle and not-so-subtle cues. Chapter 10 aims to identify these influences, so that teachers may recognize them and develop a critical perspective on them, and proposes ways in which teachers might make aesthetic aspects of mathematical values more explicit and negotiable in their classrooms. It also explores issues related to pedagogic practices, to choices that teachers and curriculum developers make in structuring the scope and sequence of mathematics learning.

A BACKGROUND NOTE

The questions and claims in this book are rooted in a philosophical commitment to pragmatism, which is an approach to conceptualizing the world that, in turn, is unequivocally rooted in aesthetics (Cherryholmes, 1999; Dewey, 1934; Shusterman, 1992). A pragmatist philosopher is interested in anticipating consequences, in asking what are the conceivable consequences of acting in certain ways and not others. But the pragmatist knows that these consequences must be evaluated, and this is where its aesthetic orientation becomes obvious, since the pragmatist necessarily must ask: Do they make life better or worse? More pleasurable or more painful? More productive or less so? These questions are evaluated in terms of beauty, satisfaction and fulfilment; they involve deciding which consequences should be desired and valued.

The etymological roots of the term *pragmatism* relate it to the Greek word *pragma*, which means "that which has been done" and "a thing right or fit to be done." The emphasis of pragmatism, and of the inquiries in this book, is both on action and on rightness of action. How can we conceive the aesthetic so that it productively describes the mathematical action? C. S. Peirce's pragmatic maxim outlines exactly how the aesthetic is to be conceived and why it will be taken as central to mathematics learning: "Consider what effects which might conceivably have practical bearings we conceive the object of our conception to have, then, our conception of these effects is the whole of our conception of the object" (1878/1992, p. 132).

One straightforward, though perhaps oversimplified approach to characterizing pragmatism is to contrast it with the tradition of analytic philosophy. Though these distinctions are more complex today, the analytic tradition distinguishes itself most emphatically by its commitment to foundationalist assumptions and distinctions, and ahistorical positive essences. In contrast, the pragmatist will not ask questions such as: What is beauty, really? Or What is truth, really? The pragmatic approach is committed to mutability, contextuality, and the sociohistorical, thereby eschewing foundationalist questions. When I use aesthetic notions such as elegance, harmony, and order, they can always be deconstructed; these notions are not meant to adhere to a formalist aesthetic that construes them as ahistorical and apersonal. The pragmatic approach is more interested in tracing the impact and consequences of granting ideas or beliefs to be true or beautiful than it is in defining them. So, for instance, I will be asking what consequences follow from mathematicians' use of aesthetic notions. Does it help them solve problems? Does it signal to others that they belong to some kind of in-group?

PART I

Beauty and Pleasure in Human Experience

In the introduction, I suggested that an aesthetic reading of events in a pedagogical setting could provide both an interesting and explanatory view of students' mathematical experiences. However, within mathematics education, little is known about the plausibility (and consequences) of such aesthetic readings. Therefore, I want to zoom out from the particular settings of the introduction and investigate possible aesthetic interpretations of much more general human experiences. Zooming out will involve considering different conceptions of the aesthetic, in a wide range of contexts and for a wide range of purposes. I will juggle with all these conceptions for the time being, until I zoom back into a mathematics context in Part II and then begin refining the notion of the aesthetic in Part III, so as to improve its appropriateness and usefulness in the mathematics learning contexts.

Chapter 2 begins the process by "reclaiming" the aesthetic from the arts, where it has evolved into a somewhat esoteric concept, and offering it as a feasible and meaningful concept in other domains of human inquiry, including mathematics. This chapter aims to illuminate the way in which the aesthetic intermingles with practical, theoretical, and logical forms of human reasoning, even in nonartistic domains. The expanded and refined conception of aesthetics that will emerge shall pave the way for the idea of a mathematical aesthetic and, eventually, to an aesthetic of mathematics learning.

While Chapter 2 considers the possibility of extending the aesthetic to domains of knowledge and inquiry beyond the arts, Chapter 3 focuses on locating aesthetic sensibilities in human embodiedness. Focusing on a more democratic access to aesthetics will raise the possibility of children possessing, evolving, and using an aesthetic sensibility in their mathematics learning.

CHAPTER 2

Reclaiming the
Aesthetic from the Arts

In both philosophical and educational discourses, the aesthetic is usually situated solely within artistic activities (and less often in experiences of nature—of sunsets, storms, and other natural phenomena). The compartmentalized view of human thinking and knowing—the logical for mathematics and the aesthetic for the arts—is partially to blame for the lack of attention to the aesthetic within mathematics learning (and the corresponding lack of attention to the logical in artistic production). In "reclaiming" the aesthetic from the arts, my goal is to support the contention that mathematical inquiry, like artistic inquiry, draws on aesthetic forms of thinking and knowing.

THE FLUIDITY OF HUMAN FACULTIES

Common parlance would cast the arts as the domain of aesthetic decisions, in contrast to that of moral decisions (ethics) or of objective decisions (science). The philosopher Mark Johnson (1987) argues that rigid separation of, say, the aesthetic from the moral is rooted in an Enlightenment view of cognition that assumes mental acts can be broken down into distinct forms of judgment. This view supposes that moral reasoning involves moral concepts and could derive determinate rules for action, whereas aesthetic judgments involve no concepts at all, only feeling and imagination. But many scholars now break down so glibly a compartmentalized view of human decision-making. According to them (e.g., Dewey, 1934; Lakoff & Johnson, 1999; Polanyi, 1958), humans do not make exclusively moral or exclusively theoretical judgments. Instead, the moral and the theoretical, as well as the aesthetic, are seen as permeating every aspect of human life.

Neuroscientific researchers such as Antonio Damasio (1994) also challenge this Enlightenment view, claiming that our rational and moral decisions necessarily call upon affective and aesthetic judgments: feelings resulting from a perception of the "body landscape" are an integral component of decision-making. Based on his research with patients who have certain brain lesions, Damasio has shown that without feelings humans are hindered in or incapable of making personal choices. Such research stands in sharp contrast to the Cartesian view that human minds are and act separately from their bodies. What are these feelings and how are they related to aesthetic responses?

Consider a scientific perspective on aesthetic response. Damasio helps answer the question using slightly different language. He differentiates between "feeling" and "emotion." A feeling is the result of the process of continuous monitoring of the changes in one's body state. An emotion is *felt*; feeling an emotion is the experience of these changes in juxtaposition with the emotion-inducing perception (the stimulus causing the emotion). As such, feelings are just as cognitive as other percepts because humans construct them and are aware of them. At a conscious level, feelings label outcomes of responses as either positive or negative and these judgments lead to deliberate avoidance or pursuit of a given response option. At a subconscious level, feelings—or "somatic markers," as Damasio calls them—act as internal guides. They provide criteria by which human beings rank the available sense images in the process of reasoning.

The function of Damasio's somatic markers as internal guides resonates with the mathematician Henri Poincaré's (1908/1956) theory of mathematical creation, in which ideas are created in the unconscious and passed through some kind of "aesthetic sieve" before emerging into the conscious mind. In fact, Damasio agrees with Poincaré that some kind of preselection is carried out, whether covertly or not. But he also implies that *all* humans rely on a preselection mechanism in all their perceptual acts. (The mathematics educator Richard Skemp [1979] has also pointed to the role of feelings in problem solving in his book *Intelligence, Learning and Action*.)

The art critic and philosopher Ernst Gombrich (1979) might argue that the criteria that guide preselection form a person's "sense of order," which modifies itself constantly as that person gains more experience in the world. That would make Poincaré's "special aesthetic sensitivity" a strongly developed sense of order with respect to mathematical objects and processes. As professional mathematicians gain experience in looking for and finding different types of ordering patterns, they concurrently develop a uniquely individual aesthetic sense, which in turn attunes them to patterns that others may not be able to discern. The philosopher Harold Osborne (1984) points to the crucial role played by such a sense of order, both as a form of beauty and as an action of the human mind attempting to come to terms with randomness, disarray, or chaos. Osborne suggests that the imposition of order—making patterns fit together in a harmonious way—gives rise to aesthetic satisfaction.

The supporting evidence for Damasio's thesis focuses primarily on the personal and social domains of decision-making rather than on the abstract-symbolic decision-making operations of artistic and scientific reasoning. Operations in the personal and social domain precede, from an evolutionary perspective, abstract-symbolic decision-making operations. These latter operations will still depend on some kind of somatic markers, though they may not be perceived as "feelings" that act covertly to highlight certain components over others. However, Damasio maintains that, whatever the nature of artistic and scientific reasoning, it interacts intimately with feeling and emotion, and is mediated by body-based signaling that is aesthetic in nature.

The research methods from which Damasio builds his thesis are those of cognitive neuroscience, and his hypotheses are each qualified by empirical testing. Further research in this field, using such scientific methods, will certainly shed more light on the nature of mathematical reasoning—a domain about which Damasio at present only speculates. However, there are other methods available to those inquiring about the nature of human reasoning (in general, but also in mathematics), which can provide insight into the abstract-symbolic domains of reasoning, including the philosophical methods of John Dewey.

Dewey (1934) argues that the aesthetic is a pervading quality of human reasoning and experience. He begins his argument by pointing out that the categories used to characterize and communicate different modes of reasoning and experience (i.e., emotional, intellectual, aesthetic) may make our descriptions and analyses of them more tractable, but that these categories impose artificial boundaries and dualisms that do not exist. As with Johnson, he bemoans theories that have accustomed us to drawing rigid separations between "logical, strictly intellectual, operations that dominate in science, the emotional and imaginative processes which dominate poetry, music, and to a lesser degree the plastic arts, and the practical doings which rule our daily life" (1925/1986, p. 104).

No matter what the domain, whether mathematics or sculpture, Dewey sees aesthetic ways of reasoning as working to establish a unity or form—a basic sense of understanding or of mastery—for otherwise unknown or undetermined things. Aesthetic reasoning brings understanding and imagination—thought and emotion—into agreement, giving rise to a feeling of fittingness of the cognitive powers. The feeling of pleasure that belongs to aesthetic responses arises because one has succeeded, seemingly against odds, in making something comprehensible, in having secured some grasp of a phenomenon. In locating the aesthetic in the everyday, in "the events and scenes that hold the attentive eye and ear of man, arousing his interest and affording him enjoyment as he looks and listens" (1934, p. 4), Dewey claims that the aesthetic is accessible to all, in the diversity of human activities, given the right conditions and opportunities.

What is this pervading aesthetic quality that Dewey talks about? Simply put, it is a quality of experience, of arranging one's world at a given point in time. Dewey maintains that humans have an inevitable tendency to arrange events and objects with reference to the demands of complete and unified perception.[1] The qualifying demand of human reasoning is a thoroughgoing unity of experience. Aesthetic experience would be impossible in either a world of only flux, where no closures were possible, or a world in which suspense and crisis were absent, and hence, where no resolutions were possible. But people can find closure and resolution despite the vicissitudes of their surroundings. They can attend to the structure, order, and coherence of an experience and impose on it, or find within it, a certain integral fulfilment. This is achieved in part by fitting together the various dimensions of experience—the practical, emotional, and intellectual—and by remaking past experiences so that "they can fit integrally into a new pattern" (1934, p. 176).

Damasio would support Dewey in contending that humans inevitably frame their understandings of "outside" events in terms of their inner desires. But Dewey goes further in saying that the aesthetic is the vehicle through which human beings ascribe meaning to experiences. To take an example from the mathematical world, the experience of reading a proof is not purely intellectual. It only gains meaning from the aesthetic act of integrating an outside truth with beliefs such as attainment of certainty, desires such as simplicity or austerity, personal understanding, and recognition of one's own state of knowing.

In linking the aesthetic to cognition as he does, Dewey precedes many others (e.g., Davis, 1996; Ernest, 1998; Lakoff & Nunez, 2000; White, 1993) in challenging the philosophies of the Platonists and the formalists who see mathematics as disembodied and immutable. Such philosophies, as the mathematicians Philip Davis and Ruben Hersh (1986) write, "cannot tell us what mathematics is, why mathematics is true, why it is beautiful, how it comes to be, or why anyone should care a fig about it" (p. 201). By viewing humans as creatures who think and learn through qualitative discriminations intended to achieve states of coherence with their environments and interactions, Dewey anticipates a much more "humanistic" conception of mathematics. Such a conception suggests that mathematics has a claim to the aesthetic that is equal to that of the arts, provided we agree that the aesthetic initially arises not only in art through manifestly aesthetic stimuli, but in *experience* at its most complex and fundamental level.

Dewey emphasizes the aesthetic as a theme in human experience, as a way that humans organize and derive meaning from everyday situations in which they find themselves. He also insists that there is an aesthetic quality that belongs to any inquiry, be it scientific or artistic: "The most elaborate philosophical or scientific inquiry and the most ambitious industrial or political enterprise has, when its different ingredients constitute an integral experience, aesthetic quality" (1934, p. 55). In the next section I focus on Dewey's theory of inquiry in more detail, as it provides compelling insights into the aesthetic nature of mathematical inquiry.

THE AESTHETIC NATURE OF INQUIRY

Dewey defines *inquiry* as "the controlled or directed transformation of an indeterminate situation into one that is so determinate in its constituents' distinctions and relations as to convert the elements of the original situation into a unified whole" (1938, p. 108). The process of inquiry that regulates problem solving in all domains, the artistic and the scientific alike, begins in problematic and uncertain situations.

In contrast to traditional epistemologies and theories of logic that dichotomize the rational and the nonrational, Dewey is careful to emphasize the necessary continuity of modes of thought and their dependence on one another, and this leads him to focus on the aesthetic nature of human inquiry. He argues that inquiry is emergent from, and pervaded by, background, noncognitive experience such as affect, intuition, and imagination. These elements feed the foreground of *qualitative thought*, which is concerned with "ideas," "concepts," "categories," and "formal logic."

Dewey refers to the background, noncognitive experience that emerges from inquiry as *qualitative reason*. Qualitative reason shapes cognitive realms in such subtle ways that it often cannot be defined, if only because the line between the affective and the cognitive can become blurred in interpretation: Human cognitive capabilities engage often without regard for precognitive influence. For instance, the background experience of rhythm, an essential organizing tool of human experience, draws attention to certain features and relations—it selects through qualitative reasoning mechanisms. Often without conscious awareness, it gives what Dewey calls a "qualitative unity" to objects or phenomena that are externally disparate and dissimilar. Such unity allows human beings to abstract discernible patterns in conjunction with the ideas and concepts at hand. However, rarely in their discernment and representations of cyclic patterns, for instance, do humans recall the rhythmic influence of their perception. These perceptions are not necessarily innate or immutable; they are guided by phenomenal and experiential factors.

What Is Qualitative Unity?

Since qualitative unity is so central to Dewey's theory of inquiry, as well as to an appreciation of the aesthetic nature of inquiry, I will illustrate the notion using a more concrete example. Suppose someone (with at least some previous exposure to fractions) is confronted for the first time with the information in Figure 2.1, which shows the color-coded decimal expansion of the fraction 1/7 (depicted here in shades of gray, but shown in full-color on the cover of this book).

Various precognitive elements can influence that person's qualitative thinking about the image, which will be aimed at making sense of this relation or juxtaposition of visual elements. I will consider three possible responses to this situation. One individual might have a predilection for, say, purple, which might lead her to *perceive* the image as equally spaced purple squares, including different shades of purple that appear close together: pink and blue. She might search for more purples, or see the images as purple diagonal stripes, or might label 1/7 as quite a purple number. Another individual might have an immediate experience of rhythm that leads her to *perceive* the image as repetitions of strings of color (that she *sees directly* or *perceives*, as opposed to *counts*). She might go back and forth between seeing predominantly black or white, but she senses repeated cycles of color. She might quantify the repetition, look for its beginning or end, or associate the fraction 1/7 with a repeating form. Alternatively, a third individual might be influenced by her imagination and *perceive*, not blocks of colors, but a staircase that goes up from bottom left to top right. Then she might look at the several different staircases and notice the fact that each one is a solid color. She might pay attention to how the staircases grow or shrink or how many there are, or she might subconsciously label the fraction 1/7 a "staircase number."

1/7 =

Figure 2.1. One visual representation of the fraction 1/7.

Each of these individuals selects different features of the image that provide them with a qualitative unity of the object under consideration. Note, however, that the selection of features is not haphazard; it follows from aesthetic choices, from sensibilities to certain forms and relationships.

Dewey insists that qualitative unity must be felt, or "had": It cannot be expressed in words. How does one come to "feel" qualitative unity? He stresses that such unity must be sparked by a directly experienced quality; a form such as *rhythm* can only operate as an immediate qualitative link for the inquirer via experience. The theories of embodied cognition—as put forth most recently by George Lakoff and Mark Johnson (1999) and which resonate strongly with both Damasio's (1994) and Dissanayake's (1992) positions on the primacy of body-based experience—propose that directly experienced qualities depend upon embodied knowledge. That is, body-based *schemata* structure human interactions, perceptions, and apprehensions. These *schemata* are not necessarily visual, nor are they exclusively propositional. Rather, they are dynamic structures for organizing ongoing experience and comprehension that emerge from bodily movements through space, our manipulations of objects and perceptual interactions. As Mark Johnson (1987) writes:

> They are gestalt structures, consisting of parts standing in relations and organized into unified wholes, by means of which our experience manifests discernible order. When we seek to comprehend this order and to reason about it, such bodily based schemata play a central role. (p. xix)

Thus, subject matter is formulated primarily by embodied knowledge through forms and patterns such as balance, symmetry, containment, and rhythm.[2] These are primarily qualitative formulations, and are apprehended as such. Of course, not all perceived qualities connect directly to body-based knowledge; they may connect to more abstract or sophisticated schemata that are the result of mappings, projections, or elaborations of body-based knowledge (see Lakoff & Nunez, 2000).

Qualitative Unity in the Process of Inquiry

Dewey's process of inquiry has three components: (1) an indeterminate situation that provokes a state of disturbed equilibrium—a state of tension; (2) the period of exploration (including the specification of the problem and the construction of hypotheses) and a movement toward restoration of equilibrium—toward release; and (3) the recovery of fulfilment or satisfaction (through the elaboration and testing of the hypotheses). The above example focused on the role of qualitative thought in an inquirer's initial encounter with a situation. But qualitative thought continues to function in the second and third phases of inquiry too.

With the following example, I want to show how a perplexing situation can give rise to the single qualitativeness that underlies further explicit reasoning. Imagine that the three individuals described previously are next confronted with the image shown in Figure 2.2. A general tension may result from the implication that the same fraction can correspond to two different visual patterns. The three individuals might even respond with exclamations such as "Oh!" Dewey views such exclamations as the simplest examples of qualitative thought and notes how they provide the impetus for most every scientific investigation. However, I want to draw attention to the way in which the qualitative unity achieved by each individual produces different tensions and, thus, different subsequent lines of reasoning.

The staircase inquirer might be the most disturbed, since her organizing quality of diagonality that was established upon seeing the previous image and used to define the fraction 1/7, has been upset. She will select and observe facts that will help her to reequilibrate that quality; hence, she might perceive the new image in terms of how far "off" the diagonal it is, and therefore wonder about restoring the diagonal or whether there is another kind of diagonal. On the other hand, the rhythmic inquirer might be surprised that the two images both correspond to 1/7, but her sense of cycling colors has not been disturbed, for the colors cycle in exactly the same way in this image as they did in the first. Finally, the third inquirer will have lost the image of staircases, and might be provoked to interpret this image as stripes, columns, or a colorful checkerboard, and therefore wonder which image is more pleasing or whether there are other kinds of positive images, too.

1/7 =

Figure 2.2. Another visual representation of the fraction 1/7.

The qualitative unity "felt" by each individual thus gives rise to a different set of questions and tensions. This unity organizes the inquiry because it shapes the conjectures, ideas, and abstractions that follow; it provides a heuristic function. However, the inquirer is aware of the quality not by itself, but as the background thread and the directive clue in which she acts. In his essay on qualitative thought, Dewey writes: "To say that I have a feeling or impression that so and so is the case is to note that the quality in question is not yet resolved into determinate terms and relations" (1930/1986, p. 248). However, following the initial sensing of a problem, during the determination of a problem situation, ideas start to appear to the inquirer as simply vague suggestions of relations and distinctions.[3] The staircase inquirer might bend her head to see whether the image has just been turned or shifted. These suggestions actually become ideas when they are examined with reference to their functional fitness—their capacity to provide a means of resolving the given situation. The suggestion of turning or shifting the image might become an idea if the inquirer sees how different transformations affect the image, how they might relate to the diagonal pattern.

Dewey points out that when a subject matter is reasonably familiar, as will be the case when mathematicians engage with their problems, relevant distinctions speedily offer themselves, and sheer qualitativeness may not remain long enough to be readily recalled. Because of this, it may be very difficult to recall the aesthetic responses that guide choices and actions. Nevertheless, this constitutes the aesthetic logic: the control of selection of detail and of modes of relation, or integration, by a qualitative whole. Such logic is often recognized in artistic thought, but seldom in mathematical thought (Polanyi, 1958). Perhaps, as Dewey suggests, the mathematician is so concerned with the mastery of symbolic or propositional forms that she fails to recognize the creative operations involved in their construction.

Typically found at the close of a successful investigation, declarations such as "How beautiful" or "How elegant" mark for Dewey the realized appreciation of a pervading quality that is now translated into a system of definite coherent terms. Such judgments of appreciation—where the evaluative role of the aesthetic operates—arise when inquiry has reached a close that fulfils the activities and conditions that led up to it. Without these affective responses, the inquirer would not have the experiential sign that the inquiry has reached a close. But aesthetic judgments can also occur during an inquiry, as a result of the resolution of tension for each subproblem. They constitute a series of landmarks in the progress of the undertaking. In fact, Dewey (1934) remarks that they are so important that "their function of being clews [sic] and giving direction that the sense of harmony which attends them is too readily taken as evidence of truth of the subject-matter involved" (p. 249). When the staircase inquirer realizes and is able to describe how to transform the second image into the first, when she is able to see what happened to the staircase and how she can make it appear again, she has perhaps achieved a resolved state. Not only has she worked through the dissonance caused by the second image; she has also understood the general relationship between these two images, and united her previously disparate perception.

CONNECTING THE AESTHETIC TO LEARNING: FIRST STEPS

In examining the aesthetic dimension of inquiry and experience, I have been dancing around the issue of student learning, never quite articulating how inquiry, experience, and learning might be seen as bound together in a way that may be relevant to mathematics education. If one takes the view, as do the educators Marton and Booth (1997), that learning is about changing one's way of experiencing a phenomenon, then the learning/experience coupling should seem natural. Moreover, if one takes the view that learning proceeds from an undifferentiated and poorly integrated understanding of the whole to an increased differentiation and integration of the whole and the parts, then the connection between Deweyian inquiry (and experience) and learning should start to become at least intuitively natural. With the following hypothetical example, I want to probe further that intuitively plausible connection, and hence articulate better the aesthetic dimension of learning. Consider the following scenario:

> A student sits in front of a piece of paper where several triangles
> have been drawn. She wants to construct the altitudes of each
> triangle. The first few examples are easy; she uses the method
> her teacher has shown and constructs a perpendicular line from a
> vertex of the triangle to its opposite side. But then she comes to a
> triangle for which that method does not work. She cannot find a
> line between the vertex and the opposite side that is even close to
> being perpendicular. She frowns.

The student's usual routines have failed; she experiences the disruption of habitual action as a feeling: tension, frustration, confusion, or doubt. She may skip that triangle and move on to the next one. But if she does not, she can no longer appeal to her habits: She must engage in conscious thought. That is, she will have to engage in a process of inquiry that can mediate between the actual (I cannot construct an altitude) and the possible (Is there another way of constructing an altitude? Do some triangles not have altitudes?).

> The teacher sees the student's problem and tells her she must extend the opposite side in both directions and use her new line to construct the perpendicular through the vertex. The student follows the instructions, and moves on to the next triangle, wondering what new trick she will encounter this time.

Has any learning taken place? Quite possibly not, if the student has not established any pattern or regularity that might have restored the elements of the original situation into a unified whole. If she has changed her way of experiencing the phenomenon of a triangle's altitudes, it is only by gathering facts and information, tackling altitudes in isolated pieces rather than maintaining an integrated whole. She has established no relations with past experiences and, moreover, has experienced no delight, no satisfaction of her previous doubts or confusion. Therefore, her process of inquiry has been stunted. This is not, however, because the teacher "told her" the answer.[4] Consider instead this scenario:

> The teacher sees the student's problem and tells her she must extend the opposite side in both directions and use her new line to construct the perpendicular through the vertex. The student extends the opposite side, and uses it to construct an altitude. She notices that the altitude and the opposite side don't actually touch—something she has never seen before—and comes to a new way of thinking about perpendicularity: two line segments can be perpendicular without even intersecting. She looks back at her first few triangles and tries to determine how this triangle is different. This new triangle has an obtuse angle, and that makes the vertex "jut out" beyond the opposite side. But this method of extending the line could be used in every case; it is more general than her previous method. Now she feels that she could do any example.

In this scenario, the teacher still "tells" the student an important fact, but this time the student has come armed with an expectation that there will be some regularity or relationships to find—an expectation that may have been aroused through the surprising interruption encountered in her task. Her qualitative reasoning has been engaged. In seeking out and establishing patterns and regularities, and in attempting to maintain an integrated whole, she has taken an aesthetic orientation to inquiry. In the end, the new regularity satisfies the doubt and confusion she previously experienced, and provides her with a feeling of organic unity that restores her habitual functioning, and thus augments her confidence to move on to the next triangle.

When the student is comparing the different triangles, she is not engaged in thought as a "pale, bloodless abstraction." Rather, her thinking is charged with an urgent desire stemming from a single qualitative impression that will take her from her current condition to one in which the triangles return to having a basis of commonality. The student has learned something; she has reorganized her experiential world in order to find a fitting way of thinking about the altitudes of a triangle. And it is the aesthetic that provides the background against which her mathematical acts can become meaningful, against which the selection and regulation of observed facts takes place. After all, I can compare an apple and an orange and observe that one is red while the other is orange. It is an aesthetic orientation that drives me to seek unity, pattern, or regularity: to see what the fruit have in common, how they can be conceived of together, and to form an image—a schematic perception—that accepts or rejects new members that I might encounter.

FITTING THE PIECES TOGETHER

Dewey construes the aesthetic as a theme in human experience, and insists that there is an aesthetic quality that belongs to any kind of human inquiry, at all stages of that inquiry. His description of inquiry will be very useful in Part II, where I turn my attention to mathematical inquiry and try to understand the different roles that the aesthetic may play in mathematical problem solving.

In contrast to Dewey, Damasio's (1994) theory of human decision-making mphasizes the aesthetic as a mode of discrimination and choice. Several scholars, as I show in the next chapter, have placed more emphasis on the aesthetic as an innate urge or capacity that, I would suggest, provides a kind of substrate to the multidimensional behavior involved in experience and decision-making. In so doing, they provide some insight into the particular forms and structures that tend to attract human attention.

CHAPTER 3

"Wired" for Beauty and Pleasure

If the aesthetic plays such an important role in experience and cognition, educators must wonder, on the one hand, what kinds of aesthetic sensibilities students have when they enter the classroom and, on the other, how these sensibilities develop? The question is still far from resolved. However, over the past couple of decades, scholars from different disciplines have been claiming that humans do possess innate aesthetic sensibilities, which they use as sense-making mechanisms in their everyday activities, including their mathematical ones.

Naturally, an innate aesthetic sensibility does not mean that everyone shares the same preferences and judgments or develops equally powerful aesthetic responses. Even mathematicians, who are notoriously conforming in their aesthetic judgments (see King, 1992)—compared with artists—frequently diverge in their personal responses and tendencies (Burton, 1999a; Wells, 1990), particularly across different cultural contexts (D'Ambrosio, 1997; Eglash, 1999; Joseph, 1992). Consider an example that several mathematicians have noted: Although some mathematicians may pursue (and impose) symmetric structures and relationships, while others may seek instances of asymmetry, both groups use symmetry as an aesthetic guide (Dyson, 1982). (This phenomenon has been described in the decorative arts as well where, for instance, many Eastern cultures prefer designs of asymmetry while Western ones tend toward symmetry.) Indeed, given the constraints of our human embodiedness, there are likely to be many such biologically based aesthetic tendencies affected by and developed within particular sociohistorical contexts.

HOMO AESTHETICUS

The scholar Ellen Dissanayake (1992) provides perhaps the most comprehensive and concentrated account of the aesthetic as a core component of human behavior. In her book *Homo Aestheticus* she argues that sensibility to the aesthetic is a characteristic human trait, equal in consequence to the other faculties typically associated with human beings, such as the cognitive or the social. She sees the human aesthetic as an innate urge to enhance everyday experiences and events, thus placing less emphasis on the aesthetic as a mode of discrimination or cognition than as a way of experiencing the world. Aesthetic responses, according to Dissanayake, derive from actions that humans take in the world in order to fulfil a fundamental biological need to "make special":

> Humans everywhere, in a manner unlike other animals, differentiate between an order, realm, mood, or state of being that is mundane, ordinary, or "natural," and one that is unusual, extra-ordinary, or "supernatural." (p. 49)

If the urge to "make special" drives aesthetic response, what provokes this urge, and how do we know it is such a panhuman, vital experience? Arguing from an evolutionary point of view, Dissanayake suggests that as early humans developed higher-level cognitive abilities (such as planning ahead or assessing causes and their consequences), they needed to make certain experiences special or extraordinary in an attempt to influence the outcome of events that were potentially uncertain and troubling. Thus came the beginning of ritual and its accompanying activities such as dancing and decorating. Interestingly, with respect to this book's focus on mathematics, the mathematician and historian Abraham Seidenberg (1962) proposes that the origins of mathematics (specifically counting, but also geometry) can also be found in ritual, arguing against the commonly held belief that mathematics arose in response to more practical, economic concerns such as taxes, allocation of resources, and trade. Based on anthropological sources, he claims that counting was frequently the central feature of a rite, and that participants in ritual were numbered. As the mathematics educator Dick Tahta elaborates[1]: "'One, two, buckle my shoe/Three, four, knock on the door.' The gods are ushered into the ceremonial, the stars majestically ride across the sky, men create numbers 'in rite order'" (p. 19).

Returning to Dissanayake, these making-special activities would seem to contradict Darwinian assumptions that humans confine themselves to behavior that simply assures adaptation to geography and livelihood. Dissanayake points to evidence showing that humans elaborate a way of life that is beyond evident necessity—one that is expressive, ritualistic, and decorative. For example, human take care to paint their faces in attractive colors and designs; they develop ritual dances that are rhythmic and graceful; and, more recently, they spend time and resources on activities which might be regarded as wasteful in terms of survival such as mowing lawns, arranging flowers, shaving body hair, and even selecting specific font styles on the computer.

In the movement from the black and white of phenomenological immediacy to the murkier search for subjective meanings, Dissanayake sees humans becoming adept at distinguishing perceptual and emotional subtleties. This, in turn, provides humans with a cognitive capacity to make judgments of quality, of what is "beautiful" or "better." As a result, not only do humans distinguish images, sounds, and tastes that appeal to their senses more than others; they also distinguish elements such as repetition, symmetry, and proportion that appeal to their cognitive faculties.

Why should such elements be cognitively appealing? Dissanayake argues that they are highly enabling, in that they provide shape and meaning while using minimal resources. For example, symmetry is highly enabling in that it allows human minds to grasp the whole of a structure or form, as well as make predictions about it, based on information from only a small part of it. It allows the mind to reduce complexity to simplicity through an act of perception. The Dutch-American mathematician Dirk Struik acknowledges the link between symmetry and understanding when he writes, "[i]ncidentally, the symmetry and harmony of forms that turn out to be most efficient . . . also strike us as more agreeable, *beautiful*" (2003, p. ix, emphasis in original).

Another distinguishing element linked to understanding involves cycles of repetition, which allow the mind to structure raw experience— changing seasons, sunrises, tides—and pattern its projections of the future. With respect to mathematical phenomena, humans record and impose rhythm on events and objects through the one, two, three, four, of counting, as well as the construction of lines and angles into geometric patterns. These perceptual and physical acts shape human comprehension, which in turn (in primal contexts) translates into mastery, and then security. Dissanayake asserts that early humans drew emotional satisfaction from the controlled behavior of structuring space and time—that is, from arranging and placing space and time into comprehensible form. Humans nowadays also draw emotional satisfaction from aesthetic perceptual acts, as evidenced by Zoe's grasp of symmetry described in the introduction and her subsequent show of pleasure.

The progression of efficient, satisfying acts into value judgments begins when elements such as symmetry and rhythm come to be perceived as "good" in and of themselves, and then iteratively continue to find their way into "making special" activities. Thus, Dissanayake finds a biological determinant to evolved structures—symmetry, repetition, and order—for expressing mathematical ideas. In this, she is supported by the mathematician Saunders Mac Lane's (1986) analysis of the practical and conceptual origins of mathematics. He points out how mathematical objects such as number, size, and order have been shaped by our human actions of counting, comparing, and noticing patterns—actions that humans take in order to control and understand their environment. Thus, mathematics, seen as a synchrony of actions such as patterning, ordering, transforming, and balancing, consists of and gives rise to qualities that are cognitively pleasing.

Dissanayake also insists, now taking a developmental stance, that humans' in-born capacities for discrimination are first exercised in aesthetic contexts—that is, in the sensory-rich and pleasurable interactions with their mothers and their environments. These interactions predispose human beings to respond to, and to seek, emotionally resonant and richly satisfying aesthetic experiences.[2] This might suggest a strong link between aesthetic and affective responses. The essential emotional component of human aesthetic responses manifests itself physically: such responses *feel* good.

The cognitive scientist Steven Pinker (1997), another scholar interested in the aesthetic dimension of human behavior, explains how human emotions become so deeply implicated in aesthetic responses. He focuses on the adaptive responses of human beings to selective pressures in an evolutionary context and, in particular, on their responses to the set of "enabling acts" that increase their ability to survive within environmental and social constraints. Some subconscious part of the mind, he argues, registers those highly enabling acts—such as using symmetry to perceive and gather information on family members or hunted animals—through a sensation of pleasure. This pleasure alerts us to, or brings to our consciousness, the advantages of such acts.

Enabling acts occur through obtaining information about the consequential objects and forces that dominate everyday lives. Whereas these may have once been acts of predicting times of rain, the location of fertile hunting grounds, or generosity in other humans, modern humans face very different situations. Nevertheless, Pinker argues that the pleasure-alerting mechanisms function in the same way. When confronted by information-rich and potentially consequential stimuli—the ominous foreign subway map separating me from my hotel, for example—I derive pleasure from being able to discern its underlying pattern. In his study of the interplay between art and science, Martin Kemp (2000) reinforces Pinker's position by contending that all human acts of artificial making (whether in the arts or in science) well up from the same inner necessities to gratify our systems of perception, cognition, and creation. In science no less than art, humans artificially activate the system of gratification and reward provided by our pleasure in "pattern, in symmetry, in order and its judicious breaking, in minutely discriminatory acts of recognition" (p. 2).

A "SENSE OF ORDER"

Pinker and Dissanayake are both concerned with the consequential dimension of human behavior—that is, the way in which "making special" and "registering enabling acts" form the basis for aesthetic sensibility. However, there are other ways of thinking about the role of the aesthetic in human experience and inquiry. For example, Edward Wilson (1998), a scientist, and Ernst Gombrich (1979), an art historian, were both interested in the causal dimension of human behavior—that is, the way in which aesthetic sensibility is used in anticipation during acts of perception and cognition. Wilson argues that humans have predictable, innate aesthetic preferences that they use in making sense of their environments. He notes that basic functioning in the environment depends on discerning patterns, such as the spatial patterns involved in perceiving surfaces and objects, and the rhythmic patterns involved in detecting temporal change.

The continued and improving ability to discern such patterns gives rise to what Wilson calls "epigenetic rules"—that is, to inherited regularities of development in anatomy, physiology, cognition, and behavior. He argues that such rules account for many aesthetic predispositions and preferences. For instance, studies in human facial recognition show that humans are particularly drawn to right-left symmetry (as opposed to up-down symmetry or no symmetry at all). Finding such symmetry provides the simplest (shortest) descriptions of faces and even of bodies—and thus makes such stimuli easier to encode and recall. It should not be surprising then that Zoe (the student described in Chapter 1), for example, exhibited an attraction to symmetry. In Part III, there will be similar examples of students showing sensibility to symmetry.

Wilson provides a concrete example of a universally shared aesthetic preference. He describes a study tracing arousal response to a variety of visual images in which the most arousing are those that cognitive psychologists call "optimally complex." Although researchers have a method for quantifying complexity, a qualitative description will suffice here: "optimally complex" designs contain enough complexity to engage the mind without overwhelming it with incomprehensible irregularity or diversity.

Gombrich pursues the same idea. For instance, a simple square grid shown in Figure 3.1 contains little or no complexity—the pattern is too redundant, too repetitive. For Gombrich, the square grid "can be taken in so easily that it leaves our perceptive process without enough work to do. . . . When the expected happens in our field of vision we cease to attend" (p. 8). However, coloring every other square in a checkerboard pattern adds one level of complexity. Distorting it in order to show a perspective view of a tiled floor adds yet another level of complexity. Finally, creating larger squares, or even rectangles with the base squares could be a further complicating—or "complexifying"—variation. If too many variations or distortions are made, such that little or no redundancy and repetition can be detected, the design moves from being too simple to being too complex to provoke arousal. However, if the stimulus is just complex enough, the perceiver is most aroused—more aesthetically pleased—since, as Gombrich explains, "delight lies somewhere between boredom and confusion" (p. 9).

Gombrich's notion of the human "sense of order" predates Wilson's notion of epigenetic rules, but they seem to have much in common. This is the elementary expectation of regularity that humans have when they probe the environment; it serves as a sounding board against which variations are detected, as well as deviations, similarities and differences, and change. Gombrich's "sense of order" acts like a searchlight. It hypothesizes order and organizes its perceptions according to that order. Humans are thus biased in their perception toward straight lines, circles, symmetry, and similarly ordered configurations rather than with the random shapes or patterns encountered in the chaotic world. Gombrich emphasizes that the order hypothesis is the condition that makes learning possible, since without some initial system, a first guess, no "sense" could be made of the millions of ambiguous stimuli incoming from the environment. The mathematician Alvin White (in Bruner, 1969) corroborates and adds to Gombrich's claim by noting that the seeking and noticing that

Figure 3.1. Square grid, checkerboard, tiled floor, rectangles.

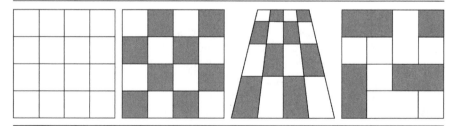

ultimately leads to learning is not random: "It is directed, selective, and persistent and it continues because it satisfies an intrinsic need to deal with the environment" (p. 89).

The optimally complex designs in Wilson's study turn out to be comparable (within the survey's metric of complexity) to abstract designs used worldwide in friezes, logos, and pictographs—a fact that would not have surprised Gombrich. These are the designs that appeal to human beings through their unexpectedness, and are therefore delightful because they can still be encoded and remembered. Such designs attract more attention; in a sense, they invite the perceiver to spend more time trying to grasp them fully, or even begin to manipulate and represent them. The notion of unexpectedness is prevalent among mathematicians' descriptions of what they find aesthetically pleasing in mathematical situations (see Burton, 2004; Hardy, 1940; King, 1992; Sinclair, 2006; Wells, 1990), and emerged frequently in the students' mathematical activity I discuss in Part III. Their aesthetic response is consistent with these arguments of Wilson and Gombrich.

In thinking about mathematics, though, it becomes apparent quickly that the attractive entities are not necessarily (and perhaps even not commonly) visual. Do the arguments that Wilson and Gombrich make apply only to visual designs? Certainly not, and it is important to recognize that the perceptual acts involved in probing the environment are also highly cognitive: they presuppose a cognitive map on which meaningful objects can be plotted as well as a capacity to decide whether or not those objects fit (Arnheim, 1969). Any perceived unexpectedness, whether in terms of temporal, aural, or mental designs, should attract humans according to the same principles as visual designs. The key is that, in order to perceive unexpectedness, the perceiver must have some expectation of regularity in the domain of perception: that is, some relevant sense of order.

The claims presented in this chapter do not specifically relate to school learning. However, the observations made about human tendencies and predispositions certainly inform learning theory, since humans learn best when they can engage their strongest and most effective responses to the environment. The educator Howard Gardner's (1983) theory of multiple intelligences loosely follows this line of reasoning, in encouraging educators to meet students' preferred and multiple ways of thinking. However, it seems to neglect the dialogical nature of human engagement. Human beings do not simply apply visual intelligence, for example, to phenomena; rather, they respond to certain patterned visual cues according to their evaluation of both visual and nonvisual complexities. Additionally, they respond only if they care somehow about the consequences or outcomes.

To summarize, based on the work of several scholars representing diverse fields of research in human behavior, I have posited four related claims. First, humans possess an aesthetic sensibility upon which they depend in their diverse modes of meaning-making. Second, there is a set of aesthetic tendencies that appear to be biologically based (or embodied) and thus universally shared. Naturally, these tendencies can be deconstructed—they refine and diverge through education and enculturation. Third, exercising these sensibilities can bring humans pleasure and, thus, humans naturally seek to do so. Fourth, humans have a "sense of order" that directs attention to particular patterns such as balance and provides the means for learning, through feedback cycles of expectation, perception, and adjustment.

The group of scholars I have cited reflect a variegated notion of the "aesthetic," one that will seem broader than common parlance usually allows. Few of these scholars actually define their use of the aesthetic. Dissanayake speaks of "making special," while Gombrich refers to a "sense of order." In the next part, I develop a more operative notion of the aesthetic—particularly as it applies to mathematical inquiry—that I will eventually use as a lens on mathematics learning.

PART II

Beauty and Pleasure in Mathematics

Having explored the aesthetic in its widest contexts, in Part II I narrow the book's investigation to the domain of mathematics; first to mathematics researchers and then to mathematics learners. While Part I drew primarily on nonempirical sources and evidence, Parts II and III consider the actual inquiries and experiences of both mathematicians and students.

I begin Chapter 4 by articulating a concept of the aesthetic that will be used in this book, and I contrast it with other conceptualizations. I then develop an aesthetic framework that identifies and illustrates the different roles the aesthetic plays in mathematical inquiry. I draw on both the experiences of research mathematicians and an analysis of a "real time" mathematical inquiry The distinct roles of the aesthetic—of which there are three, namely, the motivational, the generative, and the evaluative—will allow me to formulate the "mathematical aesthetic lens."

Chapter 5 considers the extent to which the roles of the aesthetic are necessary to mathematical inquiry. The intent of Chapter 5 is to evaluate and dispel claims that the mathematics aesthetic should be treated as an epiphenomenon in relation to learning and doing mathematics, or merely as a fanciful hobby indulged in only by illustrious mathematicians. At the end of Part II, I will have developed the concepts needed to locate, understand, and explain the mathematical aesthetic in student learning.

CHAPTER 4

Developing a Mathematical Aesthetic Lens

Before delving into *the mathematical aesthetic*, I consider first the concept of *the aesthetic* as it has been used historically and conventionally. I then outline how I intend to use the concept in this book, guided by my pragmatic goal of improving understanding of mathematics and mathematics learning. I am working toward answering the question, "What might productively be meant by the *aesthetic* in the context of mathematics and mathematics learning?", a question that emphasizes my desire to develop a conception that improves my understanding of mathematics and mathematics learning, and not one that attempts to define it objectively once and for all.

THE AESTHETIC

In common parlance, the adjective *aesthetic* is often used interchangeably with words such as *beautiful, good, harmonious*, or—especially in mathematics—*elegant*. This use of the word sometimes implies an objective philosophical orientation, where aesthetic qualities are seen to reside solely within the artifact being judged, independently of the observer or the cultural context. This was the orientation taken by formalist art theorists, such as Clive Bell and Roger Fry, whose primary aesthetic criterion was "significant form," which consisted of the optimal unity and coherence of the compositional elements. From this point of view, then, the painting is to be judged based on its shape, its colors, its composition, and so on—and any observer should, with sufficient sophistication, come to the same conclusion about its aesthetic merit. Similar to formalist art critics, the mathematician G. H. Hardy wanted to identify aesthetic criteria objectively, such as economy, surprise, and significance, which he claimed "any real mathematician could see." These criteria defined mathematical "beauty" and "elegance." One of the theorems Hardy uses to illustrate these criteria is the Euclidean proof of the infinity of primes, a theorem he considered one of the most beautiful in mathematics.[1]

In contrast, I interpret adjectives such as *beauty* and *elegance* as epithets of a feeling that might be best described as *fitting*. That which gives a sense of "fit" ultimately depends on the perceiver, as well as the sociocultural matrix binding the perceiver and the perceived. In the arts, the wide divergence of aesthetic tastes is quite obvious, but even in mathematics it is possible to find some mathematicians who are indifferent to Hardy's beloved theorem. For example, the writer David Wells's (1990) survey of mathematicians' aesthetic preferences shows quite convincingly that mathematicians can and do differ in their judgments of beauty depending on these factors: field of interest; preferences for certain mathematical entities such as problems, proofs, or theorems; past experiences or associations with particular theorems; and even mood. Wells also points out that aesthetic judgments change over time; eventually, some results are considered too obvious to elicit an aesthetic response; they may well start to look more like the square grids I used in Chapter 3 to describe Gombrich's links among complexity, comprehension, and aesthetic responses. One wonders whether the aesthetic only evolves in one direction, or might some mathematical results become *more* aesthetic? Whatever the case may be, the inferences made by Wells correspond to a *contextualist* view, and are summed up by this respondent: "beauty, even in mathematics, depends upon historical and cultural contexts, and therefore tends to elude numerical interpretation" (p. 39).

Thus, in recognizing the aesthetic as subjectively and socioculturally constructed, I am trying to discourage a common tendency—supported by linguistic usage—to describe aesthetic qualities as inherent to objects, and thus independent of perceivers. Additionally, in contrast with some philosophers of aesthetics who insist on emotional detachment being a prerequisite for aesthetic experience (see, e.g., Beardsley, 1982), my own concept of the aesthetic emphasizes the intimate connection between aesthetic responses and emotions. Aesthetic responses to artifacts, situations, and equations are always accompanied by feelings, and they are frequently feelings of pleasure.

In addition to seeing the aesthetic as a judgment regarding a sense of "fit," I also see it as a "way of knowing" that is based on perception, but not necessarily *sensory* perception.[2] Within the arts (and, especially, arts education, see Eisner, 1985), the aesthetic has been conceptualized as "a way of knowing," but this conceptualization is less commonly found outside the arts. Many might find it natural that artists would need to develop and use knowledge about how sounds and colors should fit together, but what are the analogous forms of knowledge in the mathematical sciences? After all, numbers fit together in equations following logical rules, while shapes can be defined according to formal rules. In her study of the aesthetic dimension of science, Judith Wechsler (1978) provides a helpful definition of aesthetic knowing in science. She sees it as a mode of cognition that focuses on forms and metaphors used in conceptualizing and modelling (note how she cannot help but blur the artificial boundaries among the aesthetic, cognitive, and affective categories). This definition of the aesthetic has a different emphasis than the value judgment one, in which the aesthetic acts as a guideline for the appropriateness of an expression (scientific or mathematical). Instead of focusing on final product or finished artifacts, the aesthetic as a way of knowing is process-oriented. In other words, it is involved in the actual making of, in the sensing and probing for, appropriate and evocative expressions of reality. Whether the emphasis is the process or the product, though, the common, binding theme is the underlying impulse for a sense of "fit."

In addition to aesthetic judgments, values, ways of knowing, ability, and sensibility, I have also referred to aesthetic experiences, using the term *aesthetic* to denote the quality of someone's encounter with his or her environment, one that is integrating and cumulative, and that turns disparate events and moments into memorable, satisfying, coherent *experiences*. Again, the aesthetic of an experience relates to an emotionally imbued sense of fit.

Throughout this book, I will be providing many examples that illustrate the aesthetic—as I understand it—in action, thus offering a functional rather than definitive account of it. However, if pushed, my working definition of the aesthetic—when it qualifies behavior, values, objects, feelings, and experience—has to do with a pleasurable sense of fit, which speaks about context and surroundings as well as attributes of the situation in question.

This definition provides little help to those who have not experienced the aesthetic in mathematics, or to those who question the aesthetic sophistication of students learning school mathematics. While the two stories in the introduction were intended to evoke the pleasurable sense of fit I have associated with the aesthetic, I now take a more pragmatic approach to understanding the mathematical aesthetic by tracing how it reveals itself—and what consequences it has—in the course of mathematical inquiry. Rather than trace these consequences in the world of the professional mathematician, where the aesthetic publicly appears in its ultimate and approved form, I propose instead to start with the mathematical aesthetic in a more accessible, "live" event that involves both the process and products of mathematical thinking.

THE MATHEMATICAL AESTHETIC

Mathematicians use words such as *beautiful* and *elegant* quite frequently. Sometimes exclamations such as "what an elegant theorem!" seem to mean "I understand the theorem." At other times, such statements are meant to communicate to their addressees a sense of belonging to the "in-group" of mathematicians: If I can call the theorem beautiful then it means I share a discourse with other mathematicians that sets us apart from nonmathematicians (and presumably, nonmathematicians are unable to appreciate the same mathematical elegance or beauty). What do mathematicians mean by those words, *beautiful* and *elegant*? How do these words differ from one another, if at all, and how are they different from other value judgments such as "correct" or "good" or even "true"?

In seeking to answer such questions, one can take an absolutist approach and try to determine criteria that define aesthetic appeal in mathematics. Hardy did this with his list of aesthetic qualities, which included economy and unexpectedness. However, as my story in the introduction suggests, these criteria are difficult to objectify; they depend on the person applying the criteria, the situation in which that person finds herself (in a mathematics class or on a road trip), and on cultural norms and influences. This is true even in the tight, small world of research mathematicians, as Wells's (1990) survey suggests. Thus, defining criteria may not only be very difficult, but probably quite unproductive as well. A more productive approach could be to find out how research mathematicians (and others) attend to, call upon, or even rely on aesthetic sensibilities in the course of producing mathematics (including solving problems, formulating definitions and proofs, or communicating results). As it turns out, in reading the descriptions that can be found in the literature on mathematics discovery and development, it is possible to locate specific roles of the aesthetic in mathematical production (see Sinclair, 2006).

The most obvious and public of the three roles is the *evaluative*; it concerns the aesthetic worth of mathematical products such as results or proofs and, more specifically, the judgments made about which products are most significant. Mathematicians may evaluate both their own work, as they complete a proof or solution, and that of others, as they review potential journal articles or attend conference presentations. Within the evaluative role, the discourse of aesthetic judgments and responses is most common.

The *generative* role of the aesthetic pertains to aesthetic modes of reasoning used in solving problems, as opposed to logical or even intuitive ones. I have used the term *generative* because it is described by mathematicians as being responsible for generating new ideas and insights that could not be derived by logical steps alone (see, e.g., Henri Poincaré, 1908/1956).

Lastly, the *motivational* role relates to the role of the aesthetic in attracting mathematicians to certain fields and, in turn, in stimulating them to work on certain problems. While the evaluative role operates on mathematicians' finished, public work, the motivational and generative roles of the aesthetic belong to more private, evolving facets of mathematical inquiry.

These are quite general descriptions that have been inferred from the mathematical literature and my own interactions with mathematicians (through interviews and discussion), and lack some of the details and evocation that could help connect them to actual mathematical moments. In the next section, I give more specific examples of these roles and the unique kinds of aesthetic sensibilities they engage.

THE MATHEMATICAL AESTHETIC IN ACTION

Few mathematicians have attempted to provide a pragmatic account of how the aesthetic functions in the actual work of mathematicians. Does it help them solve problems? Does it affect the fields of mathematics they choose to pursue or the problems in those fields on which they choose to work? Does it play a role in their process of contributing solutions and results to the mathematical community?

One way to find out how aesthetic sensibility affects mathematical inquiry—in a real-time way—is to pay attention to one's feelings and decisions while exploring a mathematical situation, or struggling with a problem. I once asked a small group of mathematics educators to do this at a conference. At first, many were reticent, unconvinced that the aesthetic could have much to do with their attempts to solve a rather elementary number-theory problem. However, one participant returned the next day in disbelief, with this observation: "I had worked out an equation that contained an $n - 1$ term and I didn't like that -1 part at all. It wasn't nice. I just had to tidy it up." He was surprised that a mere aversion to -1 could elicit such strong emotions and, in turn, seemingly "unmathematical" decisions—there was no straight, logical reason to get rid of the -1. I wish I had asked him where his aversion came from, what he actually did next, and how his problem turned out. Perhaps he had had previous experiences working with similar problems in which a -1 term blocked the solution path; maybe his aesthetic response had no mathematical importance in the end—perhaps it was just an arbitrary, inert occurrence. It is easy enough to believe that certain things are pleasing and others revolting, but are these responses merely epiphenomena of mathematical activity? Or do they play a more central role?

Unfortunately, it is difficult for an outside observer to capture aesthetic judgments and responses in action. Even if I had been watching the participant work on his equations, I might not have been able to infer from his actions that he was reacting to the unwanted -1. I might have asked him why he was reworking his equation, but intrusive observers can sometimes ruin the flow of activity.

Fortunately, a few research mathematicians have reported on the aesthetic dimension of their own mathematical discoveries, and some have even provided introspective analyses of their experiences that reveal the various ways in which aesthetic sensibility influences their actions and choices. Since I am primarily interested in the pragmatic role of the aesthetic, that is, in the causal and consequential effects of the aesthetic in mathematical activity, I will refine the aesthetic tripartite framework proposed above by analyzing an actual experience of a mathematical inquiry. I use my own example of mathematical inquiry in order to maximize my access to the depth and breadth of experience. Eminent mathematicians make grand claims about the inextricability of mathematics and aesthetics. This chapter aims to construct a map between the lofty ideas summoned by such claims and the prosaic realities of the mathematics classroom. My goal is to provide a vivid description of the mathematical aesthetic, one that is accessible to nonmathematicians, and one that can be useful as I turn my attention to the mathematics learner. This description should also be evocative for mathematicians, professional and recreational alike. Indeed, for those readers, I hope it will generate that feeling of "novel recognition" that one can experience upon becoming aware of a tacit, perhaps subconscious understanding that has suddenly been explicitly articulated.

I recount my mathematical discovery, from start to finish, not as you might encounter it in a professional mathematics journal, but in its full messiness. Unlike the professional mathematician's terse presentation of results, I offer the detours, false starts, frustrations, surprises, and pleasures that constituted my journey and provide the necessary basis for an aesthetic analysis. The journey unfolds in three parts, each one highlighting three different ways in which the aesthetic is involved in the process of inquiry. Each section of the journey is followed by a brief reflection, in which I identify a specific role of the aesthetic and further illustrate it using the testimonies of professional mathematicians. The mathematics involved in this journey requires no more than a high school level of understanding. I would therefore strongly discourage those readers who are tempted to skip the mathematical exposition in favor of the subsequent reflections and analyses: the aesthetic dimension of mathematical activity I am trying to expose cannot be separated from the *mathematics* that gives rise to particular responses and behaviors.

Stepping in and Exploring

A colleague brought to my attention an interesting configuration that he had constructed using the dynamic geometry software The Geometer's Sketchpad (Jackiw, 1991/2001). Start with any triangle ABC (shown shaded in Figure 4.1) and construct a square on each side of the triangle; find the center of each of the three squares and join them with three line segments to create the "centers triangle" DEF. As he was describing the configuration, I immediately thought of the famous Napoleon's theorem, which begins with a similar drawing and states that the triangle formed by joining the centers of three equilateral triangles constructed on the sides of any triangle will also be equilateral. My colleague's sketch was actually a simple variation on it, which I had never thought of, even though I had explored Napoleon's theorem on my own, and even used it in workshops and classrooms.

I was intrigued by the connection I made to a well-known theorem. I was also surprised by the seemingly arbitrary shape of the "centers triangle," which did not seem related to the initial triangle, despite being constructed via the ultraconstrained square: surely the random triangle ABC should give rise to a special derivative triangle, as is the case with Napoleon's theorem? I decided to reconstruct and explore my colleague's configuration.

Well, there was not anything special about triangle DEF. But in my initial playing around, I noticed that I could drag the vertices of triangle ABC so that they traveled inside and outside of triangle DEF. Perhaps out of habit or maybe experience, the in-between case—the boundary condition—drew my attention. I began to wonder when segment DE

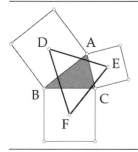

Figure 4.1. The center triangle DEF constructed from triangle ABC.

would connect with vertex A: when would A "kiss" the centers triangle? I dragged vertex A onto DE, or at least as close as the screen would allow.

The Motivational Role of the Aesthetic

Why did I choose to work on this problem? I see many Sketchpad activities, and have read many geometry textbooks, but this phenomenon seemed to invite me to explore further. I was motivated by several factors that have a strong aesthetic component. First, by making the connection to Napoleon's theorem, I established that the phenomenon had some kind of significance—it was related to a recognized area of geometry, one that I remembered Philip Davis (1997) enthusiastically describing. Second, I was surprised to realize that a configuration I had looked at and played with many times before held even more hidden treasures. And third, I enjoyed the visceral feeling of fit that I got when I pushed the vertex to the edge; and even my anthropomorphization of the event—seeing osculating triangles—shows a high level of personal involvement and commitment.

Many mathematicians, including Roger Penrose (1974) and John von Neumann (1947/1956), have noted the influential role of the aesthetic in choosing problems; this is what I call the *motivational* role of the aesthetic. In each field of mathematics, there are many open problems, and many problems waiting to be posed. How does a mathematician decide which problem to work on, which problem is worth the time, energy, and attention? While there are some mathematical problems that are more famous, and even more fashionable, it would be difficult to argue that there is an objective perspective—a mathematical reality against which the value of mathematical products can be measured. Contrast this with physics, for example, another discipline that makes strong aesthetic claims (see Farmelo, 2002; Fischer, 1999; McAllister, 1996), where questions and products can be measured up against physical reality: How well do physicists explain the shape of the universe or the behavior of light?

Mathematicians have been attracted to certain fields and certain problems as opposed to others since the dawn of mathematics. The ancient Greeks marvelled at the elegance and purity of deductive geometry, while the Chinese revelled in the balance and complementarity of magic squares and Vedic mathematicians wove transcendent theories of infinity (Joseph, 1992). Joseph shows how mathematicians' cultural contexts—their beliefs, priorities, and temperaments—have played an important role in determining their intrigues and pursuits. This implies that the presence of some kind of attraction is an essential component of mathematical activity for many mathematicians; they are not willing to work in any field, nor will they take on any problem.

However, the motivational role can act in even more subtle ways. For instance, the mathematician Wolfgang Krull (1987) describes how Ernst Kummer's work with algebraic numbers was motivated by his desire to find the kind of simplicity and regularity displayed by whole numbers, as represented by the fundamental theorem of arithmetic (which states that any whole number has a unique factorization into primes). While Kummer understood that this would be impossible in the domain of all infinite decimals, he saw an opportunity in the subdomain of "algebraic" numbers. Convinced that these algebraic numbers should have a structure just as beautiful and simple as that of ordinary whole numbers, he did not rest until he found such a structure of factorization within them. He ultimately succeeded in doing so by introducing what he called "ideal" numbers, thereby achieving his motivational aesthetic ideal.

In my own investigation, I seem to have been drawn by the *connectedness* and *fruitfulness* of the problem: I could see how it was related to other relationships I had explored and I could sense that the problem had "promise." Indeed, the mathematician Jacques Hadamard (1945) claims that one of the most important motivational aesthetic criteria is that of potential, the fruitfulness of a future result: "without knowing any further, we *feel* that such a direction of investigation is worth following; we feel that the question in *itself* deserves interest" (p. 127). Penrose, however, writes about being drawn to problems that have a *visual appeal*, such as those found in irregular tilings—which, interestingly, verge on the antisymmetric. Visual appeal seems to be a criterion that is increasingly available to mathematicians; the computer-generated images that are now being produced have bewitched many—as David Mumford and his colleagues (2002) acknowledged in their recent and colorful book *Indra's Pearls*. Another frequent source of attraction is *apparent simplicity*. The mathematician Andrew Gleason (in Albers et al., 1990) exemplifies this criteria well: "I am gripped by explicit, easily stated things . . . I'm very fond of problems in which somehow an at least very simple sounding hypothesis is sufficient to really pinch something together and make something out of it" (p. 93). As it did for me, a sense of *surprise* can also aesthetically motivate a mathematician. Surprise constantly arises in mathematics as mathematicians find things they have no reason to expect: a pattern emerging in a sequence of numbers; a point of coincidence found in a group of lines; a large change resulting from a small variation.

These criteria—connectedness, fruitfulness, visual appeal, apparent simplicity, and surprise—are not objective features of the mathematics in question. Mathematicians with different areas of expertise and different past experiences will gauge the fruitfulness of a mathematical situation in specific ways. Moreover, as Wells (1990) shows, something that may have been surprising to a mathematician 100 years ago—such as Euler's formula $e^{i\pi} + 1 = 0$—might no longer surprise the mathematician of today, and therefore no longer attract her attention.

Working with the Problem

I measured the angle of vertex A. At an accuracy of three significant digits, Sketchpad told me that angle A measured 91.031°. Though it was an "ugly" number because of those decimals, I was certain that the angle, if I could get A to lie more precisely *on* DE, would measure exactly 90°.

I needed to check out this hypothesis that, after all, was based on no "logical" evidence. First, I had to figure out how to force A to fall exactly on DE. However, every time I tried to drag A onto DE, everything would move. The vertex and the segment were chasing each other around! Then I decided that if I could *fix* the angle A at 90°, in other words, construct it as such, I could perhaps see whether A would then be kissing DE. But how would I fix A? Fortunately, I could use Thales's theorem: construct a circle (shown in Figure 4.2) using BC as the diameter, then, each point on the circle must form a 90° angle with B and C. So, by putting A *on* the circle, I could force its angle measure to *exactly* 90°.

Then came a moment of truth: Once I moved the vertex A onto the circle, it was indeed kissing DE. Moreover, even when I moved A around the circle, my triangles kept kissing: that was compelling enough visually that I did not even bother to verify whether vertex A was in fact exactly on segment DE or whether it just looked so on the sketch. But had I just found a particular relationship or was there something bigger happening?

I decided to try a slight variation of my kissing triangles. I constructed the Napoleon theorem-like configuration; it has equilateral triangles on each side of the shaded triangle (instead of squares), as shown in Figure 4.3. Perhaps when I looked at a similar situation, some kind of pattern would emerge.

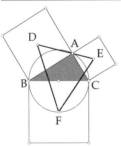

Figure 4.2. A kissing triangle. Vertex A lies both on segment DE and on the circle.

$m \angle BAC = 90.00°$

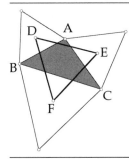

Figure 4.3. Napoleon's theorem configuration—equilateral triangles on a general triangle.

Having constructed the equilateral-triangles configuration, I could not wait to see to measure the kissing angle. Once again, Sketchpad gave me an "ugly" angle when I tried to drag vertex A onto segment DE, but it was pretty close to 120° and I felt a little rush of hope. As before, I wanted to verify my conjecture by *constructing* A to measure exactly 120°. I realized that this time Thales's theorem could not help. So I needed to figure out how to construct an arc of a circle that would allow me to look at *all* triangles with $\angle CAB = 120°$.

As I pondered this problem, I continued in pattern-detection mode and constructed another variation that I hoped would verify my emerging relationship between the outer polygon and the kissing angle measurement. (So far I had found that equilateral triangles have a kissing angle of 120° and that squares have a kissing angle of 90°.) This time I constructed a regular hexagon on triangle ABC (see Figure 4.4). Since I knew that Sketchpad would quickly give me the kissing angle, I did not waste any of my brain power—committed at the time to my two problems—on trying to guess, though I knew the number would be smaller than 90°. I soon discovered that the kissing angle for the hexagon was 60°. So the rest seemed obvious; the kissing angle is just 360° divided by the number of sides of the regular polygon, or $360°/n$. So, that meant that for a pentagon, my kissing angle would be $360°/5 = 72°$.

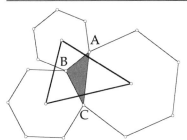

Figure 4.4. The regular hexagon case.

While I was attending to the 60° angle in the regular hexagon case, I realized I could solve my technical problem. I needed an arc through BC such that any point on that arc would subtend the chord BC with a constant angle (specifically, a 120° angle). Therefore, I needed the family of triangles BX'C constructed on BC for which the angle at X' was 120°. Obviously, this arc would be part of a circle that was somehow related to BC. I decided to go for a more "mechanical" solution: I could construct the *locus* of points X'—which would form an arc—such that angle BX'C measured 120° (see Figure 4.5). This required that the angles at B and C add up to 60°. I could use a Sketchpad parameter! By moving the geometric parameter X along the 60° arc FE, X' moved along an arc describing all the possible triangles such that ∠BX'C measured 120°. With Sketchpad's locus command, I constructed the arc BX'C.

This was not a typical Euclidean geometric method, but I did not really mind—my aesthetic sensibility did not require the kind of purity that has led some mathematicians (especially historically) to insist on using only methods appropriate to the domain of the given problem (e.g., only analytic methods, and not geometric methods, should be used to solve analytic problems). One could also argue that my aesthetic sensibility was pragmatic: My method gave me the arc I wanted. Moreover, I knew that my method would work for any angle, not just 120°. The culmination of this construction was to animate point A along the arc BX'C and to watch how point A maintained its kissing position.

The Generative Role of the Aesthetic

I have identified some of the reasons for my initial attraction to this problem, but a different set of aesthetic factors came into play as I began to explore. These factors played a *generative* role during my process of inquiry. Consider, for example, my desire for exactness. Seeing the "ugly" initial angle measurement, which was so close to a whole number in the convenient degree metric that anoints right angles with integer measures,

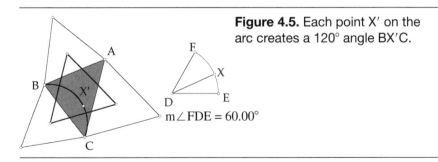

Figure 4.5. Each point X' on the arc creates a 120° angle BX'C.

m∠FDE = 60.00°

I was prompted to try to "right" it. And I wanted to accomplish that, because I would then have sure evidence of some lurking relationship—the meta-aesthetic principle has it that things do not turn out "nicely" without reason in mathematics! The aesthetic choice, one of "neatness," was to see this number as 90° and to pursue the implications. This action at once suggested and confirmed my belief that a discernible relationship existed and provided shape to the conjectures I would make as to the nature of this relationship. Had I not made this turn to neatness, I might have dismissed the kissing state as uninteresting or concluded that the angle measurement would not be involved in determining a relationship; I might even have abandoned my pursuit had the angle 93.031° turned up.

The polymath Douglas Hofstadter (1992/1997) provides a similar example of the generative role of the aesthetic in action when he shows how his attraction to analogy changed the way he perceived a geometric configuration. According to Poincaré, who was among the first mathematicians to write about this generative role of the aesthetic, mathematicians tend to focus on the ideas and relationships that are best able to "charm this special sensibility that all mathematicians know" (p. 2048). Since Poincaré does not provide any illustrative examples, some may find his claim a little mysterious and perhaps even suspicious. But an interest in analogy, a tendency to value whole numbers, or, in the case of the mathematician Doris Schattschneider (2006), a penchant for symmetry, can all be thought of as "special sensibilities" that guide certain choices and decisions during inquiry.

The aesthetic can also play a generative role in coming to a sense of conviction about mathematical ideas. I experienced a strong, visual sense of "fit" when I was able to construct the circle and "lock" it into the kissing position. By moving point A around the circle, I could set the relationships in motion and *see* that for any right-angled triangle, the kiss would persist. My conviction grew with the visceral sense of "fit"; I had not yet proved anything, nor understood exactly how the relationships I thought I saw worked, but I could *feel* that things were right and that I was onto something worth pursuing. Finally, after having looked at the hexagon case, the possibility of a framing structure was emerging, from the specific case of the square to the general case of regular polygons and possibly circles. This possibility of structure, in turn, contributed to a deeper prescient sense of fit. I was anticipating that certain relationships would emerge in a whole family of shapes. As with reading a novel, I wanted to find out what would happen next, what theme would emerge from the sequence of ideas.

I would like to highlight two other important dimensions of my discovery process, both related to the generative role that the aesthetic seems to play. The first involves my developing relationship with the mathematical entities with which I worked. Instead of seeing the objects in my configuration as isolated, abstract things, I saw them as animated by their relationships, particularly the kissing one. According to mathematician Keith Devlin (2000), mathematicians tend to see things like numbers, equations, and shapes as characters in the mathematical soap opera. That is, mathematicians seem to develop a personal, intimate relationship with the objects with which they work, as can be evidenced by the way they anthropomorphize them, or coin special names for them in an attempt to hold, to own them. For example, Hofstadter (1992) baptises his emerging object "my magic triangle" then "my hemiolic crystal." The mathematician Paul Lévy (1970) becomes possessive about the objects; he insists on referring to the focus of his investigations as "*ma courbe*," even though it is generally known as the von Koch curve. Naming these objects makes them easier to refer to and may even foreshadow its properties. Equally as important, though, it gives the mathematician some traction on the still vague territory, some way of marking what she *does* understand. The mathematician Norbert Wiener (1956) did not underestimate these attempts to operate with vague ideas; he recognizes the mathematician's power

> to operate with temporary emotional symbols and to organise out of them a semi-permanent, recallable language. If one is not able to do this, one is likely to find that his ideas evaporate from the sheer difficulty of preserving them in an as of yet unformulated shape. (p. 86)

The philosopher Verena Huber-Dyson (1998) also evokes this unformulated, tacit knowledge, making more explicit its aesthetic dimension, and the way in which it functions generatively:

> All the while you are aware of a pattern, just below the threshold of consciousness, exactly as a driver is aware of the traffic laws and of the co-ordinated efforts of his body and his jeep. That is how you find your way through the maze of mathematical possibilities to the "interesting" cases. (p. 2)

The second dimension involves my use of Sketchpad as a working tool. I cannot separate my mathematical interest from my enjoyment of working with Sketchpad. Through visual and kinaesthetic manipulation, I find that Sketchpad provides me with a body-syntonic way of creating and discerning patterns. In addition, by offering an approximation-friendly way of working (allowing me to drag things "close to" without having to construct them explicitly to be so), I can frequently find initial entry points that my mathematical imagination alone might not find. Similarly, its dynamic nature often provided striking effects that my mental screen would not have been able to simulate. Mathematicians also have tools with which they can create new mathematical objects or transform existing ones. In interviews, the mathematician Adrian Lewis has described to me the use of certain tools as part of the aesthetic dimension of enjoying his "craft," of using "well-worn tools in often routine ways, like a well-oiled piece of engineering" (in Sinclair, 2006, p. 112). What he finds beautiful is "not just the startling revelation or the philosophical wonder" of a work of mathematics, but the *craft* of it, "the inexorable sequence of simple tools at work." Though less dramatic than a startling revelation, there is something comforting in the knowledge that the careful application of a tool will produce a "perfect, fine-tuned result."

Schattschneider (2006) provides additional insight into this notion of craft when she describes the "paradigms" that mathematicians use in the course of solving problems and proving theorems. For example, a symmetry argument is used as a way to transform an unknown complex situation into a more familiar, simpler one. It may also provide insight into the structure of the unknown situation. Schattschneider views these paradigms as beautiful because of their powerful ability to simplify, or to cut across both complexity and surface differences, or to reformulate the situation in more familiar terms. Also, these paradigms may still carry vestiges of the aesthetic impact they had when the mathematician first encountered them in a proof or solution. The mathematician's appreciation for a certain tool may thus guide the way she works with or manipulates mathematical relationships.

Wrapping Up and Looking for More

I felt a certain amount of satisfaction at having resolved my technical problem, so I returned with renewed confidence to my first problem: Why should this relationship between the kissing angle and the outer polygon hold? It was time to pull out a notepad. I needed the static configuration to study what was happening and to jot things down. I also wanted to return to the square case, which seemed to me somewhat easier to work with.

Once I drew the configuration on my notepad, I noticed several new properties (see Figure 4.6). The first was that when vertex A was on segment DE, the shaded triangle seemed to be congruent to triangle NAM. In fact, if I could prove that congruence, then it would follow that the kissing angle at A had to be 90°. After several false starts—mainly looking for similar triangles—I noticed the quadrilateral CMNB and the fact that segment DE seemed to bisect both MC and NB. In fact, this was obvious (E is the midpoint of diagonal MC, since it is the intersection of the diagonals of the square on AC and similarly, D is the midpoint of diagonal NB). Therefore, CEDB is congruent to MEDN (since EM = EC; ND = DB; DE = DE, and

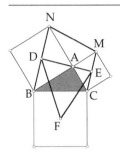

Figure 4.6. Toward a proof of the kissing angle theorem.

∠NDA = ∠BDA = ∠MEA = ∠CEA = 90°). So MN is equal in length to CB. And thus, by the SSS rule, ΔNAM is congruent to ΔACB, and so ∠NAM = ∠CAB. Since ∠MAN + ∠CAB = 180° (because ∠MAC = ∠NAB = 90°), then 2∠CAB = 180° and ∠CAB = 90°. My proof was complete!

It was complete, but still particular to the squares case. I liked the sequence of relationships that led to the final step of the proof. My proof also highlighted properties of the configuration that I had not attended to in my explorations to that point, which in turn revealed to me how the outer polygon and its center point interacted with the triangle ABC and its kissing vertex. And I had a vague idea that I could explain the other configurations in a similar way. Yet it still felt like I was missing something simple. And I had certainly only proved one case of the kissing angle theorem.

Another colleague, a little while later, helpfully pointed out the way in which AD acted as a line of symmetry in the square case. Since D was the center of the square, I thought the center of any other polygon would also create a line of symmetry with the kissing vertex. I returned to the hexagon case—I thought it would be less misleading than the square and might provide me with a fresher outlook—and examined this hypothesis.

Assuming that point A lies on segment DE, and that D is the center of the regular polygon on AB, then by definition, AD is a line of symmetry for that polygon. However, AE is also a line of symmetry for the polygon on AC (see Figure 4.7). And then I saw the hexagon BDNMEC, which had always been there, even in the square and triangle cases. (No matter what kind of polygon is used, there will always be a hexagon the vertices of which include the two nonkissing vertices of the original triangle, the two endpoints of the kissing segment on the "centers" triangle, and the two vertices of the polygon closest the kissing point.) So, the segment DAE acts as a line of symmetry through the hexagon BDNMEC. The rest was easy: ∠ABC = 180° − (∠ABD + ∠CBE) = 180° − 2∠ABD = 180° − [180°(n − 2)/n] = 360°/n.

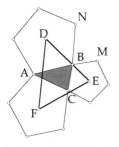

Figure 4.7. Alternate proof of the kissing triangles theorem.

Now I had really nailed the proof. Not only would it work for any polygon, but the proof also involved a powerful tool in mathematics: a symmetry argument. Moreover, it seemed shorter than my previous proof, even though it was more general. And again, I got to discover a whole new shape—the hidden hexagon—that I had not seen before.

The Evaluative Role of the Aesthetic

During this phase, I felt that I was gaining some insight into the connections; I enjoyed the emerging intelligibility of the relationships I had conjectured, and was becoming convinced they were true. The proof brought into focal awareness new relationships—I had not previously noticed the triangle NAM, or the quadrilateral CMNB—and helped me to identify the central properties of the kissing triangles. It was the center of the polygon that mattered, not the number of sides it had. The center, at least for the square case, held the key to the similarity argument in the proof. I was seeing previously disparate ideas fit together and catching a glimpse of how my particular result for the squares could belong to a more general context. I was experiencing that aesthetic moment of fit. Here I am referring to the experiential aspect of the aesthetic rather than the perceptual aspects that invited and directed my attention. As the mathematics educator John Mason (1992) writes, at the end of a similar mathematical experience, it was "like coming out on a panoramic view, producing a lightening of the spirits" (p. 15).

However, I had a nagging feeling that I had not found a very elegant proof, evidence of a powerful *evaluative* aesthetic manifesting itself. Perhaps I did not like the fact that I had to use the derivative quadrilateral CMNB in my proof. Perhaps I wanted to see more clearly how the special-case proof could extend to the general case. Perhaps the proof was simply not obvious enough. This kind of aesthetic unease often motivates mathematicians to search for better proofs (see, e.g., Davis, 1997). For example, Carl Friedrich Gauss once proved the same theorem seven times, not because any of the proofs were wrong, or misleading, but because he wanted a better—more aesthetically pleasing—way of making his argument. Even theorems or results that have been proven true for millennia can tempt mathematicians to find better, or perhaps just different, proofs, as with Tom Apostol's (2000) most recent, almost wordless proof of the irrationality of $\sqrt{2}$. As Wolfgang Krull (1987) writes: "Mathematicians are not concerned merely with finding and proving theorems; they also want to arrange and assemble the theorems so that they appear not only correct but evident and compelling" (p. 49).

Thanks to the hint my colleague gave me, the second proof proceeded along smoothly. I did not experience the excitement and pride I might have, had I figured it out all on my own, but I was able to appreciate the improvement it made over my first proof. It was shorter, more general, and somewhat clever in its use of the hidden hexagon. But it was the symmetry argument that really pleased me; that invisible line of symmetry nicely brought the whole diagram together, giving it an invariant structure it had been lacking, making up for the odd, unpredictable behavior of the center triangle. Different mathematicians may privilege some aesthetic criteria over others. While the symmetry argument really pleased me, Davis (1997), who worked on the Napoleon theorem, thinks that the most pleasing proofs are ones that are transparent; he writes:

> I wanted to append to the figure a few lines, so ingeniously placed that the whole matter would be exposed to the naked eye. I wanted to be able to say not *quod erat demonstrandum*, as did the ancient Greek mathematicians, but simply, "Lo and behold! The matter is as plain as the nose on your face."
> (p. 17)

THE AESTHETICS OF DETACHMENT

At this point, I want to take a brief detour to discuss the notion of aesthetic detachment, which has been very important in the discipline of aesthetics. Although there are several other historically important notions in aesthetics, this one deserves attention here because of its relevance to learners of school mathematics. Many aesthetic reactions came up during my journey, but I never felt the sense of emotional detachment that aestheticians, and even some mathematicians, describe as being primary in aesthetic appreciation. On the contrary!

In art criticism circles, some scholars hold that the aesthetic of detachment emerges from the subtle interplay between the real and the fictional, the authentic and the artificial. It is seen to account for, at least in part, the aesthetic experiences derived from the ugly, the violent, and the tragic (Dewey, 1934). The philosopher Monroe Beardsley (1982) also suggests that an aesthetic experience characterized by "detached affect" necessarily has its subject matter stripped of instrumental values.[3] Certainly, there is the sense in which my mathematical pursuits had no instrumental value: I was not calculating the speed of a plane or the rate of compound interest. I was fixed on things purely mathematical: triangles, angles, and polygons and the relationships between them. But I cannot say that this was a factor in my experience.

Dewey (1934) provides another perspective on the "detached affect" phenomenon in his discussion of aesthetic response to the purportedly ugly and tragic. He proposes that when a particular subject matter is removed from its practical context, the subject matter enters "into a new whole as an integral part of it" (p. 96), so that the former ugliness is contrasted with a new quality. It thus acquires a new expression on account of its new relationships. It may not be the removal itself, of emotions or subject matter, that is important, but the removal of something from its usual setting so that it becomes part of another expressive whole.

This process of *extraction* better captures my experience with the kissing triangles, and even my childhood experience with my mother's conversion trick. Those inert mathematical objects of triangles, angles, and polygons were removed from their initial setting—as disjoint, separate elements in a construction recipe—and configured into a new one which bound them together as a unit, and in my so doing, I bound myself to that unit. What is the usual setting of triangles, angles, and polygons? From my point of view, triangles are set by typical categorizations (equilateral, isosceles, and scalene) or properties (measurement formulas, special centers and lines), or relationships (congruence, similarity). The new setting bound triangles with other polygons, with inside- and outsideness, with a derived triangle, and with kissing. These features of the new setting suggest the way in which I became part of this expressive whole; I became aware of myself as observer in the investigation. In Part III, I argue that the process of extraction might be crucial for the aesthetic engagement of students who often find mathematics cold, abstract, and alienating.

CHAPTER 5

Aesthetics and the Development of Mathematics

Mathematicians talk about two stages in the mathematical process: discovery and justification. The discovery stage involves the acts of investigation and inference that convince the mathematician that something is true, while the justification stage involves the careful construction of deductive arguments that establish the truth according to the norms of the community. These two stages ignore a necessary, preliminary stage in which the mathematician selects an area of inquiry and formulates relevant premises—one where the motivational role of the aesthetic operates. Before moving on to my primary goal in this chapter—exploring the importance of the aesthetic in mathematical inquiry—I will quickly distil the important aesthetic aspects of the kissing triangles investigation described in the previous chapter.

DEBRIEFING THE KISSING TRIANGLES

My kissing triangles exploration could not have begun had I not been attracted to both the surprise and the familiarity of the geometric configuration. These aesthetic reactions motivated my work, inviting me to select a particular area of inquiry; they played a *motivational* role. As I explored—no *problem* immediately suggesting itself—these aesthetic reactions did not instantly fade away. They affected the direction of my exploration by emphasizing anomalies or facts that called for explanatory hypotheses. The Napoleon's theorem connection drew my attention to the two interacting triangles, and from there I noticed the boundary condition and posed the question about the kissing angle. My aesthetic reactions provided an initial traction, a way in, a point of access.

When doing mathematics, one consciously chooses to ignore certain mathematically trivial features of a situation, such as color perhaps, but those choices are not exhaustive—they just produce a smaller infinity of features. I could have noticed the size of the squares, and headed off into Pythagorean theorem-inspired investigations. Alternately, I could have noticed when the squares did or did not overlap. The rules of noticing cannot be entirely logical—interests, preferences, and experience insinuate themselves into what is perceived. Had I not felt surprise or familiarity, I would probably not have embarked on the exploration. However, had I been forced to investigate the situation, what would have happened? Maybe nothing. Without noticing, I do not recognize my choices, and without choices, I cannot act. So perhaps I am given a problem to solve: When do the triangles touch? And now I can get started; I have a premise to investigate and a hypothesis to make. This is the point at which the aesthetic can play a *generative* role.

After I decided to investigate the kissing triangles, I dragged the configuration to the kissing point and measured the kissing angle, which had a value of $91.031°$. Here I made an aesthetic choice, one of "neatness": I decided to "read" this number as being $90°$ and to pursue the implications. What was aesthetic about this small yet pivotal choice? It was the perception of the possibility of a nicely behaved relationship existing behind this unusual yet familiar configuration. I pursued this relationship precisely because I believed it would be interesting, more interesting than had the angle $93.407°$ turned up. The philosopher of science Michael Polanyi (1958) sees such aesthetic choices as being governed by the sense of beauty that forms the scientist's "intellectual passion." He argues that the sense of beauty has both the *motivational* function of distinguishing what is scientifically interesting from that which is not, as well as the *generative* function of guiding the scientist toward discovery. I have discussed the motivational role above, and it seems to me that my turn toward "neatness" played a heuristic, generative role in guiding me toward a possible relationship. At the beginning of Part I, I hinted at another instance of the generative role of the aesthetic: the aversion to -1 that prompted my colleague to rework his initial equation.

The generative role of the aesthetic unquestionably belongs to the discovery stage of the mathematical process. During the stage of justification, however, the aesthetic seems to play yet a different role, an *evaluative* one. When I saw the CMEB quadrilateral and the congruent triangles, I knew I had the makings of a proof. I still had to "write it up," though. I had to provide a logically flowing sequence of steps. In a way, I did not have many possibilities regarding order and word choice, but I did find myself striving to find an ever more succinct final statement. While the attention to order is logical, the desire for succinctness is aesthetic. It does not increase the truth of the proof. But it pleases me, for some reason, to be able to say it in fewer words. I place more value on the succinct form: I will remember it, I will take pride in it, and I will talk about it with (some of) my friends.

The second version of my proof brought both a similar and a different kind of aesthetic satisfaction. I was pleased at having constructed a proof that was both more general and shorter than the previous one—thus, a similar striving for succinctness. But I was also very pleased with the symmetry argument I used. The poet often strives for succinctness, but also for some organizing structure—often through rhyme or rhythm—and the symmetry argument gave my proof that kind of structure. Here again, the aesthetic has an evaluative function.

I have identified three roles—namely, motivational, generative, and evaluative—that the aesthetic plays in mathematical inquiry, and I have even shown how each role was pivotal in determining my own choices and actions. But does the aesthetic always and necessarily play such a determining role in mathematical inquiry?

THE IMPORTANCE OF THE MATHEMATICAL AESTHETIC

To reiterate from the above section: Are the roles of the aesthetic I have identified in any way central or necessary to the development of mathematical knowledge? A weaker version of this question is: Are they frequently important? Then, turning to educational concerns, do students show aesthetic sensibility that plays similar roles to those I have described above? And if so, are these roles pedagogically desirable? One could argue that if the first question is answered positively, a positive answer to the second question follows, as has been the case in similar debates: One argument for increasing problem solving in school mathematics is that problem solving is central to mathematics. I prefer to investigate the second question about students' aesthetic sensibility independently though; there certainly are some practices of mathematical activity that are central to published research mathematics, which educators would not want to encourage in the classroom—such as systematically erasing all traces of one's work when presenting results.

The Necessity of the Motivational and Evaluative Roles

I think the answer to the question of whether the aesthetic is necessary in mathematics depends on the meaning of the phrase "the development of mathematical knowledge." I have already suggested that aesthetic decisions cannot be avoided in the first stage of mathematical inquiry, which involves the selection or formulation of a problem. Unless forced to, a mathematician does not work on an arbitrary problem that has neither personal appeal nor external endorsement. John Nash frequently needed other mathematicians to "assign" him a problem, not being able to decide alone. Though his own personal aesthetic played a minimal role, if at all, the mathematical community's aesthetic was necessary; they also had to decide on the importance or significance of the problem he would propose.

The philosopher of mathematics Thomas Tymoczko (1993) points out that there exists no mathematical reality against which results, problems, or fields can be judged—as might be the case in other sciences such as physics; mathematicians have to decide how important the Riemann hypothesis is, or how important the field of "semidefinite programming" is. They cannot decide on logical grounds alone. One hypothesis may outdo another if it involves many other problems or fields, as is the case with the Riemann hypothesis—this reveals an aesthetic preference for connection over isolation. Some fields may lend themselves more to overall organization, as is the case with geometry—this reveals an aesthetic preference for ordered structures over unordered collections. The complex web of significance, elegance, and importance is almost impossible to disentangle.

However, since mathematical fields frequently change, and gain or lose importance, this web is not static; it depends on the aesthetic decisions of mathematicians participating in the community. A strong-minded mathematician may decide to pursue a problem that appeals to her alone. Depending on what she finds, and on how well she relates her findings to the community, others may come to appreciate its qualities. Therefore, in addition to playing a role in the context of discovery or selection, the aesthetic also necessarily plays a role in the context of justification. Mathematicians must find ways to convince each other that a certain result is interesting. They may appeal to its number of connections or to the order it brings to a hitherto variegated field; but they may also appeal to its brevity or to its use of a surprising method. The mathematics educator Robert Davis (1987a) wrote about "mathematics as a performing art" and although he was describing the performances of students, his phrase captures well this component of the evaluative role of the aesthetic: mathematicians will often "perform" their results or findings, and some mathematicians are better at it than others! (see Sinclair, 2006).

The Necessity of the Generative Role

I have argued that the mathematics community needs to appeal to the aesthetic to make decisions about significance, much as a country needs laws to make decisions about what is right and wrong. But what about individual citizens? And what about everyday problems that do not involve "nationwide" concerns? Let me make an analogy between moral and aesthetic decisions. Clearly, deciding whether to take the highway to work or the city streets requires little moral involvement. Similarly, calculating a derivative involves little aesthetic involvement. In each case, there is no real problem, and probably little investment in the outcome. However, deciding how to deal with parents who can no longer take care of themselves requires significant moral involvement. This is a real problem the outcome of which has personal importance. It requires moral imagination—exploring the possibilities, playing each possibility out, assessing the relative merit of each—and cannot be solved by any number of logical steps.

I could make the parallel statement about my kissing triangles: They presented me with a real problem the outcome of which mattered to me. Were aesthetic decisions necessary? I am now talking about the context of discovery, one that comes closer to the individual thinker, and thus to the student learner, than the context of justification. This is a more difficult question. While my introspective analysis revealed several instances of aesthetic behavior, how can I decide whether any of them were in any way necessary?

Several scholars have argued that solving a real problem requires some kind of extralogical act, be it intuitive or aesthetic. For example, Polanyi (1958) insists that "a real problem cannot be solved by sequential, logical steps"; a real problem requires an imaginative leap, one that can locate a potential landing spot. The literature is full of anecdotes about those elusive "aha!" moments in which the scientist has an out-of-the blue insight that catapults her to that landing spot. Poincaré (1908/1956) strongly believes that his insights are generated by an aesthetic sensibility, though one that operates primarily at the subconscious level. However, the out-of-the-blue nature of such insights, the way in which they emerge fully formed, makes it difficult—as much for the outside observer as for the mathematician—to tell what role the aesthetic plays in giving rise to them.

However, in thinking back to my kissing triangles, the aesthetic decisions I made during the discovery process were not so much about the culminating insight—there were several signposts along the way, not just one leap to a landing spot. In fact, I think the signpost metaphor works well to describe the way in which the aesthetic guided my travels through the terrain. Does the mathematical terrain need such guides? Are logical guides not enough? I believe this is where the generative role of the aesthetic needs to be considered.

In a certain sense, I solved my kissing triangles problem when I first measured the angle of vertex A. My solution was 91.031°, or perhaps *about* 91.031°. But I did not stop. I wanted to know what *exactly* the measure would be—a desire that moves me from the physical constraints of pixels to the ideal world of mathematical points and lines. Not only that, I wanted to see whether there was any regularity, an analogical relationship between polygons—would the kissing angle of the square be related to the kissing angle of the pentagon? Both these impulses are aesthetic in nature; in fact, they reveal the generative role of the aesthetic in mathematical inquiry. I see these impulses as providing the order hypotheses that Gombrich (1979) saw arising in the human "sense of order," which I described in Part I. According to Gombrich, such hypotheses make learning possible, and mathematical discovery must surely be driven by the kind of learning that ensues from an initial impression, or qualitative understanding, that can be probed and tested.

If this "sense of order" insinuates itself into every human learning endeavor, is there anything special about its role in doing or learning mathematics? At first blush, it seems plausible to say that the quest for exactness is quintessentially mathematical, as might be the quest for foundations, for finding the basic, underlying order. If this is true—and there may be other specifically mathematical aesthetic orientations—then perhaps mathematicians have developed a highly sensitive sense of exact, basic order. Certainly this is consistent with some of the earliest accounts of geometry done by ancient Greeks such as Euclid.

However, my goal is not to define the mathematician's "sense of order" exhaustively; I mainly want to outline what it might look like and what it might do. The mathematics educators Silver and Metzger (1989) recount an episode that might help fill out this picture. They observe a professional mathematician working on a number-theory problem—prove that there are no prime numbers in the infinite sequence 10001, 100010001, 1000100010001 . . . —and describe his actions in detail. At a certain point during his work, the mathematician hits upon a certain prime factorization, namely 137×73, which he describes as "wonderful with those patterns" (p. 67). He starts working with that particular factorization, using the pattern as a basis for further exploration. Silver and Metzger propose that the mathematician was responding to the near-symmetry in the numbers, which might have seemed promising, potentially generative.

In fact, it turned out to be unhelpful in solving the problem, but the episode provides another illustration of Gombrich's "sense of order"; the perceived symmetry yield a first guess that made a conjecture possible. The mathematician's verbal response to the perceived symmetry shows that his decision to follow his aesthetic impulse was at least partly conscious and most definitely emotional—he is pleased to see the pattern. (I mention this because emotional responses frequently make it possible for an outside observer to detect an aesthetic response, something on which I rely in Part III.)

Hofstadter's (1992) own introspective analysis of a mathematical discovery provides yet another illustrative example of the "sense of order." While studying a geometric configuration, Hofstadter recognizes that one object in a first configuration is related to an object of a second configuration; from there he hypothesizes that a second object in the first configuration will have some similar relationship to some second object in the second configuration. He hypothesizes order based on a potential analogy; he imposes the analogy on the situation in order to make some sense of it. He explains that his "inner compass" tells him that such an analogy will be fruitful. But Hofstadter also finds analogies beautiful in the way they can reveal deep similarities between otherwise disparate objects; finding an analogy in mathematics is thus part of the aesthetic impulse that guides his work. Had Hofstadter ignored his aesthetic impulse, he might have failed to conjecture a relationship at all. He might still have solved the problem, of course, but using analogy is part of the appeal for him. He takes pleasure both in his ability to recognize analogies and in his appreciation of the power or effectiveness of analogy in his own mathematical meaning-making.

One of the reasons Hofstadter does mathematics—or listens to music—is to satisfy his aesthetic impulse for analogy. The aesthetic is thus an animating purpose of his mathematical activity; it allows him to see the world as he likes to see it, and to experience the pleasure that perceiving analogical relationships affords him. This is a slight reversal of the "sense of order" principle: Mathematics now becomes a vehicle for satisfying aesthetic needs, for finding or creating a sense of order in one's environment.

I have been trying to determine the importance of the aesthetic in the actual discovery process. On the one hand, Gombrich's notion of the sense of order suggests a fundamental cognitive aspect of the aesthetic; it would thus seem to be a necessary searchlight in the mathematical terrain when real inquiry is required. On the other hand, Hofstadter's example points to the more psychological, motivational aspect of the aesthetic in mathematics, one that may vary in importance for different mathematicians.

FITTING THE PIECES TOGETHER

Now I can return to the second question stated in the previous section: Do students show aesthetic behavior that fulfils similar functions to the ones I have described above? And, if so, are these functions pedagogically desirable? These questions will soon be tackled, but let me first sketch out what the motivational, generative, and evaluative functions of the aesthetic might have to do with school mathematics.

In terms of the initial stage of the mathematical process where the motivational function of the aesthetic operates, students rarely choose their own problems and so rarely have a chance, or encounter the need, to make fruitful aesthetic choices, except perhaps in classrooms where problem posing is actively pursued. In terms of the final stage, where the evaluative function of the aesthetic operates, students are rarely forced to justify the significance or interest of their solutions, except in classrooms where the development of these particular normative practices is actively supported.

As it turns out, however, posing problems and judging the significance of results are both ways of "acting like a mathematician," which many researchers see as a central goal of mathematics education. And I have shown that "acting like a mathematician" involves making judgments about the significance and interest of various mathematical phenomena, ideas, and results. Therefore, the motivational and evaluative functions of the aesthetic are quite relevant to school mathematics.

The generative role carries more tentative implications. In terms of its cognitive aspect, students might have more success in problem solving—and here I refer to truly problematic problems—if they could engage their "sense of order." And perhaps this "sense of order" is something that must be explicitly evoked, developed, and nurtured. The psychological aspect of the generative role raises the question of whether students might also become aware of, or further pursue, opportunities to satisfy their aesthetic sensibility in the course of mathematical inquiry (as they may do in the course of painting, writing a poem, or other similar artistic activity). However frivolous or unlikely the question now seems, I would say that the current minimal levels of student interest in mathematics are alarming enough to warrant further consideration of the relevance of the generative function of the aesthetic to school mathematics.

It is difficult to make sense of the above implications, inferences, and even imperatives without knowing much about the kinds of aesthetic behavior students display in their school mathematical activities.[1] Thus far, mathematics education researchers have tended to focus on the cognitive and, more recently, on the affective dimensions of student mathematical learning, choosing to ignore the aesthetic dimension. It would certainly stand to reason that professional mathematicians develop and refine their aesthetic preferences and responses as they are acculturated into the community. Does that mean that young students have no aesthetic preferences and tastes in the mathematical classroom? Or do they have some, which are somehow as unsophisticated—at least compared with those of mathematicians—as are their mathematical abilities? Or do they possess very similar aesthetic preferences and responses, which they have simply not learned to use in mathematics settings? These are the questions I will address in Part III.

PART III

Focusing the Aesthetic Lens on Students

Could the mathematical aesthetic play some of the same roles in the activities and investigations of student learners as they do in the work of mathematicians? Part I has proposed the idea that students can indeed deploy their aesthetic sensibilities in a wide variety of situations if, presumably, they are not restrained from doing so. Part II outlined and exemplified the ways in which the aesthetic insinuates itself in mathematical thinking and, in particular, in motivating inquiry, in providing generative guidance during inquiry, and in evaluating the worth of mathematical entities such as solutions, proofs, and problems.

In Part III, the goal is first to consider the mathematical activity of students and examine whether these three roles of the aesthetic pertain when they are placed in situations that support aesthetic engagement. Then, it will be possible to explore how the aesthetic lens can provide insights into previously obscured or ignored aspects of mathematical learning. Chapter 6 focuses on the motivational role of the aesthetic, examining several examples of student work. Chapter 7 looks at the generative role of the aesthetic, again examining several cases of student work, and Chapter 8 focuses on the evaluative role.

CHAPTER 6

The Motivational Role
of the Aesthetic

In the next three chapters, I want to probe the mathematics activities of students with the help of the aesthetic lens I have formulated. This probing will involve a web of questions and concerns, including: Do students behave aesthetically in the mathematics classroom and, if so, under what conditions? Should students be encouraged to behave aesthetically in the mathematics classroom and, if so, toward what purposes?

Before I begin, I want to recall Dewey's concern for false dualisms. Throughout his career, Dewey was rightly concerned with identifying, diagnosing, and exorcising philosophical dualisms—such as fact/value, analytic/synthetic, and cognitive/affective—from our thinking. In some contexts he did, however, acknowledge the usefulness of *making* philosophical distinctions—between, say, facts and values—in our attempts to explain phenomena. As the philosopher Hilary Putnam (2002) makes clear, dualisms imply metaphysical dichotomies; they imply that, for example, facts and values are different categories whose members each possess an "essential" property in common. In contrast, philosophical distinctions have ranges of implication, and we are not surprised if the distinctions do not always apply. (Is the statement "exercising is good" a fact or a value?) So, when I distinguish aesthetic from cognitive or affective ways of interpreting student experiences, I am not implying that the aesthetic, cognitive, and affective dimensions of human experiences are mutually independent categories. Rather, I believe they each have more or less distinctive features and by focusing (here) on the aesthetic, I can show how our predominant attention to affect and cognition has made invisible the aesthetic dimension of students' mathematical experiences.

Each of the student examples I describe comes from an ongoing in-school research project that has involved middle school students living in several North American cities. The very act of focusing on the aesthetic dimension of their mathematical activity involves a process of interpretation, of emphasizing certain actions and utterances over others, so I do not claim that I offer objectively factual reports. Rather, I will be *interpreting* many episodes involving students' interactions and experiences in the mathematics classroom.

Clearly, in presenting the episodes in writing, based on my observations, notes, and sometimes videotapes, I am not trying to share *all* that "really" happened. I have extracted certain comments, actions, and events, as other researchers do when they (perhaps subconsciously) choose to see through a cognitive lens. Through my aesthetic lens, I understand the account as an interpretation as well—and, in fact, as the most complex of the interpretations offered. The very use of an "aesthetic lens" acknowledges that what I notice is framed by what I know: an event of noticing is always and already an event of interpretation. While I strive to be true to the details of the students' experiences, I acknowledge that what I see and hear in the classroom depends largely on my own perceptual frame. However, I am less concerned with conventional, objectivist issues of validity, reliability, and rigor than with the more feasible, and perhaps desirable, issues of relevance, reasonableness, and viability. My goal is to push "the sensibilities of readers in new directions," as Deborah Britzman (1995, p. 236) insists. I want to present reasonable arguments that show that aesthetic concerns are relevant to mathematics educators, and deserving of continued research.

Many of the examples I draw on involve computer-based learning environments. My extensive use of computer-based learning environments stems from both personal and pedagogical reasons. Computers have played a pivotal role in my own mathematical development. It was only after I had completed my undergraduate degree in mathematics that I discovered, thanks to the Internet, the breadth and richness of mathematical ideas and fields (including knot theory, fractal geometry, and topology). More importantly, computer software helped me to experience what it means to actually *do* mathematics—that is, to make up or find new problems, to conjecture and experiment, to make discoveries and find ways and means to justify them, and to communicate my findings to colleagues. Nonetheless, the pedagogical reasons are even more important. First, well-designed computer-based learning environments can offer an incomparable "window" on student meaning-making (a metaphor used by Noss & Hoyles, 1996). Students' thought processes, decisions, and reactions can be observed more readily through their physically manifested interactions with the keyboard, the mouse, and the screen. Second, the computer can provide students with visual and experimental access to mathematical ideas and relationships. This means that pictures and models that mathematicians can imagine and appreciate in their heads suddenly become concretely available and manipulable on the screen;

guesses and hunches—which may be based on intuitive or aesthetic sensibilities—can be evoked and tested.

In Part II, I drew attention to some of the aesthetic qualities of a mathematical situation that attract mathematicians to problems: connectedness, fruitfulness, apparent simplicity, visual appeal, and surprise. Here, I want to see whether there are similar kinds of qualities that can pull students into working on certain problems. Few professional mathematicians are "given" problems to work on; in contrast, students rarely have the opportunity to truly select their own problems (see Davis, 1987b, for an inspiring exception). This would seem to make it almost impossible to find evidence for the role of the aesthetic in student mathematics. However, there are two kinds of situations in which students do have some mathematical agency in this sense. In one kind of situation, students can choose to work more aggressively or persistently on some problems than on others. In another, students can sometimes come across—or pose—their own problems as they work in more open-ended environments. I will begin with an example of the former in this section and then focus on a set of examples of the latter in the next. In all cases, I am interested primarily in the qualities that "hold" rather than merely "catch" student attention (see Dewey, 1913): that is, the qualities that direct student attention to noticing certain relationships, patterns, or structures in a situation, and thereby play a *motivational* role in their mathematical activities.

THE AESTHETIC DIMENSION OF PROBLEM SELECTION

As mentioned in the introduction, I have noticed that when students are fully engaged in my mathematics classroom, they are often motivated by the ideas involved in the actual mathematics rather than by superficial motivators. Here is an example I will not forget. Tim is a student I taught for 2 years in a split grade 7-8 class at a small school in Western Canada. At the beginning of the year, I had found a stimulating Web site called Mega-mathematics (http://www.c3.lanl.gov/mega-math/), which offers a small collection of mathematical topics of current interest designed for middle school students, including graph theory, infinity, knot theory, cryptography, and the four color theorem. Nobody in my long school mathematics career, which culminated in a master's degree in mathematics, had introduced me to such compelling ideas—I felt like I was learning about a whole new kind of mathematics. So as not to deprive my own students, I planned the year so that I would have time to introduce them to these noncurriculum-related topics. The first one was the four color theorem.

I showed the class some simple maps and challenged them to color the maps using a minimum number of crayons. They made some of their own maps and we figured out an easy way to create two-color maps. Then we tried more complicated maps and developed strategies for using as few colors as possible. I then asked the students to create challenge maps for each other, maps that would require more than three colors. After a while, most of the students seemed convinced that no maps required more than four colors. Having no way to provide them with any further insights, I ended the class by telling the students a little about the Haken and Appel computer proof of the four color theorem.

Tim is not convinced. After class, he asks me more about the Haken and Appel proof, and though I confess to not really understanding it, I tell him that it involves having the computer search and test over 1000 maps that could represent *all* possible maps. He grows even more skeptical and literally spends the whole day showing me one new, complicated five-color candidate after another. At first I am impressed with his tenacity, but I soon grow tired of checking his maps, and finally tell him he will have to find two other witnesses before I will take *my* crayons out again. He persists. For a whole month, he persists.

Why was Tim so driven to work on this problem? I think several factors were involved. First, the problem seemed so simple to him; Tim was motivated by the idea that he, a middle school student, could stick his nose into a mathematical problem that challenges professional mathematicians. Problems such as Goldbach's conjecture can have the same effect on students; they are misleadingly simple and accessible at first, but ultimately intractable. As I mentioned in Chapter 4, misleadingly simple problems also attract many professional mathematicians.

Second, the problem was rooted in experiences Tim could connect with. He had seen maps being colored, and knew why adjacent countries should not share the same color: The problem had an intrinsic interest to Tim. Third, the problem involved lots of drawing and coloring; Tim spent hours creating complex, attractive maps, more carefully executed than anything else I had seen him do—whether in the mathematics or the art classroom. Compared with other factors that could have motivated Tim's inquiry, such as wanting to obtain a good mark or wanting to beat a friend to the solution, these three factors have a strong aesthetic dimension. Tim was attracted to the misleadingly simple nature of the problem, to the sensory appeal of making and looking at the maps, and to the way in which this problem connected with his own experiences.

Fourth, the problem had an epistemological interest to Tim; he could not accept that a computer had checked *all* the cases. How did the mathematicians know they had not missed a case? How could they even come up with all the possible cases for the computer to test? The more Tim worked on creating the maps, the more convinced he became of the impossibility of exhaustively enumerating them. The mathematics educator Deborah Ball has depicted a similar situation, in terms of whether it is possible to check *all* cases, arising in a classroom of second grade students who are working on the problem of whether and why two odd numbers always add up to an even number. These students eventually come to realize that it is not necessary to check *all* cases because they can assert and justify a certain property relating to *all* odd numbers (namely, that they are one more, or less, than an even number). Tim was unable to find such a general property—and, for that matter, neither was his teacher! Even if he had been able to, many people find perplexing and perhaps wondrous the very idea that it is possible to somehow circumscribe, hold on to, and work with all maps, all odd numbers, or any other infinite set of objects, and then to assert something about every single one of them.

Tim's question was not only about checking *all* cases, but also about whether the computer had made a mistake. He had been wrong many times himself—why should the computer be so right? To varying degrees, many mathematicians have the same questions about the Haken and Appel computer proof; some are concerned with the fallibility of the computer, or the program, and others with the unintelligibility of the result. (Some may even be weary of its history: first conjectured in 1852, it was incorrectly proven true using noncomputational methods, and again incorrectly proven true in 1880.) For Tim, the computer proof lacked exhaustive certainty. Not all students would show a similar epistemological desire, but Tim's curiosity about the idea of "all cases" bordered on his curiosity about infinity—an idea that frequently engrosses the human mind—because he strongly believed in the existence of an infinite number of maps.

In tackling this problem, Tim is revealing two aesthetic inclinations. One is to transform the disparate, disordered maps into some organized state, to gain some kind of unifying grasp of those maps. The other is to achieve exhaustiveness, an inclination that drives mathematicians' urge to generalize: to identify properties and relationships that work *for all*.

The fourth factor distinguishes itself from the first three: whereas the first three are based on Tim's perceptions of the problem, the fourth pertains to how Tim *wants* to perceive the problem, what form he wants to bring to it. A similar distinction applies to my kissing triangle discovery. I perceived the situation as surprising and connected, but what I *wanted* to determine was a well-defined ("exact") general relationship. Similarly, Zoe perceived disorder and *wanted* to perceive an organized set of polygons. Recall also that Hofstadter wanted to find analogy in his geometric explorations of triangle centers. In a sense, the aesthetic urge to impose structure and order, to organize and pattern, drives mathematical activity; in order for a student to *do* mathematics, she must develop that aesthetic urge.

Though compelling, the distinction between existing and desired perceptions is somewhat vague. Students perceive many things in life as disorderly and surprising; similarly, students want many things in life to be more organized (except perhaps their bedrooms) and certain. What is special about their mathematical perceptions? How do their mathematical perceptions invite aesthetic sensibility? Furthermore, while it is plausible that the concept of infinity stirs surprise and wonder in many students, and that the four color theorem is inviting to Tim's aesthetic impulse, neither infinity nor graph theory feature widely and significantly in the school mathematics curriculum. Is there anything about fractions that can be surprising? Is there anything about algebra that might invite students' aesthetic sensibility? In other words, can the aesthetic dimension of Tim's experience with the four color theorem motivate student inquiry in the more common topic areas of school mathematics?

One might also ask whether Tim and Zoe's experiences are misleading; are most students really capable of aesthetic engagement in mathematics? If so, the literature should be full of similar examples. Two facts challenge this objection. First, with few exceptions, researchers use primarily cognitive or affective lenses, and thus aesthetic behavior is rarely highlighted or reported. Second, and more importantly perhaps, certain types of learning environments are more conducive to aesthetic engagement than others and many mathematics classrooms do little to foster aesthetic behaviors and dispositions. Recall in my kissing triangles how important it was for me to be able to *extract* (the special form of detachment described in Chapter 4), and also to be able to experiment and visualize. Perhaps, if given the opportunity, more students could, in fact, engage their aesthetic sensibilities. I now examine the motivational role of the aesthetic in a computer-based problem posing context.

THE AESTHETIC DIMENSION OF PROBLEM POSING

This example is quite a bit longer than the other student examples I have presented, but I would like to provide a better account of the *evolution* of the motivational role of the aesthetic in mathematical problem posing. I pursue a more experiential aspect of the aesthetic, turning my attention from the initial perceptions that invite inquiry, such as surprise, to the aesthetic qualities of experience that sustain inquiry.

The students in this episode were part of a mixed class of grades 7 and 8, enrolled in a bilingual middle school in an eastern Canadian city. I met with this group of 15 students once a week for approximately 3 months and engaged them in a number of different computer-based activities. This episode occurred during our second session together.

Christine: Meeting Lulu

Christine is working with the Meeting Lulu microworld.[1] In this microworld, Lulu (the small circle labelled "L" in Figure 6.1) moves around on a Cartesian grid in a way that depends functionally on the movements of the object with the four arrows for up, down, right, and left. Students refer to this object in the first person as they describe its movements and locations on the grid. So as Christine moves "I," Lulu responds by moving, too. The implicit challenge is to figure out where "I" can meet Lulu, how the meeting place can be predicted, and under which conditions a meeting is possible at all. Under the default movement rule, as Christine finds out, Lulu and "I" can meet quite easily, simply by navigating "I" toward Lulu. Only one meeting spot seems possible, however, so the meeting can never occur at the park (the square near the middle, appearing blue on the computer), much to Christine's dismay. Christine does notice that Lulu always moves in the opposite direction to "I." Moreover, as one of her classmates points out, when "I" moves over by one unit, Lulu moves by two. Therefore, Lulu always moves twice in the opposite direction to "I."

On the second page of the microworld, a meeting is not initially possible (since the starting positions are different)—not until the student changes the coordinates of the starting positions of the two players.

I ask the class to find some possible starting positions for the two players in order for a meeting to be possible. Since, when both "I" and Lulu move, colored traces of the paths taken are left behind on the grid ("I"

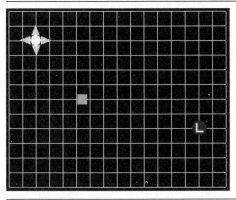

Figure 6.1. The Meeting Lulu microworld, opening page.

leaves a red trace and Lulu leaves a green one), the students can easily read the coordinates of the successful starting positions.

Christine finds one quite easily, placing Lulu at (0, 0) and "I" at (3, 0). As the other students propose their own starting positions, I encourage them to test each other's proposals and to try to determine a rule. Eventually, as a whole class, we are able to conclude that in order to meet, "I" and Lulu have to be a multiple of three units away from each other, both horizontally (in terms of the x-coordinates) and vertically (in terms of the y-coordinates). So if "I" starts at (–1, 6) and Lulu starts at (2, 0), a meeting will be possible. On the other hand, if "I" starts at (-1, 6) and Lulu starts at (0, 0), there is no way to navigate to a meeting spot. After we express this condition more algebraically, I encourage the students to investigate the other movement rules available on the third page of the microworld.

As I walk around the classroom, I notice that Christine is still working with the first movement rule. Since all the other students have already moved on, I ask Christine whether she needs help in understanding the meeting conditions developed by the class. She points to the screen, to the two traces, and tells me, "Actually, I'm looking into those shapes." Christine is no longer investigating the possibility and location of meeting Lulu, but is instead paying attention to geometrical aspects of the traces. From the way that she focuses on the traces and continues to create different shapes with the traces, it is clear that she is comparing them. Shortly after, she tells me that whatever shape "I" traces out, Lulu will trace out a similar shape, though one that is "two times more big" and "turned around halfway," that is, oriented at a 180° degree rotation.

Using her insight, she starts creating a few designs. I consider drawing her attention to the area and perimeter of the two shapes, but decide to let her play a bit more. And then finally, she switches to a different movement rule, focusing of course on the shapes traced by each player. When the players move "at right angles" to each other, she finds that the two shapes have the same size, but that they are "turned by 90°." She seems disappointed when she tries the "opposite direction" rule, probably because it is a mere simplification of the first rule, which was "twice in the opposite direction."

After having explored all the given movement rules, she asks me whether there are any others. Christine explains that she would like to have a movement rule that traces the two shapes so that they are mirror images of each other, which she illustrates by holding her hands up, palms facing me, to form a vertical reflectional symmetry. I direct her to the final page of the Meeting Lulu microworld where it is possible to create new movement rules. Using the natural language interface provided on this page (see Figure 6.2), she is able to create a "reflection" movement rule.

Figure 6.2. The natural language interface for creating movement rules.

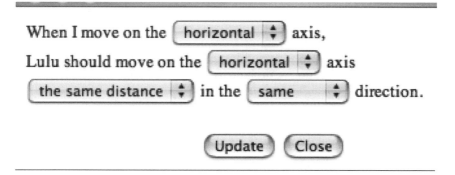

She chooses from the menus given so that when "I" move horizontally, Lulu moves horizontally by the *same* distance but in the *opposite* direction and when "I" move vertically, Lulu moves vertically by the *same* distance and in the *same* direction.

To test her rule, she places "I" at (−1, 5) and Lulu at (1, 5) and uses Lulu's arrows to trace out a staircase (see Figure 6.3). She proudly shows her design to her friends and shows them how to make their own movement rules, pointing out how they can bypass the natural language interface by working directly with the algebraic equations. Then she settles back in her chair, ready to go to work, and remarks, "Now I can make my tree." She sets both Lulu and "I" at the top of the *x*-axis and begins tracing out half the tree by moving "I," watching the other half trace itself out for free thanks to her "reflection" movement rule.

Figure 6.3. Christine's reflectional staircase (left); Christine's tree (right).

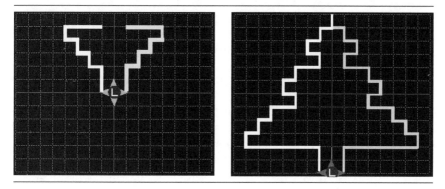

There is certainly an element of mystery involved in finding the meeting spot, but Christine seems to *grow into* her aesthetic engagement as she works with the microworld. Perhaps the kinds of aesthetic qualities that can immediately attract the mathematician—such as surprise—require more time to make themselves apparent or valuable to students. Nonetheless, Christine does notice something interesting on the grid, something that is quite unrelated to the problems we are pursuing as a class. She has been working toward the goal of finding a meeting place, but now she is free to play, to make designs with the traces. In a sense, she is free because I have invited students into a more open-ended activity. Also, she may feel greater freedom because of the expressive possibilities of the traces on the screen. One might infer that her attraction to the traces is based simply on the visual appeal of color, but I suggest that, in addition to this sensory attraction, Christine's attention has been fixed by a more cognitive interest. After all, she does not just stop there, merely noticing the pretty traces.

Christine has observed that the traces are *related*, both in terms of size and orientation. She perceives a connection between the two shapes, one that she wants to make sense of. Although the class had been concerned with the arithmetic properties of the microworld, Christine shifts her attention to its geometrical properties. In the end, she actually forges a connection between the two by finding rules for generating shapes, as if satisfying an urge to unite them. The educator David Hawkins (2000) would not find this surprising; he has argued that the school mathematics curriculum of today does children a disservice by separating the world of geometry from the world of arithmetic, worlds that were so intertwined for the Pythagorean mathematicians. He sees each world as representing two basic and contrasting human powers for understanding.

One of these is strongly spatial and pictorial, geometrical. Its grasp is that of form or pattern, of many elements related synthetically. The other is strongly analytic; it goes step by step, in time and in logic. Its process is digital: It goes like the fingers in counting.

Hawkins proposes that historically speaking, mathematics begin with the cooperation of both powers, with the union of number and form. And based on his experience, he points out that children are also good at associating a visual gestalt with the corresponding number sequence: easily learning to see, for example, three pebbles as a triangle. Since children's curiosity and investigative talents are motivated when they can engage their native understanding and their talents for extending it, Hawkins believes mathematics curricula should strive to recapitulate the synthesis of the ancient Greeks' mathematics. In contrast with many other countries, the high school curricula in the United States split the number/form synthesis quite drastically by separating topics into algebra 1, algebra 2, and geometry courses. However, the split manifests itself much earlier in the way that content standards are described and textbooks structured.

While some mathematical activities explicitly seek to provide a combined arithmetic and geometric representation of fractions, thus heeding Hawkins's call, Meeting Lulu does not. Instead, it is Christine who finds the geometric interpretation of the arithmetically defined movement rules, and Christine who experiences the pleasure of making the connection between her two powers for understanding. Rather than provide the synthesis, Meeting Lulu allows Christine's talents to seek and establish cooperation. Having made the synthesis, though, it becomes available to Christine's friends, and is quick to catch on in the classroom; soon others are investigating different geometric properties of the traced shapes, and using their own movement rules to create designs.

Returning to Hawkins, his notion of *explorative inquiry* provides additional insight into Christine's aesthetic motivation. For Hawkins, the motivation to explore is aesthetic in that it is done for its own sake. Christine enjoys making the designs; she does not stop once she has "solved" the problem of creating vertical symmetry. She makes the designs for the pleasure of making them; the making is motivating, and also sustaining of her continued interaction with the Meeting Lulu microworld.

Exploratory inquiry is aesthetic because it involves the students' desire to organize their perceptions and experiences into patterns of order, equivalence, and symmetry. When the student is exploring, she is engaging deeply in noticing; observation and experiment; pattern discernment; goal setting and goal seeking. Compare these behavioral modes with the nonaesthetic mode of taking a rule-bound or mechanical path to a goal, or being strictly constrained by a predetermined problem.

By emphasizing the role of exploratory inquiry in learning, Hawkins reveals how reform initiatives around problem posing and problem solving fail to "do justice to the humanity of essential processes of goal setting" (2000, p. 111). Goal setting is not merely problem posing, it is the result of the ongoing activity of exploration that evolves and fabricates a problem—in the eye of the inquirer. While the mathematics educators Stephen Brown and Marion Walter (1983) rightfully argue that problem posing helps reestablish the humanistic bond between problems and solutions—revealing where problems come from and why they are problematic—their "What-if-not?" strategy for problem posing can effectively neglect the crucial goal-setting phase of mathematical inquiry, particularly when it is used as a necessary and sufficient heuristic. Certainly, many good problems grow out of "What-if-not?" type approaches, but the student must first explore in order to wonder and to locate the contingent, the phenomenon that can be "What-if-notted." By creating different designs,

Christine notices the traces and their dependence on the movement rule, and only then can she wonder, "What if the movement rule was different, what would happen to the traces?"

In the narrative above, I left Christine as she started to work on her tree. In a sense, she had accomplished her mathematical mission and was now free to express herself perhaps more artistically. While one could easily dismiss her subsequent actions as trivial, I believe they reveal an important aspect of Christine's mathematics. Christine is able to use her mathematical discoveries to her own ends; she uses her reflectional symmetry rule as a tool for creating something she enjoys making and cares about. By making the tree, instead of sticking with the staircase, she can express her mathematical understanding in a more attractive way. In a way, she also escapes the usual constraints of the mathematics classroom, where students have to submit to rules and obey them; perhaps she saw possibilities for both freedom and transgression similar to those I saw in my mom's mathematics of conversion.

Her desire to create something more pleasing resonates with the desire that animates the evaluative function of the mathematical aesthetic—to express what one knows in a better way—though the criteria are somewhat different. In my kissing triangles, I used criteria commonly found in mathematics, namely succinctness, generality, and perspicuity; Christine, on the other hand, used sensory appeal. In fact, the first staircase trace she used as a test shows the reflectional symmetry very well, and in a simpler manner.

Perhaps Christine uses the sensory criterion because she is working in a mathematical domain that admits artistic expression, and surely her sense of artistic expression depends more on sensory appeal than on the simple or perspicuous. But perhaps Christine has not yet learned to identify or appreciate the criteria traditionally used in evaluating mathematical entities. If so, then learning mathematics will have to include learning to appreciate such criteria, and learning to achieve them in her own work. I will return to this suggestion in the final chapter of this book.

I do not want to imply that Christine's tree-making activities simply reveal her unsophisticated mathematical aesthetic. On the contrary, making the tree rounded out the experience for Christine, provided an intrinsically satisfying culminating point that she would not have experienced had she stopped at the testing phase, which simply ratified her movement rule equations. This kind of experience can shape a student's beliefs about and attitudes toward mathematics—as it did for me in the truck, converting miles into kilometers—and thus provide students with the kind of educative experiences that Dewey (1938) argues are conducive to further cognitive growth.

What can be said about Christine's cognitive growth in this episode. What did she learn? What does she know? The goals of problem-posing and -solving activities are rarely to teach students new concepts; rather, we want to know whether students can use, or think with, the concepts they have already encountered, and perhaps use those concepts to develop new ones. Christine showed proficiency in working with coordinates, and in identifying geometric transformations, concepts she had previously encountered. She also showed a good understanding of vertical reflection symmetry, both by her ability to determine the movement rule and in her choice of test shape. Then, initially scaffolded by the natural language interface, she was able to discover how the movement rules could be expressed and manipulated algebraically, which she subsequently showed her friends. The aesthetic may not have been directly involved in the development of her mathematical understanding; however, it provided the conditions under which Christine wanted and needed to learn.

I claimed that meaningful, pleasurable experiences could shape a student's beliefs about and attitudes toward mathematics. In a sense, this is difficult to argue with. However, with the following example, I want to show that students can decide to grapple with a mathematical problem because they anticipate such experiences—much as you might decide to listen to a certain piece of challenging music because of the qualities of experience you know it ultimately affords.

Casey, the student in this episode, is part of the same class of grade 7 and 8 students described previously. The episode occurred near the end of the year.

Casey: "I Like the Way It Feels"

The students have spent almost 3 months working with Meeting Lulu and five other Internet-based mathematical situations. For our last class together, I invite them to return to the activity of their choice and pursue further explorations independently.

When I ask Casey, who has decided to return to the Frogs problem, why she is choosing this situation over the other five, she responds, "I like the way it feels when I get the frogs going right. I know that I can do it and that I'll have a little click when I finally figure it." I watch her for a while as she tackles the frog problem. (The goal of the Frogs problem is to exchange the positions of two teams of three frogs, initially separated by one empty slot. Frogs are only permitted to slide forward into empty slots or to "leapfrog" over a frog on the opposite team into an empty slot. See Figure 7.1 on p. 101.)

In her first few attempts, she makes the same mistake as she did the first time she encountered the problem. She mutters under her breath, "This is how I got stuck before. . . . I know I know how to do this." She tries a few more times, wishing she could "remember the trick." And then, something seems to click: "Oh yeah! How could I have forgotten?" She finally remembers how the solution goes, and she seems to try to make sure it sinks in this time by doing it a few times over again.

At first glance, it would appear that Casey opts for this particular inquiry because she knows she can be successful at it. She also mentions an aesthetic response with respect to the "way it feels" when she gets the solution, probably because she remembers its rhythmic dimension. (The solution alternates in a syncopated pattern between the movement of frogs on one team and the movement of frogs on the other; and many students demonstrated a visceral sense of this patterned movement as they clicked on the appropriate frogs, swaying or nodding their heads with the "beat.") Casey remembers the satisfaction of finally hitting upon the solution after many, many tries. She wants to have that feeling again.

Some might criticize Casey for not challenging herself with a different problem, since she knew, at one time, the answer to this problem—though one might argue that she only partly knows that answer now, in the sense that she still must reconstruct it rather than simply regurgitate it. Yet Casey seems to recognize that having known the answer does not mean she still knows, or remembers, how to get to it. I have learned this lesson on the occasions where I have attempted to reconstruct proofs I already know, such as the proof for the infinity of primes. Moreover, I have seen mathematicians take delight in the opportunity to reconstruct a proof they have already seen, as if they are teasing themselves. Of course, the mathematicians depend on the affective boost of confidence—since their task is obviously doable—and are mainly left with the cognitive challenge of seeing whether they can remember how the "story" fits together. Although this does not contribute to knowledge creation within the body of mathematics, if indeed one can think of the growth of mathematics in such a way, it is a common component of mathematical practice, and perhaps a contribution—through rehearsal, through demonstration, through rhythm—to more personal forms of growth.

Actually, Casey's capacity to acknowledge the incomplete or tenuous state of her knowledge is commendable. Teachers who convey the attitude, "now, we've covered slopes" frequently do injustice to students with respect to this capacity. Such an attitude prevents students from developing a sense of mathematical integrity with which they ask themselves, "What do I understand about slopes?" It might even prevent students from imagining further learning, as the mathematics educator Anne Watson's (1992) poem ironically suggests:

> We did tables with our last teacher
> We've done computers, it's ticked off,
> miss
> We did calculators with the supply
> I don't have to do estimates, I got them
> all right last time
> I asked "What if . . . " in Year 4
> My mum says I'm not allowed to test
> my hypotheses
> We've all done rulers before . . . (p. 11)

An alternative would be to give students the sense that they have learned a great deal about slope, but that they will surely encounter it in new situations, from new perspectives which will surprise them, and which will change the way they currently understand slope.

Casey was motivated by the intelligibility and satisfaction she would gain from solving the Frogs problem again. The fact that Casey chose a problem that she had already solved should not disappoint or discourage mathematics educators. Rather, her choice suggests a possible trajectory in the development of aesthetic motivation. That is, as students gain confidence in mathematics and develop beliefs about the kinds of experiences that mathematics can offer, they may seek out more novel problems or challenges using different aesthetic criteria.

COLORING WITH NUMBERS

In this section I investigate the motivational role of the aesthetic across a large number of students using a highly visual computer-based environment. The design of the Colour Calculator (CC) was inspired by mathematicians at the Centre for Experimental and Constructive Mathematics (CECM) at Simon Fraser University, where technologies are being developed to employ the visual capacities of human perception to search for relationships and patterns in numerical distributions. Mathematicians at CECM employ these techniques to look for underlying structures of mathematical objects. I decided to modify one of their tools for use with simpler mathematical objects—fractions and their decimal representations.

In designing the tool, I hoped to encourage students to make sense of and explore these mathematical ideas using some of their aesthetic sensibilities to qualities such as symmetry, repetition, rhythm, and pattern. I also wanted to put these ideas in a new setting, removed from the properties (such as proper/improper) and operations (such as simplifying and converting) that form their usual—often repelling—context, in an effort

Figure 6.4. The Colour Calculator.

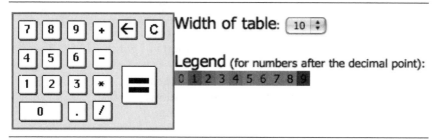

to achieve the Deweyian phenomenon of extraction (see Part I). Before reporting on the aesthetic behaviors of the students with whom I worked, I describe the tool and some of its aesthetically rich design features.

The CC is a regular, Internet-based calculator that provides numerical results, but which also offers its results in a color-coded table. Conventional operations are provided; the division operation allows users to easily generate numbers with repeating decimals while the square root operator allows users to generate irrational numbers. Each digit of the result corresponds to one of ten distinctly colored swatches—reflected in a legend—in the table. Figure 6.4 shows the Colour Calculator interface with the legend appearing in shades of gray instead of in color. On the computer, the numbers 0 through 9 correspond to the colors magenta, purple, blue, turquoise, teal, green, yellow, orange, red, and brown (see this book's cover).

The calculator operates at a maximum precision of 225 decimal digits, and thus each result is simultaneously represented by a (long) decimal string and an array or matrix of color swatches. It is possible to change the dimension, or the width, of color table to values between 1 and 30, as well as the number of decimals that appear, from 1 to 225. Thus, of particular interest in the CC are the pattern-rich real numbers because they can be *seen and understood as patterns of color*.

This graphical representation of numbers calls attention to and facilitates the perception of important classes of real numbers—terminating, periodic, eventually periodic, and nonperiodic—and some of their properties. The calculator operations (addition, subtraction, multiplication, division, and square root), as well as the changeable width of the table, enable exploratory action on the color patterns themselves.

In Figure 6.5, the operation 1/7 has been typed into the calculator with number of decimals displayed set at 100, and table width set at 10. While the figure appears in shades of gray, the CC generates the associated colored table showing the sequence of colors purple, teal, blue, red, green, orange repeating.

Figure 6.5. The Colour Calculator showing 1/7.

Equation: 1/7
Results: .142857142857142857142857142857142857142857142857142857142857

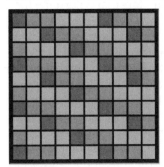

Using the button that controls the width of the table of colors, the student can select different table dimensions that result in different color patterns, some of which highlight interesting aspects of the fraction's period. Figure 6.6 shows 1/7 displayed using a table width of 18 and 17, respectively. Even in shades of gray, the striped and diagonal patterns in the table can be seen.

Given this basic environment engaging the visual capacities of human perception, what kinds of mathematical observations emerge? The types of questions that seem compelling to ask in this environment relate mostly to patterns in the decimal expansion of real numbers: What different types of patterns exist? How does the pattern depend on the number? These questions can lead to sophisticated number theory questions, especially with prime numbers, that many mathematicians find compelling.

However, they are not all necessarily the type of questions or properties compelling or suitable to middle school students. However, by beginning with this aesthetically rich situation and asking what is interesting and/or significant to know about fractions and their decimal representations—note the reversal of order—a radical departure from conventional curricular objectives might ensue. For instance, rather than emphasizing

Figure 6.6. Different representations of 1/7 in the CC.

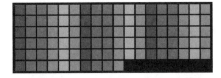 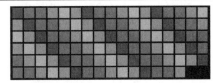

the importance of understanding fractions as parts of wholes or that of knowing how to convert fractions to decimals, the CC emphasizes the understanding of fractions as patterned objects (as representations) and the relationships between numerators and denominators that determine these patterns.

The CC environment is structured both by its mathematical and pedagogical design. The mathematical design dictates the domain of investigation: the world of numerical computation. In this domain, the square root operator represents an intentional design decision to locate the rational numbers (which give rise to repeating color tables) within a larger field in which nonrepeating patterns are equally accessible. The pedagogical design dictates how students are asked and encouraged to move through the environment. In order to help evoke aesthetic perceptions, the environment is structured to offer only minimal instructions and a few specific questions. In particular, in order to draw students into the pattern-rich rational numbers, they are asked to begin by trying a few fractions and observing the associated table of colors. The first fraction they are asked to try is 1/7, which gives a repeating, nonterminating result. They are also encouraged to change the width of the table, and then to continue experimenting with other fractions.

These minimal explanations present the students with the potential for encountering initial complexity—they have to make sense of the colors associated with 1/7, to connect the fraction to the legend provided on the screen; and that complexity has the potential to draw them into the world of CC. In fact, Stephen Brown (1993) points out that the structure of traditional classroom tasks actually gives students a false sense of aesthetic unity. By presenting students with tasks that are always as clear, coherent, and efficient as possible, they are deprived of the possibility of feelings of confusion, doubt, ambivalence, and dissonance, the very feelings that produce the tension and frustration necessary for mathematical inquiry. Without confusion or disharmony, students do not have the opportunity to bring their cognitive, aesthetic, and affective structures to "good form." As I remarked already, it is the reducing of surprise and complexity to simplicity and predictability that evokes, in learners, first reflection, then pleasure. Thus, the apparent insufficiency of textual instructions sets up trajectories of sense-making ranging from complexity/confusion to simplicity/pleasure from the outset.

Student Patterns

I interviewed 15 grade 8 students (eight boys and seven girls) of mixed ability (as rated by their regular classroom teacher). The students ranged from working class to middle class and were from small towns in North America. Each student worked through a mathematical task using the CC as I observed and asked questions. The interviews began with the student reading these instructions:

> You will be able to explore fraction and decimal number patterns with this color calculator. To get started, type a fraction like 1/7 into the calculator, then press the = button. Things to think about:
> - What do you notice in the table of colors?
> - What happens when you change the width of the table?
> - Experiment with other fractions.

After reading the instructions, the students started working while I asked some questions about the reasons behind their actions. I occasionally intervened to provide guidance, following a set sequence of prompts. These prompts were only given when I judged that the student could no longer progress either in identifying a problem or solving it. The interview continued until the student had concluded at least one exploration—that is, until the student had resolved one problem. Rather than showing a group trend, the interviews revealed enormous differences in the students' perceptions of and approaches to the mathematics of the CC, as well as in the problems they ultimately formulated and solved.

Revealing Responses

At an obvious and almost trivial level, every student expressed that they had never seen fractions or decimals like this—many of them realized for the first time that a fraction and its corresponding decimal are the same[2]—one student noting, "You never see them together like this." Every student commented on how different this type of mathematical activity was from their regular classroom work, one explaining, "You actually have to do things," while another observed, "You have to notice things."

Of the 15 students I interviewed, 13 of them showed obvious physical signs of surprise, which they expressed through one or more of the following actions: widening their eyes, sitting upright or moving forward, making a sound such as "ooh," or saying some form of "wow." Most were surprised that numbers could be displayed in this colorful way, but some were more surprised by the appeal of the colored pattern, much as they might show surprise when encountering a colorfully tiled ceiling. Whatever the source, their initial surprise caused them to want to know where the colors came from and whether other fractions would produce similar results, as indicated by their subsequent actions (asking me, trying another fraction, studying the legend).

One student, whom I will call Nadia, showed no physical surprise at all, and answered, "I don't see anything" when I asked her what she saw in the table of colors. Nadia was either completely insensitive to the patterns in the table or, due to her timidity and lack of confidence, she may have been experiencing too great of an affective barrier to even attempt to engage. (She may also have been at least partially color-blind.) The other student who showed no physical reaction was Cameron, who remarked flatly: "There are lots of colors and patterns there." I remember feeling a bit disappointed at Cameron's remark. Cameron is a good reminder that surprise is subjective; note that most students are utterly unsurprised that the three medians in a triangle always meet at a single point or that the exterior angles of a convex polygon always add up to 360°.

The aesthetic response of surprise may have drawn most students in, but I am more interested in finding out what their sense of surprise prompted them to perceive, and what kind of actions those perceptions entailed. This was easiest to observe with the more articulate students who provided a running commentary of their thought processes, like Sean:

> Okay. Ah. It looks like an abstract painting. Not exactly like a math problem. I'm trying to figure out how it calculates that. Uh. Well, it says that the results are 0.142857 and it repeats. So this is a repeating pattern. I can see it because the red sticks out and the purple, and ooh the green. They kind of go in a diagonal that shows a standard repeating pattern but I'm trying to figure out how things are working. So the number corresponds to the color.

Here Sean is not only noticing particular colors—he seems especially to like green—but is drawn in to a repeating pattern, making him want to understand where the pattern comes from and how things are working. He first realizes that each color corresponds to a number, and then, having noticed the repeating pattern, wonders whether there will always be a pattern. He tries several other fractions and eventually decides to investigate whether he can find a number that has "no pattern." Sean is looking for the pathological example; he wants to find the fraction that breaks the repeating pattern rule.

On the other hand, Ann's first observation is that "every seventh box is a purple." She also sees the repeating pattern but because she focuses on the last color of the repeating sequence, purple, she forms a more quantitative interpretation of the situation, noting that 1/7 has six repeating digits (its period is six). She "verifies" this by changing the width of the table from 10 to 6. She then begins to investigate the periods of other fractions. Anne wants to see whether there is relationship between fractions and the periods of their decimal expansions.

After seeing the result for 1/7, Kirk immediately tries 1/3, and then 1/2. He focuses on the differences between the table of colors that each fraction produces, noting that some terminate while others do not. He begins to categorize various fractions as terminating and nonterminating and then tries to figure out how he can predict to which category a fraction belongs based on its denominator of a fraction. As was the case with Zoe, Kirk's urge is to categorize, upon perceiving that fractions can be divided into two distinct groups.

Julie takes a slightly different approach; she begins by changing the width of the table of colors several times. When the width is set to 7, she remarks, "It's like a staircase." When the width is set to 3, "It's doubled up." Julie is interested in describing all the types of possible patterns 1/7 could produce. She seems particularly interested in the diagonal pattern and experiments with other fractions, trying to figure out how the grid width should be set in each case. Julie wants to see fractions as diagonals. (Interestingly, most adults prefer to find table widths that create stripes; perhaps stripes are just a bit too regular for Julie, diagonals providing some not-too-complex but welcome deviation for the teenager.)

Three other students embarked on explorations similar to the three described above. Each of these seven students in total perceived the CC's output differently, some focusing on differences, others on similarities, and others on specific patterns. Their individual perceptions, rooted perhaps in the initial surprise or appeal, gave rise to different questions, problems, and investigations. But each inquiry was motivated by an aesthetic urge: Sean was most "romantic"[3] in his desire to find the rebellious case, the bizarre and nonconforming fraction. Ann and Kirk were both more "classical" in their orientation, wanting to find some structure or order. Julie wanted to see whether she could impose a certain, personal form on each fraction.

The other 8 of the 15 students seemed more reticent to engage. They either paused, waiting for instructions, or asked me what I wanted them to do. These students might have had initial perceptions similar to the ones of Sean, Kirk, Julie, and Ann, but they needed me to ratify the significance of their perceptions. After I prompted the students, by asking them "Tell me what you see," and then assured them that what they saw was correct and interesting, each of the eight students was able to formulate a question, and all but one introduced a personal variation to their inquiry. For example, I prompted Robert to look at the kinds of fractions that were nonterminating. At one point he tried 7/9, which gave him a solid table of blue. He then decided to focus on the smaller class of fractions that produce nonterminating single-digit decimal expansions—that is, solid tables of colors.

Table 6.1 presents a list of student investigations, in their words, along with a corresponding version reformulated as a question in more conventional mathematical discourse. Each student question reveals a distinct perception that ultimately shaped the actions taken by the student, and thus their paths of inquiry.

From the questions listed in the table, it is obvious that the students investigated quite a few things about fractions and their decimal representations, as well as number theory. I want to draw attention to the fact that each problem in the table grew out of an aesthetic engagement with

Table 6.1. Problem-posing with the CC.

Student question	Reformulation
How can I make the diagonals go in the opposite direction?	How are diagonal patterns related to the period?
Maybe the period is always one less than the denominator.	How is the period of the fraction related to its denominator?
I think that all the fractions with odd numbers on the bottom will repeat.	What values of the denominator yield nonterminating decimals?
The decimals stop when there is a 2, 5, or 10 in the denominator. I wonder what happens with 8.	What values yield terminating decimals?
So with 12 on the bottom, there's an extra number before the repeating.	When is a decimal eventually periodic?
I want to take away those colors that don't fit with the rest of the pattern.	How do you move the decimal point to the right?
Aren't there some numbers that have a totally random pattern?	What kinds of numbers neither terminate nor repeat?
I want to get the table all red.	What fractions have a repeating expansion of one digit?
I wonder what happens if I try 3/7 now.	How are fractions that have the same denominator related?
So what do I get if I add 1/2 to this 1/3?	What is the effect when you add two fractions with different periods?
I think that since 1/9 has a period of 1, like 1/3 then 1/49 should have a period of 6.	What is the effect when you square a fraction that has a certain period?

the CC, first through surprise and appeal, which then led them to form various perceptions of and then hypotheses about the CC's output. Based on these perceptions, students developed interpretations and conjectures on which they could act through experimentation with the various functions of the CC.

Accessible Perceptions

Students form some kind of perception of the situations they encounter in the classroom. The problem is, is it not, that they do not notice what the teachers would like them to notice. So why did the students using the CC notice so many different, mathematically pertinent things? Why did their perceptions lead them to inquiry? To help me answer these questions, I recount a story told by the French mathematician Le Lionnais (from his 1983 book on number theory) about his first experience, at age 7, of a mathematical discovery. His discovery depends not so much on his knowledge of mathematics; rather, it depends on his aesthetic sensibilities, his perceptual interest in certain visual forms that he is able to bracket for attention.

Le Lionnais is sitting alone at the kitchen table, with a pencil and some paper, not tired enough to join the rest of his family for the afternoon siesta. For some reason, he has the idea to write down integers from 1 to 9. But instead of multiplying one integer by the others, as he has been learning about in school, he multiplies each by itself, in the row beneath:

1	2	3	4	5	6	7	8	9
1	4	9	16	25	36	49	64	81

"Suddenly," he writes, recounting the episode as he remembers it several decades later, "a veil lifts, allowing me to perceive in this otherwise dull alignment, a classically beautiful structure." But to see it, he continues, "one has to consent, without argument, to an amputation: striking out the digits in the tens decimal place, conserving only the units." This produces:

1	2	3	4	5	6	7	8	9
1	4	9	6	5	6	9	4	1

Le Lionnais admits that an ordinary adult might have found the resulting symmetry quite banal but, having discovered it himself, he is thunderstruck. He feels he has entered a "vast domain where a multitude of treasures has been hidden." Surely, he could continue mining his beautiful array simply by multiplying the digits once again (and maybe even again . . .), remembering to strike out the tens decimal places each time:

1	2	3	4	5	6	7	8	9
1	4	9	6	5	6	9	4	1
1	8	7	4	5	6	3	2	9

Hélas! The symmetry had been lost. Le Lionnais is stubborn, though, certain that "chaos could not have taken over the society of numbers, which had thus far been so well organized." And all of a sudden, he sees that the digits occupying the symmetric positions are complementary in ten: $1 + 9 = 10$; $8 + 2 = 10$; $7 + 3 + 10$; $4 + 6 = 10$. Now he can move on. What happens in the fourth row? Le Lionnais works on his rows of digits all afternoon, until he is called for dinner, finding that the sixth row reproduces the second, while the seventh reproduces the third, and so on.

When Le Lionnais looks at that second row of numbers, the row of squares, he sees something; he perceives a "beautiful" pattern possibility, audaciously ignoring the tens decimal place. When he lifts the veil and sees the symmetric structure in the row of numbers, he knows there must be more. So onward he goes to the next row, looking for the next pattern. The simple row of numbers is suggestive enough for the young Le Lionnais, and the symmetry suggested is appealing enough to drive his curiosity and satisfying enough too, in and of itself. An ordinary 7-year-old knows about symmetry, and even about sums with results bigger than ten. But would most 7-year-olds have noticed the symmetry of the second row or the balance of the third one?

Probably not. In fact, the young Le Lionnais seems to have developed an unusually acute aesthetic faculty in mathematics; he appreciates the significance of symmetry, is able to ignore things that get in the way of a "beautiful" pattern, and anticipates further "treasures."

Yet symmetry is a fundamental tool that humans constantly and successfully use to make sense of their environment. Why then would a regular 13-year-old not have noticed the hidden symmetry of the row? Perhaps humans use symmetry best when it is presented visually; children immediately see the symmetry of faces, logos, and shapes (recall how quickly Zoe saw the symmetry of the polygons). Yet numbers are not objects that are usually used or considered in terms of their symmetry, and it takes quite a perceptual leap to consider a whole *row* of numbers. When Le Lionnais noticed the complementarity of the third row, he perceived balance, another fundamental tool humans use to make sense of the environment. But again, balance is primarily used in physical contexts: balancing your arms as you walk across a beam, balancing your body on a teeter-totter.

Le Lionnais might not need visual cues but most students, who are less aesthetically developed, probably do. In fact, I believe it was the visual interface of the CC that gave students the opportunity to perceive the structuring forms—not symmetry *per se*, but the rhythm of the repeating pattern, the diagonals, stripes, and checkerboards—which are less accessible in their numeric representations. These forms were compelling enough, perhaps revealing enough that the students even perceived them as adequately significant to initiate further exploration, much as the young Le Lionnais saw symmetry as significant enough to propel his inquiry.

In order to notice symmetry and balance, though, the young Le Lionnais had to focus his attention on the numbers, see them as interesting and potentially satisfying objects to play with. The initial surprise felt by the students using the CC drew their attention, made them believe, at least for a while, that there was something interesting to play with. Imagine what would have happened if the students had been asked to convert 1/7 into a decimal number? Unless numbers already fascinated the students, little would have drawn their attention, or piqued their curiosity, demanded interpretation—the mechanical demands of long division being so heavy. The scope of their perceptions would have been reduced, funnelled into a numerical, mechanical approach. And finally, their possibilities for action, for satisfying their aesthetic urges, would have been severely restricted: it would become onerous to experiment with lots of fractions, and especially complex ones; the possibility of changing the fraction's representation would have been unfathomable.

Learning and Aesthetic Engagement

So far, I have emphasized the surprising, visual, and experimental features of the CC as being central to its power to aesthetically engage students. The latter features derive primarily from the computer-based nature of the CC: the computer is good at performing calculations with big numbers as well as manipulating and displaying data. The computer is also particularly good at providing visual representations of data. And although I believe that the computer is especially well-suited to evoking students' aesthetic behavior, a belief I will substantiate later, there are other ways to encourage children to use and build on their aesthetic sensibilities.

For example, in their book *Creative Mathematics*, Upitis, Phillips, and Higginson (1997) show how students can be aesthetically stimulated when given sensorial, pattern-rich encounters with mathematics. In one example, grade five students are presented with a bucket full of ceramic tiles. These students need no prompting: They immediately attempt to determine how the tiles can fit together. William Higginson notes that the aesthetic appeal of tessellation—like that of jigsaw puzzles—seems to be a "direct offshoot of a common and powerful human aesthetic urge, that of 'fitting'" (p. 49). The students' aesthetic urge to fit, similar to the case with Zoe's aesthetic urge to classify, drew their attention to the relevant properties of the shapes. In fact, the students subsequently also reveal their own urge to classify when they try to work out which shapes will tessellate and which will not.

Many mathematics educators have attempted to appeal to students' artistic and creative urges by linking mathematics to the arts: the golden ratio through Mondrian paintings, transformations through Escher drawings, ratios through music, and so forth. For example, the mathematics educator Robert Jamison (1997) suggests that engaging students in discrete mathematics activities with an artistic connection (for example, modular arithmetic in music and regular polygons in eurythmy) will stimulate their aesthetic sense, pique their mathematical curiosity, and reveal the artistic spirit in mathematics. Although I do not wish to deny its virtues, such linking utilizes student interest in other domains to coax them into mathematics. A pernicious consequence of appealing to students' love of something else (whether in the arts, sports, or money) in the hopes of engaging them is that it endorses the belief that mathematics itself is an aesthetically sterile domain, or at least one in which its potentialities are only realized through engagement with external domains of interest. As Dewey (1913) would say, they catch student attention through the external domain, but ultimately fail to hold it in the mathematics.

Both the CC and the tessellations, however, try to evoke the aesthetic, expressive, and transformative possibilities of mathematics itself. Instead of counting on students' sensibility and attraction to the arts to help them appreciate mathematics, their aesthetic urges are directed to contexts that are themselves mathematical: seeking patterns in rational numbers, identifying shapes that can fit together. The colorful patterns produced by both the CC and the tessellations "catch" student attention, but also manage to "hold" in the mathematics because the aesthetic urge becomes a mathematical one.

In comparison with the examples I discussed in the previous section, the power of students' initial perceptions was especially obvious with the CC, where slightly different ways of grasping the situation resulted in quite different inferences and actions. However, not all 15 students were equally aesthetically engaged. I am tempted to say that some of the less aesthetically engaged were blocked by their previous experiences in mathematics. I would have the evidence of the many researchers who have shown that students will eventually start ignoring their feelings and impressions, having been taught that they do not belong in the rational, formal mathematics classroom (e.g., Boaler, 1997; Gordon, 1965; Turkle & Papert, 1992). If, by providing students with "aesthetically rich" learning environments, we manage to enable half of them to engage in the process of mathematical inquiry, we are at least progressing.

Readers might be wondering, *Well yes, they inquired, but what did they learn?* Admittedly, I was not trying to teach the students a specific skill or concept. Rather, I wanted to see whether the students could "act as mathematicians," that is, formulate and solve a problem using various mathematical strategies. I was interested in what the mathematics educator Robert Davis (1992) has described as the *residue* of mathematics:

> Instead of starting with mathematical ideas, and then applying them, we [teachers] should start with problems or tasks, and as a result of working on these problems the children would be left with a residue of mathematics . . . that mathematics is what you have left over after you have worked on problems. (Davis, 1992, p. 237)

The students each learned something new by virtue of their inquiries, not all of which were directly related to the middle school curriculum or to the concept of fractions *per se*. This was part of the *residue* but, also, the mathematics that is "left over" encompasses much more than concepts or solutions and includes ways of behaving in mathematical problem-solving contexts. Davis's notion of *residue* may also encompass the contextually complex understandings that I have elsewhere referred to as "thicker" understanding (see Liljedahl, Sinclair, & Zazkis, 2006). I appropriate this use of the adjective *thick* from anthropology (see Geertz, 1973), where it applies to descriptions of events or social scenes that are layered, rich, and contextual. In ethnographic research, thick descriptions value modest observations—small, specific happenings, instead of ambitious theories addressing broad issues. Moral philosophy has also adopted the adjective; "thin" terms such as *good* and *bad* denote abstract ethical concepts, whereas "thick" terms such as *generous* and *cruel* have a heavy descriptive content—they are world-guided in that they depend on what the world is actually like.

In the context of learning, I use the adjective *thick* to describe the cognitive and emotional multidimensionality of a learner's understanding of a mathematical concept. For example, a *thin* understanding of square numbers might consist of the propositional knowledge that a square number is of the form $n \times n$, like 4, 25, and 100. A thicker understanding might include the experience of drawing square numbers geometrically, as "perfect" squares instead of rectangles. It might also involve having noticed that square numbers have an odd number of factors, or, having compared areas of whole-number rectangles and whole-number squares. A thicker understanding of square numbers might also involve observing how they are distributed—that they get farther and farther apart as one hops down the number line from one square number to the next—differently than other kinds of numbers such as primes. The properties that I have mentioned as part of a thicker understanding of square numbers are, of course, all implied by the initial thin description. However, they belong to certain contexts (drawing shapes, using number lines) and experiences (looking at opaque properties, solving problems) that can be triggered in future thinking. They are more context-dependent, more descriptive, and more resonant with the world in which learners live.

Having "thick" experiences with mathematical ideas and entities builds the learner's distinctive power of imagination; it furnishes the "imagic store," as the educator Harry Broudy (1977) calls it. Broudy argues that this imagic store contains the raw materials for all concepts and possibilities, and thus forms the basis for all cognition, judgment, and action. When Broudy makes this argument, he is talking about reading, and showing how even the most basic sentence—"This is a tree"—requires that the reader instantiate a relevant context of meaning, which is built up of visual, tactile, olfactory, and auditory images. A mechanical skill of reading allows the reader to decipher the words, but not to access the meanings encased in the written language. It is with our imagination that we construe a sentence such as "We are working around the clock."

How does Broudy's argument apply to learning mathematics, which is about refining, reducing, and abstracting the imagic store into precise concepts and relationships? The mathematician does not reduce and abstract from nothing. Consider the notion of the derivative, which, as the mathematician William Thurston (1995) points out, has at least a dozen definitions, or associated contexts. A "microscopic" way of conceiving the derivative (the limit of what you get by looking at it under a microscope of higher and higher power) might ultimately become reconciled with an "approximation" way (the best linear approximation to the function near a point). There may be a single public "abstract" definition (see Schiralli & Sinclair, 2003) of the derivative, which can be seen as abstracted and reduced, but it is not one with which mathematicians actually think. When thinking about the concept of the derivative in problem solving, a vague image of a prototypical derivative may be "seen" in the mathematician's mind. But as soon as she tries to focus on it, to attend to it carefully, she finds she is considering a specific kind of derivative—perhaps the tangent to the curve—or even a suite of images of derivatives including symbolically represented ones. Even though she may be working with a highly abstract concept, she must constantly draw on her rich imagic store, on the many trigger points she has attached to the derivative through her thick experiences.

In emphasizing the development of thicker understanding (gained in the residue of mathematics) over the mastery of discrete, well-defined concepts (gained through explicit teaching), a major shift has taken place. The emphasis I argue for here focuses on *meaning*, on whether the learner can appreciate the motivations for doing something a certain way as well as whether the learner can associate images and experiences to concepts. This emphasis has an impact on the many decisions that educators must make about the content and context of mathematics teaching. Although I have only scratched the surface of investigating the relationship between the aesthetic and mathematics learning, and its impact on curriculum and teaching decisions, I want to postpone those discussions until I have probed the generative and evaluative roles of the aesthetic in student mathematics.

FITTING THE PIECES TOGETHER

The experiences of Zoe, Tim, Christine, and Casey each suggest ways in which the aesthetic plays a selective and motivational role in the mathematical inquiry of middle school students. By engaging their aesthetic sensibilities and calling upon their aesthetic urges, the mathematical situations presented to the students became starting points for problem posing and problem solving. Tim's example highlighted the way in which apparent simplicity, visual appeal, connectedness, and mystery can draw a student into a problem, much as it does for the professional mathematician. With Christine, a different kind of connectedness became apparent— the relations between different modes of thinking, and her interest in or desire to connect them. The very process of goal-setting through play and explorative inquiry also revealed the aesthetic impulse in which Hawkins (2000) was interested. Dewey (1938) writes that all processes of inquiry begin in tension, in the perception of obstacles, uncertainty, or discord. While agreeing with Dewey on the important role of tension in inquiry, Hawkins rightly points out that Dewey fails to acknowledge the importance of exploratory activity in motivating learning. For Hawkins, exploratory activity is a "mode of behavior in which the distinction between ends and means collapses. . . . Or rather the reinforcement comes to [the distinction] because of what is found along the pathways of exploration" (2000, p. 116).

Finally, Casey's example drew attention to an aspect of the motivational role of the aesthetic that I had not yet discussed, but which can also be found among mathematicians. Indeed, Peter Hilton (1992), Roger Penrose (1974), and André Weil (1992) all claim that they do mathematics precisely for those "good feelings" they get when they solve a problem, for those perhaps infrequent, but sustaining experiences. Burton (1999b) sums up this view as follows, referring to the 70 mathematicians she interviewed:

> Mathematical activity for many of these mathematicians was driven by curiosity and the resultant pleasure when something was resolved. . . . Far from understanding being something which is only driven by knowledge, there is both a need to know and an associated *pleasure* in knowing which is its own reward. (p. 29; emphasis in original)

Can these examples serve a teacher or curriculum developer in any way? Based on observations of individual learners, mathematics education researchers have developed very sophisticated models of student learning, including some that are able to prescribe the structuring and ordering of materials through which students will most likely be able to learn concepts. As I have said before, these researchers have focused on the cognitive dimension of learning. However, I believe that the experiences of Zoe, Tim, Christine, and Casey can similarly contribute to helping researchers develop learning environments that can best evoke and activate a student's aesthetic sensibility and behavior.

Thus far, I have only considered the motivational role. It is perhaps most closely connected to current issues in mathematics education, as it involves student motivation and interest—an area that concerns many educators, particularly at the middle school level.[4] However, though perhaps more subtly, the generative and evaluative roles of the aesthetic are both pertinent to school mathematics learning too. They involve ways of thinking and reasoning that are difficult to articulate, as well as values that underlie the very nature of mathematics, including its methods and results. In the next two chapters, I will explore these two roles of the aesthetic in the mathematical activities of students. Following that, I return to examine some of the impact that the aesthetic analysis of student activity has on curriculum and teaching decisions.

CHAPTER 7

The Generative Role
of the Aesthetic

Since it occurs over such a potentially long period of time, with infrequent observable manifestations, the generative role of the aesthetic is the most difficult of the three to identify. A penchant for neatness, or symmetry, or an aversion to –1—these can greatly influence the decisions that are made during problem solving, but they are often fleeting, and perhaps even below the threshold of awareness. Indeed, Poincaré insisted that this role of the aesthetic functioned at a subconscious level in the work of mathematicians, a claim that was later challenged by Papert (1978).

Actually, Papert challenges Poincaré on two counts. First, he wants to show that the mathematical aesthetic sensibility does not belong exclusively to the "very creative" mathematician, but can be found in the more elementary mathematical thinking of nonmathematicians. Second, he wants to show that we can be made consciously aware of our aesthetic responses through the feelings they engender. To do so, Papert asks a group of nonmathematicians to consider the theorem asserting the irrationality of $\sqrt{2}$. He begins by presenting only the initial statement in the proof, the claim to be rejected, that $\sqrt{2} = p/q$. He then asks the subjects to generate transformations of this equation, giving them no indication of what direction to take or what the goal may be. After having generated a half-dozen equations, the subjects hit upon the equation $p^2 = 2q^2$, at which point Papert reports that they show unmistakable signs of excitement and pleasure at having generated this result.

Although this is indeed the next step in the proof of the theorem, Papert assures us that the subjects are not consciously aware of where this equation will eventually lead. Therefore, although pleasure is often experienced when one achieves a desired solution, Papert argues that the pleasure in this case is of a more aesthetic, rather than functional, nature. Furthermore, the reaction of the subjects is more than affective since the subjects scarcely consider the other equations, having somehow identified the equation $p^2 = 2q^2$ as the interesting one. Papert conjectures that eliminating the ugly square root sign from the initial equation might have caused their pleasurable charge, though it might just as well have come from eliminating the fraction—that anxiety-producing mathematical monster. He also conjectures that the experience of transforming the initial equation, whose main actor is the quantity $\sqrt{2}$, into the second equation, which suddenly reveals p as an actor in relationship with q, resonates with the "peekaboo" experience that so often pleases infants. In any case, the students' aesthetic responses guide them to an equation with which they find easier to work, perhaps a clearer one that better reveals for them the relationship between the terms. Papert's goal is not to identify the certain cause of the pleasurable charge, but to point out that the nonmathematicians in his informal study proceeded with a mode of thought that has at least as much claim to be called aesthetic as logical. He shows that an aesthetic response to a certain configuration is *generative*, in that it leads the inquirer down a certain path of inquiry, because then she *feels* that the appealing configuration should reveal some insight or fact.

Where Poincaré relegates the aesthetic to a mathematical unconscious, Papert suggests that his subjects might be consciously aware of their aesthetic responses, just as my colleague—in reacting to the –1 in his equation—was aware of his feeling of aversion. Without meaning to, he also illustrates how mathematicians must believe in, and trust, their feelings in order to exploit the generative role of the aesthetic. They must view mathematics as a domain of inquiry where phenomena such as feelings play an important role alongside hard work and logical reasoning.

THREE EXAMPLES OF THE GENERATIVE ROLE

In this chapter, I will analyze three examples of student mathematical activity, using each to highlight a slightly different aesthetic response that can be seen as playing a generative role. These examples will support Papert's claim about the level of awareness involved in an aesthetic response. They will also provide a broader sense of the kinds of aesthetic responses that students can have, and the different levels of sophistication, with respect to professional mathematicians, with which students are able to make use of these responses in their inquiries.

Casey: "I See Symmetry"

I have previously talked about Casey, the girl who chose to work on the Frogs problem again. Now I want to back up to the first time Casey encountered the Frogs. I have argued that Casey's choice to return to this

Figure 7.1. The Frogs problem, solved by moving $B_1B_2B_3$ $R_1R_2R_3$ to $R_1R_2R_3$ $B_1B_2B_3$.

15 moves:

microworld was motivated by her desire to experience the pleasure of solving the problem again; she was motivated by an anticipated aesthetic quality of experience. But the first time Casey worked on the Frogs, she drew on a different kind of aesthetic, one that played a generative rather than a motivational role.

Casey has "solved" the Frogs problem many times, but each time the computer told her she could do it in fewer moves. Finally, she hits upon a sequence that only required 15 moves. I ask the class to think about why 15 is the minimum number of moves that is required to switch the positions of the frogs on the left with the frogs on the right (shown, already switched, in Figure 7.1—on the computer the frogs on the left are blue and those on the right are red). This seems to be a difficult problem, and one that is less concrete than the one the students have just solved. I see that Casey is repeatedly doing the 15 moves somewhat mechanically. In fact, she seems to have reached an impasse; she tells me that she does not even know where to start.

Directly beneath the frogs, a sequence of colors appears, representing the individual moves made by the frogs. In Figure 7.1, these colors appear in shades of gray representing the sequence of 15 moves $R_1 B_3 B_2 R_1 R_2 R_3$ $B_3 B_2 B_1 R_1 R_2 R_3 B_2 B_3 R_3$. The colored sequences are easier to interpret than the shades of gray shown here.

I realize that Casey has not actually noticed the sequence of colors, so I ask her to look at it and to complete the sentence "It seems to me that..." This draws her attention away from the number 15, and even away from the frogs. She tells me what she sees in the sequence of colors: "There's a pattern in these colors, they go one blue then two red and then three blue and then three red, then. . . ." Though unable to articulate it, she seems to have developed a sense of the pattern.

A few moments later, she exclaims, "Oh, it goes up one way and then comes back down the opposite way." Casey now sees the symmetry in the color sequence and explains that it shows how "first the frogs get all tangled up, then they get untangled again." Then she resets the frogs to the starting position and watches the color swatches as they progressively appear for each move, this time starting with a blue frog rather than a red one. "I think I know why it's fifteen," she tells me.

It is difficult to say how Casey made the leap from the symmetry to the solution. Her next statement includes the observation that the starting team will have one more color than the other team—the last move merely rounding out the symmetry. Perhaps the symmetry allows her to think only about either the tangling or the untangling, thereby reducing the complexity of the problem. She certainly had more work to do to solve the problem; symmetry is not the last piece in the puzzle. Nonetheless, being able to discern the symmetry gives Casey a new way of tackling the problem; it gives her a qualitative grasp of the whole sequence of moves. She knew about symmetry before, of course, but had perhaps never thought that looking for symmetry would be helpful. Maybe she had even noticed the symmetry before, but my intervention seemed to allow Casey to recognize, value, and trust it as a productive, relevant way of organizing the situation. Recall that the young Le Lionnais, upon noticing the symmetry of his row of numbers, was quite willing to trust his feelings of pleasure as indications of "right" and "generative" paths to follow. He had already developed confidence—which Casey may have lacked—in what the mathematics educator Caleb Gattegno (1974) calls his "logics of feeling."

My prompt was an attempt to engage Casey overtly in the kind of "ponderings, what ifs, it seems to be thats, and it feels as thoughs" that Burton (1999b) recommends for inviting intuitive thinking.[1] Such prompts explicitly invite feelings into the process of problem solving, including those that announce pleasure and aversion. They also release students from narrow foci to more global, qualitative framings where fresh ways of seeing are possible, as are more integral, synoptic ones. In contrast with the mathematician George Polyà's (1957) problem-solving heuristics, my prompt specifically draws Casey *away* from the mechanics of the problem (the unknowns, the data, and the conditions), and toward the perceivable qualitative relations. In addition to inviting intuitive thinking, it also gives Casey a chance to engage her aesthetic sensibilities. As soon as she grasped that symmetry, she did not let go; it provided her with a pleasing, generative way of tackling the problem. The aesthetic behavior here is not just perceiving the symmetry, but also experiencing pleasure in the way that it makes the situation a "fitting" one.

Several examples have featured symmetry so far: Zoe and her categorizing, the young Le Lionnais, and now Casey. Symmetry is a highly visual and enabling way of perceiving (though it can also be misleading, as the Silver and Metzger example indicated); it is even a topic that is explicitly taught in school geometry, though more as a property than as a heuristic in problem solving. However, there are several other types of aesthetic guides that insinuate themselves into inquiry, as Papert's example above shows. While an aversion to square roots or to fractions may seem somewhat mathematically unsophisticated, I think that Papert wants to underline the fact that aesthetic responses to certain forms, at whatever degree of sophistication, can be productive. Indeed, it is said that Paul Dirac's commitment to his equation describing the behavior of electrons (the Dirac equation)—despite some serious experimental contradictions—was supported by his aesthetic response to its simplicity. Dirac neatly summarizes his commitment (in retrospect, I might add) with a statement that "it is more important to have beauty in one's equations than to have them fit experiment" (1963, p. 47).

To symmetry, then, we can add the notion of liberating form. Whether Papert's students were afraid of the square root or of the fraction, they ultimately found $p^2 = 2q^2$ a more useful, inviting equation. A third type of aesthetic guide emerged in my kissing triangles discovery. Recall that I was directed to investigate the kissing angle because I saw the possibility for a "pretty" result; in fact, turning the "ugly" 91.031° into the "neat" 90° turned out to be an effective problem-solving heuristic. This quest for exactness may in fact be the paradigmatic mathematical aesthetic, or just the one that mathematics lets humans experience most closely. As with Papert, though, I do not believe it belongs only in the world of the professional (and creative!) mathematician. The following example shows it in action, squarely in the world of the school student. It features four grade-eight students with whom I worked once per week over the course of an entire school year. They were at a small, independent middle school in North America attended by students with a wide variety of mathematical competence. The students needed help and guidance since they were trying to complete a geometry course in an independent setting, using the textbook *Discovering Geometry* (Serra, 1994). My role was to supplement their textbook activity with computer-based activities. This episode occurred in our third session together.

Sara: I Want It "Exactly There"

Sara is trying to reproduce Theo van Doesburg's painting *Arithmetic Composition 1* (shown in Figure 7.2) using The Geometer's Sketchpad. She has already constructed the framing square ABCD, and has created a custom "square" tool for any other square she might need to construct in the future. She is trying to figure out how to construct the largest of the tilted black squares. Using her custom tool, she decides to construct an "approximating" square with one vertex V on BC and another vertex W on CD (see Figure 7.2). She then slides the two vertices V and W along their segments until the tilted square "looks right."

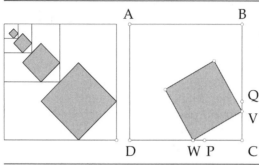

Figure 7.2. Van Doesburg's *Arithmetic Composition 1* (left); Sara's first step (right).

Choosing these locations heuristically—rather than by analytic derivation—allows Sara to at least get started on the problem. But Sara soon grows unhappy. If V and W could be dragged to the right locations, could they also not be dragged to terribly wrong locations? Based on the approximate location of W, Sara infers that W should be two thirds of the way from D to C. So she asks me whether there is any way to make a W that will "stick exactly there," pointing to the screen. As it happens, Sketchpad allows us to fix a ratio, which I show her how to do. This allows her to construct point P, as well as Q, and then to construct the tilted square on PQ using her custom tool.

Sara is happier with her new, fixed tilted square, and turns her attention to the bracket (which corresponds to the next horizontal square) that will hold the next tilted square. By repeating her procedure, she successfully recreates the van Doesburg painting.

With her square on VW, Sara had a functionally useful approximation to the tilted square. Yet she was not satisfied. Her insistence on moving from a dragged approximation to a more stable configuration reminds me of some ancient Greek geometers' aversion to *neusis*, or verging constructions. (Such constructions involve marking a certain length on a ruler, which is then slid into place in a diagram; these constructions, while functionally useful for trisecting the square, among other problems, came to be seen as suspicious—perhaps too mechanical—by ancient Greek geometers.) Sara wants to find the exact, stable location for the vertices of her square, which requires a more analytic approach. That aesthetic predilection draws her away from the contingency of the screen to the determinacy of mathematics. And it allows her to satisfy the quintessential human desire to experience exactness, the fitting moment when "a certain position of the bolt . . . positively closes the lock," in the words of the poet Paul Valéry.

In Sara's case, the goal was clear: She wanted to reconstruct the van Doesburg painting. The possibility of approximation acted as a heuristic in her problem-solving process while her aesthetic urge dictated the means through which she would express her solution. For Casey, the aesthetic provided a generative way of seeing the problem with which she had been grappling. In both cases, then, the aesthetic functioned within the preestablished goals of the student inquirer. With the next example, I want to illustrate the way in which the aesthetic can play a generative function, even when no specific problem exists. And unlike the situation with Casey, the student in this next example recognizes and values his aesthetic perception without my intervention. The setting will be familiar: the Colour Calculator.

John: "Nine Is a Magic Number"

John is using the CC to find a fraction that starts orange, blue (which corresponds to 7, 2). He tries several fractions, many of which seem like wild guesses: 2/7, 5/6, and finally 7/10. I thought he had made a breakthrough, perhaps recalling all his knowledge about the decimal system, but his next attempt is 72/10 . . . Seeing that 72/10 yields a number that is too big, he methodically increases the denominator, first to 80—he knows he needs a "fraction" (a number less than 1)—and then increasing by 1 until he hits upon 72/99. This fraction produces the pattern in Figure 7.3, which shows the pattern in two shades of gray, the lighter corresponding to 7 and the darker to 2.

He is surprised at this sudden emergence of pattern; 72/98 is a mess in comparison! But he also notices that the repeating colors in the pattern corresponds exactly to the numbers in the denominator and announces to me, "Nine is a magic number."

Results: .727272727272727272727272   **Figure 7.3.** 72/99: A fraction that begins orange, blue.

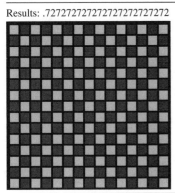

Equation: 0123456789/ 9999999999   **Figure 7.4.** "I made a rainbow."
Results: .123456789012345678901234567890

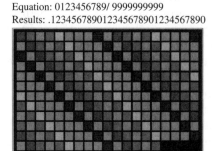

In the previous class, he had seen that a denominator of seven also creates a repeating pattern, but since the pattern seemed in no way related to the numerator, he had moved on to other fractions. But 72/99 is intriguing to him. He tries a few other cases, such as 34/99 and 59/99 and then tries 123/99. The last fraction is disappointing, but he does not give up. He makes a reasonable conjecture and tries 123/999. He sits up in his chair, with a big smile, and tells me, "I can make a rainbow." And, sure enough, he uses the "magical" properties of 9 to create a repeating sequence of colors. Figure 7.4 shows the pattern John found in shades of gray: Every swatch of gray shown in the legend of Figure 6.4 shows up in this "rainbow."

John was initially trying to find a fraction that started orange, blue. He found it, and could easily have stopped. He might also have tried to find other fractions that also start orange, blue. But John saw something he liked, something generative. One example (72/99) was enough to convince him that 9 was a magic number; he had already "deduced" that 9 would have powers outside that single example, though he was curious enough to actually check with 34/99 and 59/99. Where did that conviction come from?

It came from the same place as the mathematician's conviction (discussed in Part II), that the factorization 137 × 73 was a generative, "beautiful" pattern. Both John and the mathematician were charmed, as if such nice patterns cannot be accidental in mathematics. And because of this, John set off to see what else he could find, much like the young Le Lionnais set off to see what patterns were lurking in the third row of his numbers. It is here that one can detect another aesthetic urge: to see how a single interesting case (72/99) fits into a larger picture, to seek a more general, encompassing rule. After all, seeing one isolated case is somewhat disconcerting—one case rarely predicts or identifies the regulating principle?

He found a general rule about denominators with nines in them: If there is a fraction where the numerator has the same number of digits as the number of nines in the denominator, the repeating pattern of the decimal expansion will consist exactly of the string of digits in the numerator. And with this rule, he was able to create his rainbow. I am unsure when John had the idea to create a rainbow. I would guess that it was not until he saw what happened with 123/999. If creating the rainbow was the "solution," then it grew out of John's aesthetic response to the pattern-making power of the number 9 (relative to base 10). But one senses that John's interaction with the CC was not so teleological in spirit; rather, he was engaged in an exploratory inquiry that was fostered both by his aesthetic response and by his self-absorption in the CC world.

Saying that John was aesthetically motivated by a pattern is misleading. Ironically, since mathematics teachers often ask students to look for patterns, students come to expect that they will find one: Finding a pattern in and of itself can be quite an aesthetically sterile experience. Here is an example: I had asked a group of students to investigate how many right angles a polygon can have. They found that a triangle could only have 1 right angle, that a quadrilateral could have 4, but that a pentagon could only have 3. They thought this quite strange. "There must be a pattern" one boy muttered as he pondered the sequence 1, 4, 3. I was pleased by this assertion, interpreting it as a motivating belief about the treasures that could be found in mathematics. But my pleasure soured when I asked about the source of his conviction: "Well, this is math class; you wouldn't give us a problem that didn't have a pattern."

The difference with John is that the pattern was not the goal; the pattern was the beginning, and understanding the pattern was the means to his rainbow. I should not say that John understood the pattern; rather, he understood how it worked and how to manipulate it. And despite his interest in using the pattern, he did not ask why it worked. And when I put that question to him, he had to take out his paper and pencil, and move away from the delights of the screen.

In the three examples I have described, the students were working in computer-supported environments. Because of this, their process of inquiry was more accessible to me, as I could directly observe their actions and reactions. Moreover, the highly visual and experimental nature of the computer-supported environments may well have helped evoke aesthetic responses, and make qualitative ways of perceiving mathematical entities more accessible. In fact, as the mathematics educator Paul Goldenberg (1989) notes, computer-supported environments can foster the development and use of qualitative reasoning. Such environments, in their concreteness, open up the possibility for students to draw on visual, informal, and experimental methods in their explorations, important methods that are not dependent on symbolic-deductive techniques. John's case shows that symbolic-deductive techniques cannot—and should not—be entirely ignored. However, as the mathematics educator Michael de Villiers (1990) has argued, students will most need to use those techniques when they have asked the "Why?" question, which they can only really do once they have satisfied themselves that there actually exists a repeatable, trustworthy phenomenon that needs explaining.

MINDFUL MATHEMATICS

A mathematical situation, as any other, will have a multitude of qualities, some more overtly "mathematical" than others. Students are regularly told to ignore many of these qualities through statements from their teachers such as: "The color doesn't matter," "Mathematics is about thinking logically," and even "Just reason step by step: Don't bring your emotions into this." Teachers who instruct in this way may think that "extralogical" qualities have little to do with the solution of a problem. In so doing, however, students are encouraged solely to attend to the properties and relations relevant to the current, particular problem.

Certainly, there are instances when the color really does not matter with respect to the correct solution of the problem. But sometimes noticing the colors will provide the student with the opportunity to discern an organizing quality. More importantly, learning how to do mathematics is partly about learning how to notice and select the features of a situation worthwhile focusing on. When teachers overly restrict the class in terms of features worthy of attention, students are robbed of both an educative experience and of a possible route to further understanding.

The psychologist Ellen Langer (1998) has shown how a seemingly trivial mode of speaking can be restrictive to the point of actually damaging students' attention (and thus, their capacity to notice and select), to say nothing of their potential for imaginative thinking. She shows how traditional ways of imparting information—that is, speaking as if something is absolutely true, independent of context—deprives one of the need or impetus to notice anything. Such a style "closes down invitations to further thought," as Brent Davis (1995) writes. On the other hand, imparting information in a more conditional, contextual way ensures an appreciation of uncertainty, which increases one's tendency to notice things, see them from different perspectives, and to devote further consideration to them.

Let me demonstrate Langer's point using a mathematics example. Consider the teacher who tells her students, *The three medians of a triangle meet in one point.* Each student retains this fact, but probably misses the surprisingness of it, as well as the reasons for and implications of it. The statement does not invite further noticing. Now consider the teacher who tells students, *In an equilateral triangle, the three medians of a triangle will meet somewhere in the triangle.* Providing this context might incite the student to wonder what happens in scalene triangles, or to wonder whether meeting happens two by two or whether there is a unique meeting spot, or wonder whether there is anything special about the location of the meeting spot as well as the perhaps more technical question of how to find out where it is. While the first piece of information is precise, true, and general, it is restricted to the essential property under consideration. However, the second piece of information is less precise and general, but still true. It invites the student to consider the contingency of the statement.

Recognizing or grasping a qualitative unity, and therefore being sensitive to aesthetic modes of thinking, depends on being able to notice things about a situation. Of course, language changes are not the only means by which to nurture aesthetic engagement in students. As Brown (1993) suggests, educators also need to question the false sense of aesthetic unity perpetuated by the values of clarity and coherence found in teaching materials, teaching practices, and even, ironically, in problem-solving activities in the mathematics classroom. Day after day, students are faced with and asked to solve problems that all "work out nicely." Brown argues that this false sense of aesthetic unity is a major barrier to the development of aesthetic sensibilities, and is counterproductive to the educational goals of helping students learn how to cope with the doubts, ambivalences, and disharmonies they encounter in their fragmentary, haphazard, and incomplete lives. The irony, for Brown, is that where problem solving is supposed to be an activity involving a state of doubt, hesitation, perplexity, ambiguity, and mental difficulty, the problems that students face in mathematics classrooms are usually constructed and presented clearly and coherently, precisely in order to discourage such states. Instead of being given problems with aesthetic unity—already prepackaged—students need to be given opportunities to establish their own forms of certainty and clarity out of perplexing situations.

FITTING THE PIECES TOGETHER

In this section, I wanted to probe the various ways in which the aesthetic functions heuristically in the course of inquiry. The examples of Sara and

John revealed how very human aesthetic urges shape the goals of inquiry: looking for exactness or precision and trying to see how the particular fits into the general. In these cases, the aesthetic invites action. On the other hand, the aesthetic can also invite understanding, as it did for Casey. By being able to grasp the Frogs problem as a whole, through the symmetry of the frogs' movements, Casey was able to grasp the inaccessible situation in a more holistic, qualitative way.

In addition, the aesthetic also revealed itself as a characteristic quality in the mathematical experiences of these students. Casey explicitly sought this out by returning to the Frogs problem. But we see it more clearly in the experience of John, who engages in aesthetically driven exploratory activity. It is in this example, where John makes a rainbow, that the mathematics is most subordinated to the ultimate, expressive goal: John uses his mathematical insights to construct not a solution or a proof, but a final product. Perhaps there is a utilitarian aesthetic encompassing his inquiry: John values knowing that denominators of nines produce repeating patterns of digits because it allows him to make his rainbow. It is also in this example that the rigid distinctions between problem posing and problem solving break down, where the process of inquiry has its most cohesive shape—starting and ending in play.

I am unsure whether "utilitarian aesthetic" is the right construct, though. Certainly John uses his mathematics toward a more artistic end (as does Christine, when she makes her tree), but I wonder if it is not the expressiveness of the artistic end that is the significant factor. Both the tree and the rainbow are *personal* expressions of meaning, of mathematical understanding, that are available as part of the computer-supported environment. Actually, compared with computer-supported environments such as Boxer and The Geometer's Sketchpad, the expressiveness of the CC and Meeting Lulu microworlds is quite limited. But they do offer specialized expressive possibilities that are unavailable in the equivalent pencil-and-paper environments. For example, consider a pencil-and-paper version of the Meeting Lulu problem. Many of the mathematical questions are still relevant: Where do the players meet? When do they meet? But without the traces, which the computer automatically generates, the geometric representations remain inaccessible and the design possibilities unfathomable.

In Christine's example, I discussed the possible, implicit evaluative function played by the aesthetic; I mainly highlighted how her final product may have lacked some of the aesthetic criteria typically prized in mathematics. Zoe, on the other hand, in her more explicit evaluation of the different methods for categorizing polygons, employed familiar aesthetic criteria. She articulated them because I asked her, but she had clearly already used them, if only on a subconscious level. What purposes might they have served? In Chapter 8, I will chart out the types of criteria used by students and, more importantly, the purposes of these criteria: When and why do students evaluate mathematical entities using aesthetic criteria?

CHAPTER 8

The Evaluative Role
of the Aesthetic

The evaluative role of the aesthetic stands out as the most cited and explicit of the three functions, particularly in the world of the professional mathematician, where words such as "beautiful" and "elegant" are regularly used to distinguish good from not-so-good results and proofs. These judgments can determine whether or not a result gets published or accepted into the mathematical canon. Its influence, as well as its more public nature,[1] may account for the reason why many of the researchers who have explicitly considered the aesthetic dimension of school mathematics focus largely on this evaluative function of the aesthetic. These researchers tend to adopt a mathematics-centric justification argument, arguing that "one of the major goals of mathematics teaching is to lead students to appreciate the powers and beauty of mathematical thought" (Dreyfus & Eisenberg, 1986, p. 2). Although Dreyfus and Eisenberg acknowledge a wider presence of the aesthetic in mathematics, they believe that educators need to concern themselves first and foremost with the aesthetic dimension of problem solving—that is, with helping students develop an appreciation for the aesthetic appeal of a mathematical solution or proof.

However, students seem to have a long way to go in terms of developing this kind of appreciation. Dreyfus and Eisenberg designed a study in which they investigated whether college students were able to appreciate elegant solutions. They gave the students a set of problems to solve that were judged to have the potential to elicit elegant solutions. Their choice of problems was predicated upon whether problems had multiple solutions, nonobvious solutions, and solutions that would require only a high-school level of mathematics. Dreyfus and Eisenberg claim that students fail to appreciate the elegance of solutions judged to be elegant by "experts" and that moreover, students do not judge the solutions which are later presented to them any more attractive than the ones they have come up with on their own. Such a finding would not surprise the mathematics educator Ernst von Glasersfeld (1985), who stresses that we cannot expect children to show an appreciation for the beauty of mathematics as easily as they do for natural beauty. As I have shown, though, Dreyfus and Eisenberg, as well as von Glasersfeld, are wrongly equating the lack of agreement between students' and mathematicians' aesthetic responses with students' lack of aesthetic sense.

Ten years later, in a 1996 paper devoted to the issue of the nature of mathematical thinking, Dreyfus and Eisenberg state that there are two schools of thought on the issue of aesthetics in mathematics education. The first believes in the importance of developing aesthetic thought and attempts to introduce students to it by comparing elegant and nonelegant solutions in school-level problems (as per the 1986 recommendation). Members of the second school of thought instead find that while the aesthetic plays an integral role in the work of mathematicians, it is impossible to incorporate it into school mathematics, given students' difficulties with the most basic skills. Though Dreyfus and Eisenberg should, according to their earlier work, belong to the first school, they use the bulk of this 1996 paper to discuss the nature of mathematical thinking without mentioning the aesthetic again.

This issue of "the basics" might conceivably resonate with many mathematics educators who see the aesthetic dimension of mathematical activity either as too far up the hierarchy of mathematical ability or as an epiphenomenon—and thus dismissible, given more urgent "core" priorities. The former view finds support in the mathematics educator V. A. Krutetskii's (1976) work with gifted children, which claims to show that only mathematically capable students are sensitive to the elegance of mathematical solutions and capable of attending to a solution's clarity, simplicity, and economy. However, those who believe that aesthetic considerations should be postponed until "the basics" are covered often fail to define what is "basic," why and for whom. They also assume that the aesthetic can be separated from the cognitive and locate the development of mathematics skills solely in cognitive activity. Their educational theories of mathematics assume that only already established mathematical structures—largely numerical and logical, as opposed to spatial and visual—dictate the basic guidelines for identifying the "math basics."

In addition to the "basics" issue, there is a deeper, epistemological issue at work here. When mathematicians evaluate entities such as proofs and solutions, they do so for two reasons: One, to establish personal value; and two, to establish collective value. As the mathematics educators Alibert and Thomas (1991) note, these two purposes are often absent in school mathematics, where "the subject matter is presented as finished theory, where all is calm . . . and certain" (p. 215). Students approach mathematics as something to be accepted and learned while mathematicians approach it as something to be evaluated and negotiated—two disconnected epistemologies at work. Alibert and Thomas are particularly concerned with the problems produced by this disconnection when it comes to proofs in the mathematics classroom. While mathematicians use proofs to convince (both themselves and others), students see proofs as difficult, formal, and sometimes arbitrary things. Ironically, Alibert and Thomas believe that the perceived need to preserve the precision and the beauty of mathematics—by emphasizing the rigor of formal proofs in the classroom—may compromise students' concern for meaning and value, as well as their appreciation for the functional role of proof. In other words, why would students exhibit their preferences for one type of proof over another if they see proof as only having already-established truths? That would be an epistemological category mistake.

But what happens in classrooms where students do not see proofs strictly as formal necessities required by the teacher? In their study, Dreyfus and Eisenberg implicitly communicate the possibility that proofs can have an aesthetic value. However, they take an objectivist view of aesthetics—that a certain solution is elegant in and of itself—and, in considering students' evaluations, look primarily for aesthetic preferences that match those of professional mathematicians. Since they do not find these, they conclude that students do not show aesthetic appreciation. Yet perhaps these students are showing and exercising quite different aesthetic preferences, which suit their own current goals and needs.

For example, Stephen Brown (1973) describes what might be called a "naturalistic" conception of beauty manifest in the work of his graduate students. He recounts showing them Gauss's possibly apocryphal encounter with the famous arithmetic series: $1 + 2 + 3 + \ldots + 99 + 100$ which the young Gauss is said to have cleverly calculated as $(101 \times 100)/2$. Brown asks his students to spend some time investigating variations of the general scheme (that the sum of the first n natural numbers can be expressed as $[n \times (n + 1)]/2$. They come up with many geometric and algebraic approaches and formulations, each equivalent but expressed in various ways with equations and diagrams. Brown asks them to discuss their approaches in terms of aesthetic appeal.

Surprisingly, many of his students prefer the rather messy, difficult-to-remember formulations to Gauss's neat and simple one. Theirs are original, raw, and tangible. Brown conjectures that the messy formulations do a good job of encapsulating the students' personal history with the problem, as well as its genealogy, and that the students want to remember the struggle more than the neat end product. This is in clear opposition to the way that mathematicians like to present their results: They are almost always devoid of any of the guesses, supporting sketches, and history of the solution process. Brown's observation highlights how the contrasting goals, partly culturally imposed, of the mathematician and the student lead to different aesthetic criteria.

The question that must be addressed is whether or not the goal of nurturing such preferences is to align them with those of professional mathematicians. In contrast with Dreyfus and Eisenberg, who want to initiate students into an established system of mathematical aesthetics, I propose that educators nurture students' development of aesthetic preferences according to the animating purposes of aesthetic evaluation in school mathematics activity. The starting point would not be to train students to adopt aesthetic judgments that are in agreement with "experts" in terms of elegance and beauty. Rather, the impetus would come from providing students with opportunities in which they want to—and can—engage in personal and social negotiation of the worth of a particular idea, as I did with Zoe, Luke, and Alex—the polygon classifiers from the introductory chapter. Most importantly, students would need to operate within the terms of engagement that both allow and encourage them to look for solutions that *they* like. These solutions, as well as the aesthetic choices promoting them, may be similar to mathematicians' choices, but they also reflect their own specific concerns and preferences.

The mathematics educator Gaynor Williams (1994) has described a high school classroom setting that nurtures an appreciation for aesthetically appealing ways of expressing ideas and solving problems. In her classroom, students are not taught to pursue "elegant" or concise ideas in any objectivist definition of those terms. Rather, she both models her own aesthetic appreciation and gives her students opportunities to develop and discuss desirable values that emerge from and apply to their own work. By organizing her classroom around group work, students are able and encouraged to discuss differences among different solutions and to identify criteria that might make a certain solution better than another one. She writes:

> Students have realised there are many ways to approach the same problem. Right from the beginning of the year, even in aspects of the course where I did the teaching, it has been understood that, if anyone can see a neater, faster way to get to the same answer, we want to know about it. . . . They value responses from groups who have found an original and elegant way to approach a solution and will question until they understand the process. (p. 452)

Some students may learn to appreciate the elegance and simplicity of certain arguments or explanations, while others might appreciate solutions that correspond to their own particular thinking styles. Williams wants students to struggle with their problems, noting that when they have struggled with something for some time, and thought about possible alternative ways of solving it, they are better able to appreciate an approach that takes a different perspective and results in a simpler and possibly easier-to-understand solution. Regardless of the specific aesthetic preferences they exhibit, they will try to defend their choice within the particular culture of their classroom.

Williams explicitly emphasizes the evaluative function of the aesthetic in her classroom by encouraging the students to appreciate the value of solutions that might be more original, succinct, convincing, or clever. By modelling her own aesthetic appreciation, she must surely influence the criteria that her students value, which perhaps helps initiate them into the norms of the mathematics community. But it seems to be in the classroom negotiation that the aesthetic judgments emerge, as students are given the opportunity to compare their solutions—and not just on the basis of "truth."

WHICH SOLUTION IS BETTER?

This kind of value-oriented negotiation need not be restricted to the high school classroom. Indeed, in the following example, two middle school students who are asked to compare their solutions also draw on aesthetic criteria. Instead of asking the students to explain their solutions to each other—a frequent request in the mathematics classroom—I ask them to consider which solution is better. Of course, this requires some explanation, but the explanation has a persuasive function; it is not merely undertaken to satisfy the teacher's request. The ensuing negotiation illustrates that students take the value question seriously, and have some strong aesthetic preferences when it comes to their mathematical evaluations, some of which are perhaps surprisingly contiguous with those of the mathematical community.

John and Nora: "My Solution Is Better Than Yours"

After many tries, John figures out how to create a table of colors that starts orange, blue using the fraction 72/99. Sitting behind him, Nora also hits on a solution to the problem: 72/100 (See Figure 8.1—the light gray corresponds to orange [7] and the dark gray to blue [2]). Seeing both of these solutions on their screens, I draw them to the students' attention. When John sees Nora's screen, he hits his forehead, and says, "Oh, I should have thought of that . . . I forgot but it's just going the other way, isn't it?" Nora raises her eyebrows when she sees John's screen. I ask them which fraction is "better."

Figure 8.1. John's solution (on left) and Nora's (on right).

Equation: 72/99	Equation: 72/100
Results: .727272727272727272727272727272	Results: .72

John argues that his fraction actually gives him a method to get any initial sequence of colors; if he wants a decimal expansion that begins with 338, for example, he can use his "9's method" to come up with a correct solution of 338/999. Nora counters that her method is just as generative; an initial sequence of 338 can be provided through her decimal-based method with the fraction 338/1000.

Then John responds that his fraction is "nicer looking," since it produces a whole table of repeating colors, rather than a small sequence, and that it is "cooler," since it uses the properties of "my magic number." This seems to convince Nora, since she turns around and starts experimenting with John's method.

With little prompting, Nora and John negotiate the value of their respective solutions using several different criteria. The first criterion John invokes is that of *generativity*; he has realized that his solution reveals a generalizable pattern and he seems to value the idea that his particular solution can be extended to have a more general application. The appreciation of generativity, which both Nora and John show, is actually quite mathematically sophisticated. The mathematician G. H. Hardy (1940) mentions it explicitly in his discussion of the criteria for mathematical beauty, citing as an example the Euclidean proof that $\sqrt{2}$ is an irrational number (a proof that can easily be extended to other prime numbers).

In addition to the criterion of generativity, John also invokes a more personal criterion—his solution uses a *novel* method that he himself discovered—that might have better encapsulated his process, much like in

Brown's example of $[n \times (n + 1)]/2$. When I saw his reaction to Nora's solution—he groaned in a way that expressed the sentiment "I should have known that"—I thought he would prefer hers. But John clearly treasures his magic number 9 and his solution exploits properties he has newly discovered. In contrast, Nora had found her solution 72/100 quite easily and was perhaps not as invested in the properties she had exploited as John was in his. She might also have failed to recognize the extent to which her method uses the not-so-magical, yet still quite solid and easy-to-explain decimal place-value system. Neither John nor Nora placed much emphasis here on the criterion of transparency; they both end up preferring John's method, even though they might not be able to explain why it works, whereas they both understand why Nora's method works.

And finally, Nora and John both subscribed to the criterion of *visual appeal*; indeed, this seems to be the criterion that ultimately convinces Nora. Mathematicians rarely mention this criterion, perhaps because they communicate most of their work in nonvisual modes (and are often more than somewhat suspicious of relying on visual supports to reasoning). This might be changing somewhat, given the advent of powerful computers, as illustrated in several new books and on many websites, which use carefully chosen and aesthetically pleasing images to communicate mathematical ideas.

In the course of their negotiation, Nora and John invoked three aesthetic criteria: generativity, novelty, and visual appeal. These illustrate an already strongly developed sensibility to the aesthetic qualities that can be associated with mathematical solutions—though perhaps not a conscious awareness of them. Through John's persuasion, Nora became curious about the magic number 9 as well and decided to turn her attention to a new investigation involving nines. She did not merely accept John's solution—rather, she became convinced that his solution was interesting enough to warrant her further investigation. That might well mirror one of the most important functions of the aesthetic in the day-to-day work of mathematicians, as one tries to convince another that some solution, result, or definition is interesting enough to warrant further work, for *both*.

My prompt to negotiate the "better" solution invited Nora and John to adopt a different epistemological stance, in which mathematics is to be evaluated and negotiated. I propose that the microworld itself also contributed to affording this orientation. The computer provided Nora and John with the feedback they needed to establish that they had found correct solutions. No longer was the teacher the final arbitrator of right/wrong. Instead, I could initiate a genuine conversation about the meaning and value of their solutions. I say genuine, because my ulterior motive was not to work out issues of right and wrong, which is often the case in classroom discussions where students are invited to share and compare their solutions. Many educators have advocated the use of problems with multiple solution paths as a way of encouraging—or allowing—students to draw on different modes of reasoning. Such problems also intend to communicate to students that the process of reasoning is at least as important as the solution, or rather, that there is no right and wrong when it comes to the way a student chooses to get the solution.

So far I have focused on solutions and proofs as objects of aesthetic evaluation. But, as Le Lionnais points out, mathematicians will also judge the aesthetic value of many other mathematical entities, including definitions, diagrams, theories, methods, and algorithms. In fact, the recent discovery (in August 2002) of a new method for determining whether a number is prime illustrates how important the aesthetic value of an algorithm can be. Although existing tests for prime numbers were equally fast, this new method made headlines around the world. Why? Not because it was faster, or more accurate—these being the twin goals of most computer algorithms—but because it was more "elegant." The Agrawal-Kayal-Saxena algorithm was described by mathematicians as "straightforward," "easy to prove," "a novel approach," "simple," and "easy to improve upon." In fact, the algorithm can be written in 12 lines, which is impressively short, and it "requires only simple tools of algebra," as its authors write (Agrawal, Kayal, & Saxena, 2002, p. 2). Moreover, the algorithm does not assume the still unproven but widely believed Riemann Hypothesis, as other prime-detecting algorithms do, and thus its proof is entirely self-contained.

Obviously proofs and solutions are not the only currency in mathematics. But as is the case with proofs, students are presented with definitions, diagrams, methods, algorithms, and theories, as if, echoing Alibert and Thomas, they were finished—all being calm and certain. Students accept the division algorithm and the definition of a quadrilateral without being invited to consider, "Is it good? Is there a better one? Do I like what it does?" In the following example, I invite a group of four middle school students to consider these questions about a method for constructing a square. Once again, the invitation does not appear unusual to them, and the students hold remarkably strong opinions.

Aleah, Becca, Sara, and Zhavain: "It's More Perfect"

The four students Aleah, Becca, Sara, and Zhavain are attempting to construct their first square using Sketchpad. Constructing a square in Sketchpad is not a trivial matter; one must first know what defines a square, and then know how to use the appropriate tools. Most students start by using the segment tool to draw four equal sides (the salient property of the square) and then attempt, when the time comes, to put the segments at right angles (the more tacit property). I let the students draw squares using only the segment tool, and then show them how to use the circle tool to construct equal segments. Since they have already learned to construct perpendicular and parallel lines, they are then able to construct their container squares. Except Aleah. She is stuck on her horizontal segment, insisting on "turning it" up to a vertical position—not wanting, perhaps, to bother with circles and perpendicular lines. I show her how to turn her segment using the rotate command. Once she has completed her square, she proudly shows the technique to Sara.

I ask Sara which technique she prefers—Aleah's rotation method or her own "compass and straightedge" one? Sara thinks the rotation method is much easier and much quicker to perform (given the grammar of Sketchpad's tools at least, where rotation is a one-step action). But she describes the compass and straightedge method as "more perfect and more mathematical." I ask her what she means by "perfect," and she tells me that the compass and straightedge gives a better construction, because she knows that the "points are at the right place." Sara manages to convince Becca and Zhavain of her opinion, but not Aleah.

I then show the students how to create a custom tool that would allow subsequent squares to be created effortlessly. Sketchpad's custom tools are accompanied by scripts, which provide a symbolic representation of the steps involved in the construction associated with the tool (see Figure 8.2). Aleah thinks that the brevity of her script—only six steps, compared with ten—will help convince her classmates of the rotation method's superiority, but alas, they are stubbornly committed.

Figure 8.2. Scripts for constructing a square.

Aleah's square tool

> **Given:**
> 1. Point A
> 2. Point B
>
> **Steps:**
> 1. Let **j** = segment between A and B.
> 2. Let **B'** = rotation of Point B by 90.0° about center A.
> 3. Let **j'** = rotation of Segment j by 90.0° about center A.
> 4. Let **A'** = rotation of Point A by 90.0° about center B'.
> 5. Let $\overline{A'B'}$ = segment between A' and B'.
> 6. Let $\overline{A'B}$ = segment between A' and B.

Sara's square tool

> **Given:**
> 1. Point A
> 2. Point B
>
> **Steps:**
> 1. Let $\overline{AB}$ = segment between A and B.
> 2. Let $\odot AB$ = circle centered at A passing through B (hidden).
> 3. Let **k** = line perpendicular to $\overline{AB}$ passing through A (hidden).
> 4. Let **j** = line perpendicular to $\overline{AB}$ passing through B (hidden).
> 5. Let **A** = intersection of Perpendicular Line k and $\odot AB$.
> 6. Let $\odot BA$ = circle centered at B passing through A (hidden).
> 7. Let **B** = intersection of Perpendicular Line j and $\odot BA$.
> 8. Let $\overline{AA}$ = segment between A and A.
> 9. Let $\overline{AB}$ = segment between A and B.
> 10. Let $\overline{BB}$ = segment between B and B.

As with the previous episode, this one shows different aesthetic preferences emerging from the students' negotiation. Sara seems to have a classical orientation, preferring the Euclidean approach to constructing a square. But perhaps she had been enculturated into believing that things that are more technical, more complicated are, in turn, more mathematical. In fact, I was initially surprised at Sara's answer, convinced that she would prefer Aleah's method. But Sara also seems convinced that the compass and straightedge construction is somehow more precise. This may be due to the sense of determinacy that points of intersection provide; after all, she constructs each vertex by finding the point where a circle and a perpendicular line intersect (see Figure 8.3).

The rotation method does not have the same sense of determinacy, but of course it also provides a precise location for each vertex. Since Aleah never actually followed Sara's method, she may not have experienced that sense of determinacy that comes from finding a point of intersection.

Aleah's penchant for the rotation method has several sources. First, the rotation method is *hers*; she is the one who discovered it. Second, the rotation method grew out of her particular way of seeing a square. Even when I showed the students how to use the circle as a compass, Aleah had a specific idea about how the square should evolve that did not involve circles and perpendicular lines. She knew she wanted to rotate; all I did was to show her that Sketchpad could help her accomplish her goal. So not only was Aleah's method her own, but it answered the particular question that *she* had about making a square. In contrast, since the other students had not seen the square as Aleah did, as rotated segments, Aleah's method answered a question they did not ask.

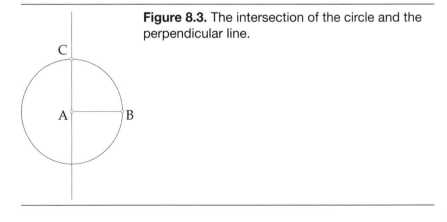

Figure 8.3. The intersection of the circle and the perpendicular line.

Lastly, Aleah seems to adopt a familiar mathematical aesthetic for simplicity and economy; she uses both as criteria for evaluating the two solutions. Her rotation method is simpler because it does not require using the circle as a compass tool, and it also essentially repeats the same step over and over, instead of requiring several constructions that are not transparently related to the square (what does a circle have to do with a square?). Her solution has more economy because it literally takes fewer steps, and saves Aleah from having to hide extra geometric objects. (In Sara's method, the circles and line segments used to determine the vertices need to be hidden and replaced with segments, as can be seen in the script shown in Figure 8.2.)

I do wonder whether Aleah actually prefers her method because it is hers and merely appeals to the criteria of simplicity and economy as less subjective-sounding reasons. Professional mathematicians might be accused of doing the same thing—ultimately preferring their own discoveries and solutions. In fact, Wells (1988) raises this issue, suggesting that they might indeed be "aesthetically biased, as many artists seem to be, toward their own fields and their own works" (p. 39). As with Aleah, professional mathematicians might also invoke aesthetic criteria such as simplicity and economy when trying to convince colleagues of the significance of their work. They may well also, as Schattschneider (2006) describes in her work on tessellations, admit to a lack of aesthetic appeal.

The first and second sources of Aleah's preference for the rotation method match Brown's suggestion that some students prefer their own solutions. However, where Brown emphasizes the students' solution process, and the attachment they feel to their solution paths, I believe Aleah's preference is not so much about the process as it is about the relationship between the problem and the solution. Aleah's method *fit* her problem, which happened to be slightly different from her classmates' problem. The mathematics she was doing connected to her own values and her own understanding, and brought to a satisfying culmination her overall experience with the construction of a square. Here the aesthetic plays a slightly more experiential role, since the "sense of fit" straddles the process of inquiry instead of operating only at the final phase.

Contexts of Negotiation. Unlike the previous case with John and Nora, the four students here do not come to a consensus, nor does their exchange lead to further investigation. However, each student develops a sense of the value of their different square-constructing methods, much as they might develop a sense of the value of a poem or book, thus establishing a personal connection with some of the mathematical ideas they will continue using in the classroom. Both episodes show quite clearly that middle school students can draw on some of the important aesthetic criteria used by professional mathematicians, something that may seem surprising given Dreyfus and Eisenberg's research cited at the beginning of this section. The apparently conflicting conclusions reveal different assumptions and goals for aesthetic appreciation.

In Dreyfus and Eisenberg's study, students who had already found their own solutions for a problem were presented with an outside, "expert" one; this set up a very different context of negotiation than the one in the two episodes I reported here. The "more elegant" solutions were essentially presented as the *right* solutions, eliciting responses from the students such as "Oh, that's how you do it." The students even became defensive: "My way works, too." Furthermore, it is not clear that the students really understood the "aesthetically superior" solutions; in fact, Dreyfus and Eisenberg report that the students wanted to "pick up the pencil and start working—without first reflecting upon different solutions paths" (1986, p. 7). This slight condemnation reflects Dreyfus and Eisenberg's belief that aesthetic judgments can be made based on objectively accessible features that determine the "aesthetic merit" of a solution, which would be agreed upon by the "experts."

However, Wells showed that some mathematicians need to "live through" a solution or proof again in order to describe its aesthetic appeal. By wanting to pick up their pencils, Dreyfus and Eisenberg's students were showing that they needed to familiarize themselves better with the different solution path before being able to compare it with their own: they could not make spontaneous value judgments.

Instead of a right versus wrong context of negotiation, the students in the two episodes were invited into a value-oriented context of negotiation. Through the process of negotiation, they were given the opportunity to familiarize themselves with each other's solutions, instead of having to make immediate judgments. I have claimed that these students appealed to aesthetic criteria that are similar to ones used by mathematicians but, for two reasons, I have not focused on whether "experts" would have agreed with any of the students' preferences. First, I follow Wells in questioning whether there is in fact a singly, unitary agreed-upon "expert" opinion and whether there is an aesthetic metric[2]—some hierarchical combination of aesthetic criteria—that could produce an "expert" opinion. After all, criteria such as simplicity, cleverness, perspicuity, and generativity may often be at odds with each other: A clever solution might be less perspicuous or a little more complex. Instead of determining whether students' judgments match those of mathematicians, I believe that more can be learned about students' mathematical aesthetic by investigating the variety of aesthetic criteria used by mathematicians and students, as well as the similarities and differences.

Second, and more importantly, students usually work with mathematical ideas that are so familiar and evident to mathematicians that they fail to elicit any aesthetic response from the latter. But even if a professional mathematician is not surprised by or drawn to the "magical" properties of 9, that does not mean the idea is unworthy of aesthetic consideration. Surely, educators cannot hope to help students appreciate the "elegance" of the Pythagorean proof of the infinity of primes without first helping them make value judgments on their own mathematics. That said, I do not believe that the primary goal of inviting aesthetic evaluation into the mathematics classroom should be to initiate students into the aesthetic norms of the mathematics community. Certainly, students need to see that the mathematical community *tends* to value aesthetic ideals such as certainty, exactness, and succinctness, so that they can understand the emphasis on rigor, proof, and terse symbolic representation in the mathematics classroom. But there is no reason to coerce students into adopting some ideal mathematical aesthetic interpreted in a metric that, say, Dreyfus and Eisenberg might use.

I have already mentioned a primary goal of inviting aesthetic evaluation into the classroom: encouraging students to develop a value-oriented sense of mathematics. In addition to presenting students with a more genuine image of mathematics as professional mathematicians practice it, a value-oriented sense of mathematics can help engage students at a more personal, humanistic level, thus making their experiences in the classroom more memorable and meaningful. After all, as Johnson (1987) argues in his book *The Body in the Mind: The Bodily Basis of Meaning, Imagination, and Reason*, the aesthetic provides the very "means by which we are able to have coherent experience that we can make some sense of" (p. xx). A value-oriented sense of mathematics should also provoke metacognitive activity since aesthetic evaluation draws on reflections of one's feelings and beliefs about mathematical ideas.

Wells (1988) offers yet another reason for inviting aesthetic evaluation into the mathematics classroom. He points out that teachers might have much to gain in probing students' aesthetic judgments by helping them adapt classroom teaching toward their students' perceptions. For instance, based on the example with Zoe (from the introductory chapter), a teacher might adapt future teaching by looking for ideas or tasks that are based on symmetry. Similarly, based on Aleah's perception of squares, a teacher might try to invite Aleah to construct other shapes using transformational geometry tools. I suggest that in probing students' aesthetic judgments, teachers might also gain insight into students' ways of thinking and feeling, which can help them adapt the conditions of classroom learning. The following example illustrates this by showing how middle school students' aesthetic reactions to the discovery of two different mathematical ideas reveal preferences about the way in which those discoveries are made. It features three grade eight students—Emma, Justin, and Aaron (classmates of Aleah), with whom I did geometry once per week over the course of an entire school year.

Emma, Justin, and Aaron: The Banality of Discovery Learning

The students have already "learned" about the sum of the interior angles of polygons. That is, they can just about remember the formula for any polygon, but definitely know what happens for triangles and quadrilaterals. So I introduce them to the idea of exterior angles. This requires a little drawing since the students do not see why exterior angles are not just the "opposite" of the interior ones (that is, the 360° complement). Once we establish that the exterior angle is what they prefer to call "the turning angle," I ask the students to investigate the exterior angles of a polygon of their choice using Sketchpad, and also show them how to construct rays and measure angles. But first, I ask them to predict what they will find. Quite reasonably, they predict that the "turning angles" will have some similarities to the interior ones—that is, have a sum that depends on the number of sides.

Before they get started, I ask the students to calculate the sum of their "turning angles" *as they measure them* so that they see the sum of the first two "turning angles" and then the sum of the first three, and so on.

The three students each pick a different polygon and proceed to construct and measure the "turning angles." This takes some time. They calculate the sums progressively. Emma announces that the sum of all five of her turning angles is 360°. Aaron says that the sum of all six of his turning angles is 429.65°; meanwhile, Emma has noticed that the sum remains 360° only when her pentagon is convex. Finally, Justin announces that the sum of his six turning angles is also 360°. We all look at Aaron's sketch and find that he has used one wrong angle in his sketch. He recalculates and finds that the sum becomes 360°.

I ask the students what they make of their original predictions. Aaron responds, "I guess we were wrong—the angles just add to 360." Since we have only looked at pentagons and hexagons, I ask them why they think the same relationship will hold for other polygons. They shrug their shoulders, then all agree that it will. Emma, always the first to question, asks why. So I show them, by "walking around a path" that when I return to my starting position I have "swept out" a whole circle, no matter how many steps I take, which is simply 360°. "Oh yeah, that makes sense," says Aaron.

Since there seemed to be nothing more to be said, I return to the question they had asked at the beginning of the class, how to make the Pythagorean tree (shown in Figure 8.4). With the 5 minutes remaining, I show them. First, you start with a square, and then you have to construct a right-angled triangle whose hypotenuse is one side of the square. I then realize that in order to do this, I need to use the "inscribed angle theorem," which states that if an inscribed angle of a circle intercepts a diameter, then the angle is a right angle. I apologize for having to introduce this new theorem so quickly and promise them that we will return to it later in the year. I then construct the circle centered on the midpoint of AC and use that circle to construct the right-angled triangle ABC (see Figure 8.4).

Before I can move on to the next step, Aaron grabs the mouse from me, saying, "Wait, that can't be true all the time." In particular, he seems worried about the cases when the point B is close to the end points A and C of the diameter. He drags B around and sees that the angle measure remains at 90°. I hear a chorus of "cool" and "neat." Since they seem interested, I tell them that this theorem can be used in designing seating for concert stages. If all the seats are placed on a semicircle in front of the stage (which acts as the diameter of the circle), every audience member will have the same viewing angle. More choruses of "cool" and "neat" ensue from all three students. I then finish the Pythagorean tree. The students stare at the screen and declare their surprise at how easily and quickly this "complicated-looking thing" could be made.

Figure 8.4. Making the Pythagorean tree fractal.

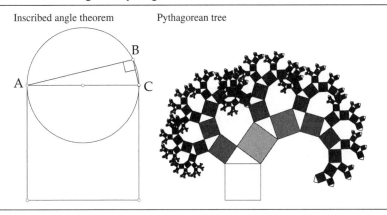

The students were quite unmoved upon discovering that the sum of the exterior angles of a polygon remains constant (the Sum of Exterior Angles, or SEA, theorem). I had tried to build up their expectations—by asking them to predict—in order to set them up for a surprise, but they failed to show any such signs of it. I had also tried to provide them with a sense of fit by having them calculate the nonconstant intermediate sums, so that the last angle would fit, like a tessellating tile, into the remaining space. By contrast, the inscribed angle theorem, which is also about a constant measure, elicited both surprise and interest. This was unexpected for me, since I had felt uncomfortable about having to introduce the theorem in such an out-of-the-blue manner and had simply hoped that the students would nod it by, anxious as they were to see the final construction.

Why were the students aesthetically numb to the apparently personally engaging and surprising discovery, yet aroused and intrigued by a haphazard discovery the importance of which I had even tried to downplay? In retrospect, I wondered whether they had sensed a higher degree of purposiveness in the inscribed angle theorem, since it had the functional value of leading us to the construction of the Pythagorean tree. If functionality can be seen as an aesthetic criterion—and the modernist movement in architecture would certainly warrant it—then perhaps the students valued it more than the criteria of surprise and fit that I had tried to evoke.

When I asked the students about their reactions a few days later, they offered other reasons. Actually, at first they were reluctant to admit their curiosity about the inscribed angle theorem. But when I reminded them of their excitement over that theorem, Aaron explained why the SEA discovery had not elicited any reactions for him: "When you know how it works, the theories behind it and why it happens, it's not so surprising." With the inscribed angle theorem, though, he explained: "But I never thought that would happen, I never even thought of those things, so when you showed us it really was surprising." Emma added that the SEA discovery had been a little tedious to do and that "when it takes a long time to get it all together, you sort of lose the surprise." Then she added, "Anyway, we know that we'll discover something at the end because it's math class." Justin nodded his head at this comment, and added his own explanation: "And we know that angles do tricks because of the inner angles thing, but that circle thing was something that we had never seen before and it was all in one picture."

Since the students had not mentioned it, I probed my own hypothesis about functionality. They seem unconvinced, claiming that their interest in the inscribed angle theorem was completely separate from their enchantment with the Pythagorean tree. But perhaps their anticipation to see how the Pythagorean tree was constructed acted as an affective and aesthetic primer, putting the students in a state of expectancy and attentiveness that allowed them to appreciate the inscribed angle theorem. If so, the students are right in dismissing the functionality hypothesis, yet the Pythagorean tree does serve a purpose. It provides both the cognitive and emotional context for the inscribed angle theorem.

Finally, I asked the students whether they would prefer it if I always just told them theorems, given their preference for out-of-the-blue surprises. Aaron quickly replied, "It's tricky, because we learn better when we do it ourselves, probably I'll always remember the exterior angles thing." Trying to be helpful, Emma proposed that, "You mix things so that sometimes we discover and sometimes you tell us."

While acknowledging its pedagogical limitations, the students express a distinct preference for the way they learned the inscribed angle theorem over the way they learned the SEA theorem. To those who lament the "canned" nature of many guided discovery activities, this may not be surprising. Emma's comment suggests that the guided discovery approach to the SEA theorem can be accused of having a "false sense of aesthetic unity." As Aaron notes, students may remember the theorems better, perhaps even understand why they work; however, they are robbed of the feelings of doubt and messiness that characterize mathematical inquiry.

WONDER AND THE AESTHETIC

Aaron's comment ("When you know how it works, the theories behind it and why it happens, it's not so surprising") brings to fore once again the relationship between wonder and learning discussed by Aristotle, Descartes and, more recently, Fisher (1998) in his book *Wonder, the Rainbow and the Aesthetics of Rare Experiences*. Aaron intimates that things he knows and understands, as well as things with which he has grown familiar, cannot evoke surprise and wonder. Fisher agrees, arguing that only that which we see as if for the first time can evoke wonder. But Fisher also relates wonder to learning, claiming, along with Socrates, that all learning begins in wonder. Fisher's view of learning is that it proceeds from sequences of small steps of wonder, sequences of surprising moments when prior experience is momentarily upset, but which that same prior experience prepares us to understand. Building on Descartes's view, Fisher argues that wonder is primarily characterized by surprise, by its unexpectedness and suddenness. Yet surprise by itself is not enough; there also has to be simultaneous certainty and a sense of realization that joins the surprise. The realization is the learning, and it is marked—recorded—by a feeling of pleasure. Without the certainty, there is no sense of wonder. He says "The mind says 'aha!' in the aesthetic moment when the spirit says 'ah!'" (p. 31).

Justin's comment about the inscribed angle theorem being "all in one picture" as well as being "something we had never seen before," certainly reflects the visual nature of his experience in addition to the sense of unexpectedness. Justin may not have understood why the inscribed angle had to be 90°, yet, according to Fisher, his immediate feeling of pleasure after realizing "this is so" indicates that he has learned it.

Educators might well wonder how teachers are to succeed in constantly evoking student wonder; surely math class cannot be entirely visual and unexpected. But Fisher is not concerned here with formal instruction and offers no help in this direction. Instead he cautions, with Descartes, that wonder declines with familiarity and that one has to work to keep alert in order to notice extraordinary things, and to avoid becoming "addicted to even trivial differences" without reflective pursuit of knowledge. Indeed, even the more complex patterns evoked by Gombrich in Figure 3.1 can become boring. Clearly, the three students had become too familiar both with the guided discovery approach and with the routine of adding up the angles of the polygon. Would the students have reacted differently had we done the SEA theorem a few weeks later? Would the students have reacted differently had I just told them the result?

I find it strange that Emma, who complained about the drudgery of the guided discovery approach, was the one who was curious enough to explore the concave case—without my prompting—and to propose that the SEA theorem only holds for convex polygons. From Fisher's perspective, once released from the predetermined path expected in the math class, having discovered that the sum of the exterior angles is constant, Emma was finally free to notice the extraordinary circumstance brought on by dragging one vertex of her pentagon. Would she have been more surprised by the SEA theorem had I instructed her to *start* with a concave polygon, one that does not "work out" as she would expect?

I do not have any sure answers to the hypothetical questions posed above. However, the aesthetic analysis occasioned by the students' experiences with two different ways of learning at least suggests the kinds of alternatives that a teacher could try as she struggles to adapt teaching strategies toward her students' ways of thinking and feeling. It is worth keeping in mind, though, that the capacity to wonder is also an attitude toward experience. If novelty is a necessary ingredient of wonder, as well as surprise, what are its precursors? What makes us capable of wondering?

The educator Tom Green (1971) argues that one precursor is the sense of contingency, the awareness that things need not be as they are. He writes, "Wonder is the product, not of ignorance, but of the knowledge that facts are problematic" (p. 197).

Mathematics is a world in which the struggle between the dependable and the contingent crystallize; in which dependable facts abound as a result of strict assumptions. But what if we *could* divide by 0, what if we threw away the parallel postulate, what if irrational numbers were our counting blocks, what if we really could have staircases like those drawn by M. C. Escher, what if we could redefine differentiability to cope with some kinds of discontinuity? The capacity to wonder also involves a confession of limitation or ignorance. To wonder is to acknowledge one's ignorance—not in a state of despair or passivity, but in the pleasurable pursuit of further knowledge.

How would Fisher talk to those for whom explanation of the science of the rainbow appears to spoil their delight? He uses the emergence of curiosity after an experience of wonder as a bridge between wonder and thought: the process of wondering. Perhaps those who have had an explanation of the rainbow thrust upon them, before they wondered about it independently, *wanting* an explanation, would find scientific description to be anticlimactic . . . unless they find scientific explanation wonderful in its own terms. This may very well be how Aaron felt about the SEA theorem. In a sense, this suggests a distinction between different types of wonder. When I wonder *why* the rainbow appears, or *how* it appears, my wonder will cease when I find the answer—my curiosity will be satisfied. Yet I can also continue to wonder *at* the rainbow. How can it be that there is a rainbow? This question will not be resolved through investigation; instead, it shows that I stand astonished before the contingency of the rainbow, even though I know how it works. Clearly, Aaron does not feel this way about the SEA theorem. In fact, he had access to neither type of wonder during the guided discovery activity, whereas the inscribed angle theorem at least provided him with the first type. And since I did not explain how the inscribed angle theorem works, perhaps he was even left wondering *at* it.

VALUING THE AESTHETIC

It is tempting, for one who takes pleasure in and values the beauty and elegance of certain mathematical entities, to view aesthetic appreciation as a goal in and of itself. Taken into an educational context, the temptation can turn into a conviction that students should be able to take pleasure in and value the beauty and elegance of mathematical solutions and proofs—as is sometimes found in some curriculum guides (e.g., the mathematics framework for the Canadian Atlantic Provinces [Atlantic Provinces Educational Foundation, 1996] includes "Aesthetic Expression" as one of the six "essential graduation learnings"). By showing that students often fail to perceive supposed beauty in a fruitful solution or elegance in a succinct proof, Dreyfus and Eisenberg's study suggests that students may not be able to engage in aesthetic evaluation for the same self-fulfilling purposes that motivate many mathematicians. In contrast, however, the examples above have illustrated that students can and do behave aesthetically in the mathematics classroom, but that their aesthetic behaviors have very functional, although pedagogically desirable, purposes: establishing personal and social value.

In each example, aesthetic behavior was elicited by inviting students to consider the value of the mathematical entities with which they were working. In the first two examples, the value-oriented approach provided a framework for the comparison of students' own solutions. Note that the students were not simply presenting their solutions to an audience—rather, they were engaged in persuading their audience that their solutions had value.[3] This involvement appeals to qualitative and ultimately more subjective criteria that rarely enter into negotiations of correctness. And though various aesthetic criteria were called upon, personal attachments seemed to dominate, as might be expected given the moral and emotional development of middle school students. I have found that older students tend to reach a level of detachment that privileges a certain set of aesthetic criteria pervasive in the mathematics community.

The third example involved a comparison of mathematical ideas presented to students, and thus avoided the bias engendered by a student's investment in his or her own work. In a sense, this third example provided the most insight into the aesthetic dimension of student learning. We know that a student's understanding of an idea will depend on the way in which it is presented and explained, but this example underlined how a student's appreciation of an idea—and interest in an idea—can depend on the way she encounters it.

We rarely ask students *what* they would like to learn or get better at; the rigidity of the curriculum makes it difficult for teachers to adapt content to the interests of students. In contrast, we might be able to ask *how* they would like to learn. Teaching strategies and methods, though influenced by teaching philosophies and histories, seem more flexible and thus more adaptable to students' ways of thinking and feeling. And perhaps, by probing their students' perceptions, teachers might gain access to their students' sense of wonder.

FITTING THE PIECES TOGETHER: AESTHETICS AND INQUIRY

This chapter concludes my empirical investigation into student mathematics. Using an aesthetic lens, I have revealed the three ways in which the aesthetic can and does function in the mathematical activities of middle school students. I have also discussed some of the challenges that educators will face in trying to evoke and nurture students' aesthetic abilities. I want to emphasize that these examples present only an "existence proof" of the roles of the aesthetic in student mathematics, and constitute but a first step toward designing and studying aesthetically rich learning environments.

However, the aesthetic lens has also provided a powerful tool with which teachers and researchers can understand what goes on in mathematics classrooms. It helps us see what can all too often seem like familiar behavior and activity in a new and generative way.

The various ways in which both mathematicians and student mathematicians become attracted to mathematical situations and problems—where the motivational role of the aesthetic was seen to operate—do not only serve an affective motivational purpose. They also contribute to providing the learner with what Dewey calls *qualitative unity*, which affects the choices and decisions made by the learner as a problem becomes determined and hypotheses are generated—where the generative role of the aesthetic was seen to operate. This was evident in both the kissing triangles' mathematical discovery of Chapter 4, and in, for example, Christine's discovery with Meeting Lulu, mentioned in Chapter 6. In the latter case, though, it seemed that the line between the motivational and generative functions of the aesthetic was particularly blurred. Dewey's account explains why this should be so: The aesthetic attraction to a problem plays a part in shaping the inquiry by influencing the discernment and selection of features in a situation, and thereby directing the thought patterns of the inquirer. Therefore, it is not necessary for students to actually select their own problems, as do mathematicians, in order to prompt the motivational role of the aesthetic, though problem selection could certainly help evoke students' attentiveness to certain qualitative features.

The generative role of the aesthetic is more difficult—even impossible—to evoke without the learner's initial attraction and attention to a qualitative unity. After all, the aesthetic choices made in the course of inquiry depend on the qualitative apprehensions, and operate on vague suggestions of relations and distinctions rather than on firm propositional knowledge. And if one is truly solving a problem or exploring new territory, vague suggestions of relations and distinctions are all there is to go on—for mathematicians and students alike. These relations and distinctions are discerned patterns—such as rhythm or symmetry—that can be imposed on one's understanding of a situation. Identifying such patterns depends upon one's attentiveness to the emerging sense of an enveloping whole, a sense of whole that guides the further selection and manipulation of component parts.

The various strategies involved in the generative function of the aesthetic (playing or "getting a feel for," establishing intimacy, and enjoying the craft) may all help the mathematical inquirer work with these relations and distinctions in establishing some unifying structure. They are not strategies that generate propositional knowledge; rather, they allow an inquirer to finds ways of directly experiencing qualities of a situation, and thus reestablishing some kind of qualitative unity. In a sense, the strategies help the inquirer enter into the subject-matter anew, with fresh perspectives and newly cued prior experiences.

Moving away from the specific roles to the more general flow of inquiry helps focus the intimate connection between the motivational and the generative roles of the aesthetic. They are codependent and coevolving: Though the motivational is initiated in the first stages of mathematical inquiry, giving rise to Dewey's required, *felt* tension, it shapes the selections and actions that follow, thereby taking on a heuristic character. Now it is apparent why Burton's (1999b) "ponderings, what ifs, it seems to be thats, and it feels as thoughs" strategy succeeded in eliciting an aesthetic response in Casey. It gave her the chance to reestablish a qualitative unity of the situation, and thus a new basis on which to make selections and actions.

Both the motivational and the generative are living in and sustaining of inquiry, in contrast with the often more reflective and after-the-fact evaluative role of the aesthetic. The aesthetic judgments constituting the evaluative character of the aesthetic seem to be made as one considers the fitness of one's ideas, whether they achieve some compelling form or whether they have succeeded in translating a pervasive quality into a system of definite coherent terms. The way in which Dewey characterizes the close of an investigation in the process of inquiry leaves open the possibility for two forms of aesthetic evaluations in mathematics. On the one hand, there is the immediate, experiential aesthetic response to the qualitative unity of a solution. This kind of aesthetic response includes a distinctly affective component, which helps announce the close of an inquiry: Recall, for example, John's emotional reaction when he created his rainbow. On the other, there is the evolving, purposeful, aesthetic appraisal that shapes the presentation of the solution, the "write-up" of a solution. I discussed this kind of aesthetic appraisal earlier when I quoted Wolfgang Krull's claim that mathematicians "also want to arrange and assemble the theorems so that they appear not only correct but evident and compelling" (1987, p. 49). The process of writing up a solution may yield an immediate, experiential aesthetic response as well, when one, for instance, has found the "perfect" way—enlightening, clever, parsimonious, and so on—of communicating the solution.

The roles of the aesthetic vitalize the personal creation of knowledge. They involve the learner's attention to aesthetic qualities of a situation, and the learner's desire to achieve a sense of "fit." However, I suggested in Part II that the evaluative aesthetic also operates—in addition to the two ways articulated above—in the social creation of mathematical knowledge, in the negotiation of significance within a mathematical community. This was especially apparent in the analyses of student activity, where aesthetic *values* emerged most markedly when the students attempted to negotiate the worth of their solutions or ideas among themselves. Aesthetic values do not follow so much from individual discernment and desire. Instead, they are defined and shaped by a community, and accepted or adopted by members of that community. In order to become participants in the mathematical community, learners need to become aware of the prevalent aesthetic values, which means that they will have to learn to appreciate the importance of the aesthetic criteria professional mathematicians adopt. Therefore, while experience and socioculturally mediated values will have some impact on the three roles of the aesthetic in inquiry, it is perhaps in the postinquiry evaluative role that enculturation will be most significant—an issue I will pursue in Chapter 9.

PART IV

Aesthetic Enculturation

Both Part II and Part III focused an aesthetic lens on the actions, decisions, and experiences of *individuals*—including mathematicians, students, and learners. In these instances, the roles of the mathematical aesthetic were played out in distinct, personal ways for each of these individuals. However, the aesthetic sensibility drawn upon by each individual was shaped by contextual factors, as was often intimated in this book. In particular, it was influenced by cultural values that may operate within both large groups such as the community of professional mathematicians and smaller groups such as a ninth grade classroom in Kalamazoo.

In Part IV, however, I seek to develop a *social* rather than individual lens on the mathematical aesthetic. Chapter 9 explores the aesthetic dimension of the values associated with the mathematics culture, and the impact that these values have had on the discipline itself. Chapter 10 begins by investigating the extent to which those values manifest themselves in the broad context of mathematics education (specifically, in curriculum-dictated topics and in the tasks and tools used by teachers and learners), then explores how mathematical values are communicated to students—explicitly or not—in the classroom. The ultimate goals of Part IV are to identify the ways in which aesthetic enculturation already occurs in the mathematics classroom, to determine what effect this process of enculturation has on the beliefs and actions of teachers and students, and to point to contexts and forms of communication that might productively support students' appreciation of the aesthetic dimension of mathematical values. I draw extensively here on the work of other mathematics education researchers, in conjunction with the aesthetic lens developed in this book, to reflect upon and sometimes refine their insights.

CHAPTER 9

Peering Inside
the Mathematics Culture

As I have argued throughout this book, aesthetic sensibility can help engage students in mathematical exploration, guide their process of inquiry, and establish personal meanings about their mathematical work. The aesthetic operates in the personal domain of the individual learner, where the learner is responding to qualities of her environment. However, as was made clear in my discussion of the evaluative role of the aesthetic, in their aesthetic responses, individuals are influenced by the values found in a particular culture, such as the culture of research mathematics. As a culture, mathematics is driven by a distinct set of values—of which some specifically pertain to the aesthetic—that distinguish it from other human domains of inquiry in terms of the production, perception, and communication of knowledge, as well as its organization for posterity. These values are responsible for the way in which the very human practice of doing mathematics gives rise to abstract, dehumanized ideas.

FROM OUTSIDE TO INSIDE THE CULTURE

Even though mathematicians do not always agree on the specifics of their aesthetic responses and preferences, they have been enculturated into a community where values shape their mathematical investigations and the ways in which they communicate the results of their work. Individual mathematicians may engage their aesthetic sensibility to a greater or lesser degree, but the culture in which they work has developed a set of values that circumscribe them all. Those outside the mathematics culture, interested in peering in, will need to understand how these values are interwoven into the fabric of the discipline and how they are communicated within the discipline, among its practitioners and between its novices and experts.

Many current and past students of mathematics—who live and have lived outside this culture—might be surprised to learn that mathematics is not a value-free subject. They might assume that mathematical truths are objective, unchanging, and absolute in the sense that they would always turn out the same, no matter which particular people are creating them. Yet mathematical values are implicit in almost every set of curriculum expectation; even the seemingly innocuous teacher imperative to "check your work" hints at the intricate set of actions and goals that are valued in mathematics.

Given the focus of this book, I want to identify some of the *aesthetic* aspects of the values inherent in the mathematics culture and to understand how these values shape both the discipline and its teaching. It is often difficult for those outside a particular culture to perceive and understand the values that shape it—many people experience this when visiting foreign countries.[1] Most mathematics teachers, despite their fluency with the subject, actually also live outside the mathematics culture, as do almost all of their students. This makes the task of educating students mathematically—which includes enculturating them—quite challenging.

Fortunately, Alan Bishop (1991), who has studied the social and cultural aspects of the mathematics community extensively, has been able to identify six principal relationships to knowledge valued by the mathematics culture, in terms of both historical and contemporary standpoints. Not all of these values are explicitly related to the aesthetic interests of this book, so I will focus more on some than on others. My goal is to determine the aesthetic implications of these values in order to help those outside the culture to appreciate them, understand them, and perhaps even develop a critical stance toward them. It will then be possible to consider mathematics enculturation from an aesthetic point of view, and propose ways in which teachers might attend to the creation and negotiation of aesthetically relevant values in their classrooms.

WHAT DO MATHEMATICIANS VALUE?

Bishop identifies three pairs of principal values historically associated with mathematics: rationalism and objectivism, control and progress, and openness and mystery. These six values may or may not be exhaustive, but they certainly provide substantial enough insight into the culture of mathematics for the purposes of this chapter. They also have varying degrees of relation to the aesthetic. Each pair of values is set in opposition, but is also linked, thus reflecting well the complex emotional, social, and ideological composition of values and indicating strongly that values are not truths, nor are they necessarily good or bad.

Rationalism and Objectivism

The rationalism value, according to Bishop, takes deductive reasoning as the only true way of achieving satisfactory explanations and conclusions; it shuns other forms of explanation that betray their human creators, such as trial-and-error pragmatism, rules of practice, traditional wisdom, and inductive or analogic reasoning. In everyday discourse, to be *rational* is to seek logical connections between ideas, thus overcoming the inconsistencies, disagreements, or incongruities that may arise from personal interpretations of situations or ideas. Rational reasoning is often seen as a good thing, except in cases where people overrationalize or appeal to logical arguments in order to defend their desires (as in, "I rationalize eating more chocolate because it contains important minerals"). Bishop writes that people are guided by and uphold the everyday rationalism value "when we disprove a hypothesis, when we find a counterexample, when we pursue a line of reasoning to a "logical conclusion" and find it is a contradiction to something known to be true, and when we reconcile an argument" (1991, p. 63). But rationalism is not, in and of itself, good; however, in mathematics, it is valued as a form of justification more than in any other domain.

The objectivism value is paired with rationalism, and characterizes a worldview dominated by images of material objects, free from the interpretations and machinations of humans. In particular, the kind of objectivism that drives mathematics, as Bishop points out, is one in which ideas can be given objective meanings, thereby enabling them to be dealt with *as if* they were objects, and *as if* there were an objective mathematical reality. This focus on objects detracts from that of process: it constantly insists on reifying behavior (e.g., the process of adding) into atomistic things, or objects (the concept of sum).[2] Objectivism and rationalism together seem to give mathematics its foundationalist bent—that is, its tendency to search for the essential building blocks of theories and proofs (or the axioms and postulates, in the case of Euclidean geometry).[3] Benjamin Bloom's extensive study during the 1930s of the personal and family history of North American prodigies in a variety of fields (including mathematics) identified a number of characteristic personality traits. Some that were identified in the mathematical subjects included a "penchant for solitude" and a "desire for precision" (see Gustin, 1985), as well as being independent-minded. The mathematicians also made frequent references to enjoying being able to "derive from scratch," as well as what could be called a *fundationalist tendency*, a desire to get to the bottom of things.

Control and Progress

Bishop's next pair of values is that of control and progress. The control value is associated with the desire to predict, which in turn is associated with a quest for security and mastery. Mathematics seeks to control, and to make abstract objects behave predictably, according to the well-formulated rules dictated by mathematicians, and this provides more security than do authoritative examples, alternate interpretations, or selective evidence.

The progress value, an attitude complementary to that of control, includes feelings of growth, development, change, and the desire to make the unknown known—the value is a dynamic one compared with the static, security-seeking value of control. Progress can be valued in mathematics because things that were unknown before are known now and will remain known in the future. The roots of the tree or the foundations of the building are secure and, therefore, the impetus can always lead toward new knowing, new branches, and new floors of the building. Compare this disciplinary value to that found in literary criticism, where scholars constantly return to old knowledge for reinterpretation or reconsideration. Given the attitude that new knowledge can be created, checked, and proved useful, it is rarely the case that mathematicians need to reconsider the truth of the Pythagorean theorem, for example.

Openness and Mystery

The final set of values proposed by Bishop is that of openness and mystery. Openness is concerned with the fact that "Mathematical truths, propositions and ideas generally, are open to examination by all" (p. 75) and that they are, therefore, not apparently dependent on opinion, politics, cultural differences, or beliefs. Of course, anyone who has opened a mathematics journal published in the past century knows that the mathematics there is hardly open to examination *by all*. As Bishop points out, one must first know the conventions and symbols being used, and second, find the ideas appealing enough to attempt to make sense of them. Thus, the openness value might better describe the desire to achieve universal and "pure" knowledge which, in principle, can be openly verifiable—independently of psychological or political issues.[4] In order to be universal, such knowledge—the demonstrations and proofs—must be formalized into declarations that admit no subjective interpretations, and which make ideas explicit and open to criticism and objective analysis.

Of course, the process of formalization also requires dehumanization; the facts must, so to speak, be made to "speak for themselves." To this point, the mathematician Gian-Carlo Rota has written that mathematical proof becomes a form of "pretending," since the language of proof produces a striking gap between "the written version of a mathematical result and the discourse that is required in order to understand the same result" (p. 142). Thus, understanding is compromised, or rather, exchanged for a kind of functional language, one where "Clarity has been sacrificed to such shibboleths as consistency of notation, brevity of argument and the contrived linearity of inferential reasoning" (p. 142). Rota's claim suggests that the openness value that shapes mathematical language has compromised human understanding and perhaps, indeed, concealed it.

Finally, the mystery value: From a historical point of view, mathematicians have long been associated with astrology, alchemy, *gematria*, and magic; and, from a more contemporary point of view, questions such as the following continue to mystify the ordinary citizen: What is mathematics? Who does mathematics, why, and for what ends? Bishop argues that mathematical mystery originated partly in the ancient Greek cultivation of exclusiveness. Mathematicians took steps to preserve their mystery by making mathematics that was abstract and removed from everyday life. The Pythagorean pledge of secrecy can be seen as a quest for exclusivity in the close connection between mystery and mysticism. More contemporary practices in mathematics—in which one mathematician's work is intelligible to and learnable by only a handful of colleagues—continue to uphold this tradition, whether consciously and deliberately or not.

In linking pairs of values, Bishop rightly reflects the fact that they intermingle in ways that produce certain characteristic, and sometimes contradictory, traits in mathematics. I want to consider one of the most important of these traits, namely, the unique form and language of justification—that of mathematical proof. I see mathematical proof as stemming from the interplay between several of Bishop's values. The mathematics educator Nicolas Balacheff (1988) provides a helpful set of characteristics of the language of mathematics that includes decontextualization, depersonalization, and detemporalization. These characteristics can be described, respectively, as detaching mathematical objects from their circumstances, detaching actions from the ones who acted upon them, and turning actions that occur over time into timeless objects. These acts are motivated quite clearly by the six values described above. For example, depersonalization and decontextualization avoid the psychological or political disagreements that openness seeks to avoid. The act of detemporalization satisfies well those who value objectivism. And many other links can probably be made. I introduce Balacheff's three "de's" because they provide a good example of how the six values have contributed to shaping mathematics, but also because the effect of the values on the language of mathematical proof has an interesting aesthetic dimension, as I will show in the next section.

THE AESTHETIC DIMENSION OF MATHEMATICAL VALUES

There are many ways in which the values described above affect the teaching and learning of mathematics, and Bishop traces some of these in his book. Naturally, the mathematics discipline morphs somewhat under pedagogical influences; however, it is still worth probing the extent to which mathematical values reveal themselves—whether explicitly, but more often implicitly—in contemporary teaching practices, and to consider whether they should or could be more present in mathematics classrooms. Of course, I am particularly interested in the aesthetic dimension of these values, how the process of enculturation currently evolves, and how it might potentially evolve. I consider each of Bishop's value in turn, probing first its aesthetic aspect, and then look for evidence of its manifestation in mathematics education.

The aesthetic dimension of the rationalism value relates to the sense of completeness and wholeness that adheres to a logical argument. The opposite aesthetic orientation might value fuzziness, imprecision, and loose ends—which are often praised in artistic production, but are banished in public mathematics, where clarity, consistency, containment, and cohesion find greater endorsement. The mathematician's desire for such aesthetic qualities is about a discomfort with graded truths: It is claimed that logical conclusions, like cohesion and consistency, do not admit degrees. Arguments are, on the one hand, either logical or not, and on the other, either consistent or not.

The rationalism value prevails today, particularly in the public sphere, in the way mathematics is communicated within the culture (in journals and conferences) and in the way it is communicated to those outside the culture (in education and media). However, so are examples of mathematical undertakings that hint at different aesthetics, such as applied mathematics and fuzzy logic or the bottomless complexity of fractals and the limitless slipperiness of post-Gödelian logic. Therefore, while mathematics is dominated by rationalism, one can imagine other forms of mathematical inquiry, and this is the sense in which rationalism is considered a value rather than a truth or simply a fact.

The mathematician François Le Lionnais (1948/1986) points to an alternative aesthetic in the mathematics culture—one absent in Bishop's analysis—that seems also to conflict with the rationalism value. Le Lionnais's relates more to the psychological than to the disciplinary.

He evokes this alternative aesthetic—a "romantic" as opposed to a "classical" one—by comparing two styles of human endeavor: on the one hand, a desire for equilibrium, harmony, and order; on the other, a yearning for lack of balance, form obliteration, and pathology.[5] The mathematician Wolfgang Krull (1987) suggests a very similar line of division: the concrete (instead of the romantic) versus the abstract (instead of the classical). He sees mathematicians with concrete inclinations as being attracted to "diversity, variegation, and the like," comparing these inclinations to the ones that find heavily ornamented buildings attractive. In contrast, those with an abstract orientation prefer "simplicity, clarity, and great 'line'" (p. 52).

The classical or abstract style cannot be equated with the rationalism value, though the similarities are apparent, but the romantic or concrete style certainly seems to stand in opposition to rationalism, especially when Le Lionnais begins to describe it in relation to mathematical objects, such as imaginary numbers, which impress through "le culte des émotions violentes, du non-conformisme et de la bizarrerie" [the cult of violent emotions, of nonconformism and of the bizarre] (p. 444). In contrast, a classical style tends to the austerity of, for example, magic squares or Pascal's triangle, and to mastery over diversity. In orienting his description of the mathematical aesthetic, Le Lionnais is careful to emphasize values not as objective truths; instead, he shows how different mathematicians exercise their values.

This chapter, however, is concerned with the mathematics culture as a whole, and not with the idiosyncrasies of individual mathematicians. Nonetheless, in calling attention to several examples in which mathematicians articulate a romantic style, Le Lionnais's insight into the mathematics culture provides a more complex view of the rationalism value, and one that might have interesting consequences in terms of school enculturation. I will return to these shortly, after considering the way in which Bishop's rationalism value manifests itself in school mathematics.

The aesthetic dimension of the rationalism value can be detected in the goals, structure, and progression of any mathematics program or curriculum, in the striving for consistency, containment, and cohesion. For example, I know of no curriculum that is designed with the intention that students encounter the quadratic formula without first having worked with square roots, and of no curriculum in which students learn how to multiply using base-ten system and divide using the base-two system. It may seem to the reader that things could be no other way, but I suggest that school mathematics curricula are being guided by the values of the mathematics culture, and that it would be possible (though perhaps strange) to think of school curricula as much less cohesive or consistent.[6]

In the classroom, a teacher's imperatives to "write your solution clearly" or "consider all the possible cases" can be seen as implicitly reflecting an aesthetic dimension of rationalism, as can the pedagogical tendency discussed by Brown (1993) of giving students tasks that are always clear and coherent. One aspect of reform teaching that challenges the rationalism value involves encouraging students to use trial-and-error approaches in their problem solving, as well as inductive or analogic reasoning. While these forms of solutions are encouraged, particularly in earlier grades, I think that deductive reasoning is still seen as the epitome of mathematics, as something students should eventually achieve—leaving them perhaps to wonder whether other forms of reasoning are not mathematical at all. Many mathematics educators have argued for the importance and prevalence of analogic and metaphoric reasoning (see, e.g., English, 2004). Their arguments have aimed to show either how supporting such forms of reasoning can improve student understanding or that such forms of reasoning are ubiquitous in mathematical thinking. Here, I am more concerned with how the use, or lack thereof, of such forms of thinking in the classroom communicates to students the values of the mathematical community.

Though the aesthetic dimension of objectivism is less apparent to me than that of rationalism, an aesthetic desire for simplicity and purity can be detected in objectivism's goals. Theories that are built on a small set of fundamental axioms have an attractive simplicity, while objectifying processes—dehumanizing and decomplexifying them—betray a quest for "pure" ideas that have been tamed enough to provide order, regularity, and predictability. The mathematician does not necessarily want to dehumanize mathematical ideas; rather, the desire is to bracket (separate ideas from their nonmathematical contexts) and purify them, and this requires extracting them from the complex flux of the human scene.

I note two examples of the objectivism value in mathematics education. First, the continued and irrevocable movement toward reification, at an earlier and earlier age (e.g., mathematical functions move quickly from being processes in which an input is linked to an output to being static symbolic equations and graphical entities) implicitly echoes the objectivist desire for bracketing and freezing (or detemporalizing, as Balacheff might say). Again, what would be the implications of starting with the graphical object and investigating the process that gave rise to it? Second, in terms of teaching materials, the effect of atomism is striking: Mathematical ideas get sliced up, torn apart, isolated, and delivered as separate curriculum objectives. Here, mathematics certainly lends itself well to such parcelling out, but current educational policies act as effective accomplices.

Now with the control value, and its desire for security, it is hard to ignore the role of algorithms in mathematics, which can offer feelings of refuge—from uncertainty and change—by providing foolproof methods. In fact, as Bishop notes, the algorithm may even give rise to an aesthetic pleasure stemming from the satisfaction of revealing a sense of order in a previously disorganized or unstructured mess (my mother's conversion method, described in the introduction, gave me that pleasure). Bishop also notes how mathematical rules and symbols can even function as security blankets for some people, gaining such familiarity that they take on a certain kind of friendliness. For example, for the calculating wizard Wim Klein, "Numbers are friends to me" (p. 261, in Devlin, 2000). Taking the number 3,844 as an example, he says, "For you it's just a 3 and an 8 and a 4 and a 4. But I say, 'Hi, 62 squared!'"

In valuing control, mathematics also exhibits an aesthetic preference for detachment, timelessness, and permanence. As the mathematician Brian Rotman points out, the desire embedded in the discourse of mathematicians involves a fantasy that things will not change and where questions can be answered once and for all:

> The desire's object is a pure, timeless unchanging discourse, where assertions proved stay proved forever (and must somehow always have been true), where all the questions are determinate, and all the answers totally certain. (quoted in Walkerdine, 1988, pp. 187–188)

It seems to me that desire and control also form part of the matrix of mathematical activity that professional mathematicians describe as *craft*—that is, the expert and considerate use of mathematical tools (such as algorithms, but also proof methods such as *reductio ad absurdum* or principles such as symmetry). For example, the physicist Freeman Dyson writes about the "aesthetic pleasure of the craftsmanship of performance" in mathematics and describes the delicate and tacit expertise involved in craft (in a way that resonates with more commonly known acknowledged craft such as woodworking and pottery):

> And if one is handling mathematical tools with some sophistication it is a very nonverbal and a very, very pleasurable experience just to know how to handle the tools well. It's a great joy. (Dyson et al., 1982, p. 139)

In my own teaching, I have seen students treat mathematical tools with a similar expertise and consideration. I recall, for example, a grade 8 student working on textbook exercises involving the multiplication of binomials. Mathematics was not her favorite, nor her most successful, subject, so I was surprised to see her work so intently and satisfyingly on problem after problem. When I asked the student why she was so engaged, she explained that these were problems she *knew* how to do, using the FOIL method (First, Outer, Inner, Last), and could get right *every* time. She could control her mathematics—the algorithm or rule was like a helpful friend. This kind of relationship to mathematical tools is interesting to consider in the light of debates in mathematics education about procedural versus conceptual understanding. I assume that Dyson, like other mathematicians, understands well the workings of the tools he so delights in using, but it seems that his enjoyment is more related to the design of the tool, to its impeccable, unwavering ability to produce a result, than to his own conceptual understanding of it.

Teaching Mathematical Values

In the previous section, I brought up Balacheff's three "de's," which are three forms of detachment, and connected them to the control value. The notion of detachment has been important in traditional philosophy, where emotional detachment was thought to be a prerequisite of aesthetic experience. The aesthetics of detachment that have shaped mathematics can be seen very clearly in many mathematics classrooms.

For example, in an article on students' investigations with the dragon curve fractal, Jackiw and Sinclair (2002) documented the process through which students moved from concrete, gestural, informal, and diverse descriptions of the fractal to descriptions that were increasingly decontextualized, depersonalized, and detemporalized. We started by folding strips of paper to create increasing iterations of the dragon curve, and then gave these spatial configurations the geographical descriptors of "mountains" and "valleys." The actual strips of paper, and their evolution over time, were eventually discarded and students began creating and analyzing sequences of M's and V's so that, eventually, they could determine whether a given sequence, such as MVVMVVM, corresponded to a "legal" dragon curve, based on both the number of terms in the sequence and the symmetries of letters within the sequence. In the end, the students had created a succinct notational system that could be used both to describe and predict the behavior of a previously ambiguous situation. We applauded their efforts for many reasons, not least for the way in which their work was mathematical: It had moved away from acts of folding paper (which had produced individual dragon curves, individually touched) to sequences of symbols that could exist independently of any physical objects.

However, we never explicitly brought this mathematical process to the students' attention, nor did we point out the values—and the advantages and drawbacks—involved in this process that we had encouraged. Nor did we point out that the notational system they had developed, while still carrying vestiges of their physically bound mountains and valleys, would appear completely detached to others. The use of M's and V's had sprung from their geographical interpretation of the paper strips, but others would likely find those signs to be empty of meaning.

My point here is to consider ways in which students encounter mathematical values in the classroom and to consider how values can be made more explicit. Do students appreciate what might be gained from the three "de" processes? Do they appreciate what might be lost? As with Bishop (1991) and Davis (1995), I believe that part of learning mathematics should involve becoming aware of and being able to develop a critical stance toward its values and their effects on both personal experiences and social norms. In pursuing the value of openness, I have strayed somewhat from the aesthetic concerns of this book. However, the aesthetic assertively nudges itself into the complex of beliefs that constitute the urge for greater detachment.

Are there any classroom practices that do not promote control in the classroom, or that invite students to consider these values critically? It seems that the reform-based practice of inviting students to develop their own alternate algorithms or solutions to problems may allow them to wrest some control away from the usual authorities, namely the teacher, the textbook, and the discipline itself. Whereas mathematicians value the sort of control that belongs to the discipline, which manifests itself in tools that are equally accessible and perfect, this pedagogical practice seems to exalt a different form of control, one that may well give rise to the more messy desire for appropriateness. Here, I recall the discussion in Part III of the evaluative role of the aesthetic, and the notion that students' individual solutions or idiosyncratic algorithms should go through a classroom process of evaluation, so as to make explicit what can and should be valued in mathematical activity, and how student or teacher values may conflict with those of the mathematical community.

Progress, Mystery, and Openness

The progress value, which is paired with that of control, can also be detected in mathematics education. Bishop identifies one form of it in the structure of the curriculum. Arithmetic operations, for example, or algebraic functions, are presented in a certain order with the assumption that knowing how to multiply will evolve from knowing how to add and that knowing how to solve quadratic equations will evolve from knowing how to solve linear ones. Moreover, the set of exercises at the end of a unit are meant to establish that if students can solve many particular examples of addition or solving linear equations, they can solve *all* such examples.

It seems doubtful to me that students' perceptions of the mathematics curriculum are guided by a progress value. Students certainly develop a feeling that mathematics keeps getting harder, and many struggle with their teachers' exhortations to apply learned algorithms or ideas to help them solve new problems. Nonetheless, they do come to believe that mathematics is a well-organized structure in which the upper levels are only accessible by assiduously and sequentially climbing from the very bottom. When adults make statements such as, "I never really understood fractions" or "I got lost in the seventh grade," they allude to the belief that once you have missed a level, any part of the upper reaches is forever lost in the clouds. Students may even be overly devoted to this structure.

A colleague of mine who teaches undergraduate mathematics classes used the scientific metaphor of polymerization to describe his students' aversion to playing with the structure of mathematics. Polymers are easy to grow by simply attaching one monomer to the next to form a straight-line dendrite. However, a polymer is only useful if those dendrites are cross-linked—that is, if the straight-line dendrites are somehow connected. Unfortunately, cross-linking is chemically challenging. Similarly, his students find any movement away from the upward climb anathema. He claims they are intellectually unwilling to do the harder work of making connections to other parts of the mathematical structure, but perhaps they have taken to heart the narrow sense of linear progress encountered in their school mathematics.

Although the aesthetic dimension of the progress value seems to me less obvious than that of control, the particular interaction of the two values with social and economic concerns has some aesthetic relevance. Mathematics is extremely committed to abstraction, and this commitment gives it an ability to retain control and propel its movement toward progress. No one can deny the seductive power of isolating and abstracting. According to the social critic Ivan Illich (1994), this extreme abstraction is one of the root causes of social malaise in the modern world, which is moving farther and farther away from a worldview that is sensitive to the proportions between human beings and nature. In his lecture, Illich argued that the growing mathematization of science and the desire to quantify—to separate, abstract, detach—has reduced our capacity to judge appropriateness and to attend to, as well as to return to, the particularities and proportions of local meanings. The aesthetic sense of "fit" to which Illich is referring can be compromised by an untempered fixation on control and progress. Turning to the classroom, I see greater potential for the "connections" process standard of the NCTM (National Council of Teachers of Mathematics). Helping students make connections between diverse areas of mathematics may well further their conceptual understanding, but engaging in the type of cross-linking described above leads to a form of enculturation in which connections are valued in mathematics, as are continued attempts to seek appropriate, fitting uses for new mathematical ideas.

The openness value, with its psychological and political neutrality, leads to the aesthetic so prized by the mathematician Bertrand Russell, who wrote that mathematics possesses a "supreme beauty—a beauty cold and austere" (1917, p. 57). But Bishop's notion of openness is evident in the mathematics classroom, too. Students are instructed to write proofs that a mathematician or a classmate could verify. They are introduced to the special, often arcane, words used in mathematical language. This impresses upon them, albeit implicitly, the importance of openness in mathematical communication. Students are also frequently offered visualizations and explanations that help make formulas, concepts, and theorems more understandable. The pedagogical nature of these attempts at transparency may well give students the impression that they are somehow nonmathematical crutches, or at least that mathematicians have some kind of depersonalized and decontextualized way of knowing mathematical truths.

Would celebrating the unrigorous, fractional approach of Leibniz's calculus provide students with a glimpse of the personal and intuitive way that mathematicians think, and also give them a more explicit encounter with the mathematical values that make mathematicians prize Leibniz's calculus while hiding its roots? Many similar topics would be available in grade school mathematics, including, for example, the use of graphs and functions. In his book *Proofs and Refutations*, philosopher Imre Lakatos (1976) studied the mathematical process by which an intuitively conceptualized phenomenon—essentially, the development of Euler's formula, which states the relationship between the number of vertices, faces, and edges of three-dimensional shapes—is then made increasingly rigorous, precise, and open. Euler's formula is often introduced to students at the middle school level, usually framed as a pattern-searching task. To me, it seems that giving students the formula and asking them to consider how to define the shapes that it applies to would provide them with a richer mathematical experience, one that would invite explicit discussion about values such as openness.

In the final pair, the mystery value is linked with openness and, in contrasting the values, I see secretiveness and exclusiveness as being the primary characteristics of the mystery value. By defining a community with access to special knowledge, mathematics simultaneously defines a community—a much larger community!—that is *excluded* from this knowledge. While mathematicians today, unlike the mystical Pythagoreans, do not purposely hide knowledge, the techniques they have developed for sharing information *inside* their community (their special language, methods, and forms of communication) make them appear all the stranger to people *outside* their community.

This duality is alive and well among school students today, judging from attitudes toward and beliefs about mathematics. The common perception of mathematics as "a gatekeeper" (to higher education, to intellectual stature) explicitly invokes this sense of exclusion (caught outside the gate) and inclusion (passing through it). A telling study, conducted by the mathematician John Berry and his colleague Susan Picker, showed that middle school students hold disturbing notions of mathematicians and their work. By asking students to draw images of mathematicians, Picker and Berry (2001) found that "[t]he average picture was of a scruffy person, probably with pens in his shirt pocket, holes in his clothes, and equations written on his arms." According to these students, mathematicians usually have "no friends except other mathematicians" and are "very unstylish." These beliefs speak to the exclusivity of mathematics in both identifying a community (mathematicians consorting only with other mathematicians) and distancing themselves from it through expressions of aesthetic repulsion.

The flip side of exclusivity reveals itself in classrooms when students temporarily gain the stature of members of the mathematical community. Mathematical insight confers a stature almost as palpable as a magician's wand. There is something quite distinct that happens in the mathematics classroom, compared with other school subjects, when teachers "pass their wands" over to other students: "Okay, Nick, now you explain it to the class." Nick's understanding of a mathematical idea allows him to occupy an exclusive position in the classroom, as one who knows. This transfer anoints him with the power to explain his knowledge to those who do not know. Sometimes, students can also be anointed with the power to *demonstrate*—that is, to choose how to perform their mathematical knowledge for others. (As I elaborate in Chapter 10, this might involve giving students the answer to a problem and asking them to create a *demonstration* of the solution.) The pleasure that students take in such demonstrations lies in the magician's power both to conceal and to reveal.

CHAPTER 10

Mathematical Values in Teaching

The previous chapter examined values inherent in the mathematics culture and pointed to some influences that the aesthetic dimension of these values has had on pedagogical practices. This chapter is driven by the realization, shared by a growing number of researchers, that *educating* students mathematically means enculturating them, namely, immersing students in the mathematical culture and the values inherent in it (see Bauersfeld, 1993; Bishop, 1991; Voigt, 1995). Enculturation involves, at least in part, the development and use of certain normative understandings of what counts as mathematical (Yackel & Cobb, 1996). In this view, educating students mathematically is much more than teaching mathematical tools and techniques; it is about recognizing, absorbing, and critically judging mathematical values. If the mathematical aesthetic is an important component of the mathematics, educators must find ways to make students aware of the aesthetic dimension of the values of that culture at an earlier point in their education.

This chapter consists of two primary sections. The first considers the broad context of mathematics education in which curricular and pedagogical choices are made, and considers these choices in terms of the aesthetic nature of the mathematical values they reveal. The second section looks more closely at the context of the classroom, and at the way in which aesthetic aspects of mathematical values are communicated and negotiated between teachers and students. In both sections, my primary intent is to expose the frequently tacit presence of aesthetically related values in mathematics education, and in so doing, I hope to assist teachers in making choices that nurture a more explicit aesthetic enculturation.

REVEALING VALUES IN TOPICS, TASKS, AND TOOLS

Chapter 9 described several examples of how the aesthetic dimension of mathematical values is communicated to students. Those very specific examples were intended to illustrate Bishop's six values, so as to evoke further more relevant or familiar examples for teachers. In this section, I attempt to be more systematic in reflecting on mathematical values in teaching mathematics by analyzing an educational context that includes the topics, tasks, and tools (such as manipulatives and computer-based technologies) used in the classroom. The reader may have already observed similarities, in terms of topics, tasks and tools, to the vignettes analyzed in Part III. In particular, the vignettes often featured non-standard tasks (such as coloring decimals, reproducing paintings), and prevalent use of computer-based environments (such as Meeting Lulu, Sketchpad). By drawing on a larger set of topics, tasks, and tools proposed by other mathematics educators who have been concerned with promoting aesthetic values—either directly or indirectly—my goal in this section is to consider the characteristics of learning situations that might help students to gain more familiarity with the aesthetic dimension of mathematical values.

I begin at a point that may seem impossibly far from the everyday choices made by teachers about what to teach on Monday morning and how to teach it, by asking: What is worth knowing? This question—and the implication that currently enacted responses to it might be changed—may strike many as overwhelming, given the constraints already established in school mathematics. Moreover, few teachers have the opportunity to start from scratch in deciding what and how to teach: The mathematics curriculum is notoriously unchanging, as well as demanding. Nonetheless, I begin here in part because, as pointed out in the introductory chapter, beliefs about what is worth knowing have shaped at least one set of recommendations (the NCTM *Standards 2000* document) about the importance of aesthetic appreciation in mathematics learning. In that document, aesthetic appreciation is linked to awareness of cultural achievements, and the implication is that those achievements constitute what is worth knowing. I begin here also because mathematical values, which have shaped the mathematics "canon"—that is, what is worth knowing to mathematicians—must play into the fabric of school mathematics—and what is worth knowing for students.

The educator Jerome Bruner's (1969) answer to the question of what is worth knowing is not so linked to cultural achievements: "Whether the knowledge gives a sense of delight and whether it bestows the gift of intellectual travel beyond the information given, in the sense of containing within it the basis of generalization" (p. 39). For the mathematics teacher (or the curriculum developer), Bruner's commendation could involve choosing mathematical topics that relate to intrinsically delightful ideas, such as infinity, or that relate to symmetry, which contains within it the basis of generalization. However, Bruner's commendation could also involve choosing tasks—ways of encountering or exploring topics—that lead to a sense of delight and an intellectual journey. For example, few would argue that plotting points leads to an intellectual journey, but might the task that involves formulating a symbolic notion to describe locations of Lulu on a grid provide the basis for generalization? Pushing the boundaries a little more, Bruner's commendation might also involve simple ways of inviting students to experience certain topics. For example, a teacher using a reform-based curriculum might well provoke delight in her students should she decide, one day, to bypass her usual approach (through group work, or contextualization, or investigation) and just say, "The formula is $C = 2\pi r$. Let's go from there."

In reflecting on the contexts described in Part III, such as Meeting Lulu, I find Bruner's answer difficult to apply. If Meeting Lulu is about plotting points, the possibilities of an intellectual journey, for example, seem to me to be quite limited. Yet there seems to be something worthwhile about the task. The mathematics educator Paul Goldenberg (1989) provides a vision of curriculum that is sympathetic to that of Bruner— including what is worth knowing—that I find helpful in characterizing mathematical contexts: "*Doing* mathematics and *mathematics* worth doing" (p. 192, emphasis in original). He cites fractal geometry as an example of a mathematial topic worth doing. However, he focuses more on what is worth *doing* than what is worth *knowing*, a focus that relates clearly to inquiry and to the roles of the mathematical aesthetic I have explored in this book. Specifically, Goldenberg sets out the following goals for mathematics education: fostering a spirit of self-propelled inquiry, enabling mathematical generativity, and developing a strong and personal interest in mathematics learning. I see components of these goals reflecting the constellation of mathematics values described in Chapter 9.

In examining the many contexts that mathematics educators have proposed, the notions of *doing mathematics* and *mathematics worth doing* are pervasive, and seem to be entangled with aesthetically related values— perhaps unsurprisingly. I will consider a few examples of such contexts and use them to identify common characteristics of "aesthetically rich" learning contexts.

Characteristics of Aesthetically Rich Learning Contexts

One of the precursors to aesthetically rich learning contexts can be seen in the work of the early 20th-century mathematics educator Edith Somervell, who was a proponent of children's use of string designs. In her book *A Rhythmic Approach to Mathematics* (1906/1975), she describes tasks in which students create various types of curve drawings using pins and thread. These relatively easy-to-make drawings can generate parabolas— not typical elementary school fare—as well as less-well-known curves in all of school mathematics such as spirals, nephroids, and cardioids.[1]

In addition to promoting the sensory aspects of her approach, in which the kinesthetic and visual dimensions of mathematical activity are deployed, Somervell also draws attention to the pleasure that students can have in creating curve drawings and the intuition they can develop to help with more advanced mathematics. According to her, students will see the algebraic and graphical mathematical treatment of their curves, which they eventually must encounter, as an "orderly explanation of experiences long familiar" (Somervell, 1906/1975, p. 17).

In addition to the sense of pleasure associated with the creation of artistic artifacts, I am interested in the pleasure and surprise that students might experience in seeing how organic thought sequences (setting rules for moving thread from one pin to another, as shown in the first three frames of Figure 10.1) can be connected to the evolution of harmonious forms (the parabola that emerges after several repetitions of the rule). The process of connecting the pins with thread fades into the background and the emergent mathematical shape, now detemporalized, takes over.

I see two characteristic ways in which Somervell's approach promotes aesthetic aspects of mathematics values: *intellectual appeal* and *significant expression*. Before further articulating these two characteristics, or even defending their relation to aesthetics or the mathematical values of Chapter 9,

Figure 10.1. Creating a parabola with pins and thread.

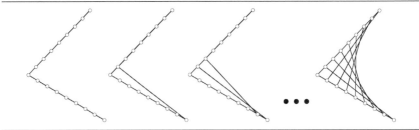

I describe another aesthetically rich learning context, this time at the high school level.

As mentioned before, Goldenberg (1989) advocates the inclusion of fractal geometry in the high school curriculum because it possesses a certain visual appeal that can attract students to "the intellectual beauty of the mathematics," and opportunities for inquiry through which "it is possible to make dramatic and fundamental changes in students' engagement in mathematics" (p. 169). Goldenberg emphasizes the fact that despite not being a part of the traditional structure of high school geometry, fractal geometry connects to and introduces other areas of mathematics. For instance, fractal geometry can connect various parts of algebra and geometry while introducing students to chaotic dynamical systems. By *intellectual beauty*, Goldenberg seems to be referring to the mathematical ideas of noninteger dimensions and infinite self-similarity, as well as to the artistic appeal of the actual fractal images that are created. In advocating the topic of fractal geometry, Goldenberg emphasizes a computer-based visual and experimental approach, which he sees as supporting worthwhile forms of reasoning not found in static, symbolic learning environments.

From these two brief descriptions, Goldenberg's and Somervell's proposals can be seen to overlap in terms of promoting aesthetic aspects of mathematics values. Both propose topics that are somewhat nonstandard and both invoke tools (pins and thread, and computer software) that can mediate the relevant mathematical ideas or forms of reasoning. I will return to these two similarities, but first I will develop further the two characteristics of intellectual appeal and significant expression.

Intellectual Appeal

I mentioned before the intellectual appeal in Somervell's rhythmic approach, by which I was referring to the surprising feeling many people get when a step-by-step, linearly applied rule gives rise to a rounded, continuous shape. Goldenberg's example of fractal geometry involves a consonant idea, namely that the repeated iteration of a rule defined on linear objects can give rise to an organic, supple shape (as in the Koch curve shown in Figure 10.2), the segments gradually turning into a fallen snowflakes. Papert (1980) also describes the intellectual appeal of the dance between the linear, step-by-step and the continuous whole when children generate circles in the computer program Logo by telling their turtles to repeat the rule of taking a step forward and then turning a little to the right.

Obviously, not all curricular topics lend themselves well to this form of intellectual appeal. However, might teachers be able to choose tasks that

Figure 10.2. Steps in creating a Koch curve.

have some similar sort of intellectual appeal? And is it reasonable to expect that a whole classroom of students will respond to the same forms of intellectual appeal? While being sensitive to the personal, context-bound nature of aesthetic responses, I have elsewhere suggested (see Sinclair & Watson, 2001) that certain ideas, such as infinity, seem to appeal to students reliably. Upon reflection, in my own experience, many of the ideas that have appealed to students have involved some play with infinity. And Caleb Gattegno's observation that mathematics is shot through with infinity suggests that all mathematical ideas are somehow connected to the infinite. For example, Tim encountered the infinite when coloring his maps by trying to grasp the idea that *all* of them would require no more than four colors. John encountered the infinite with his "magic" number 9—dividing a numerator by 9, 99, or any sequence of 9's could produce for him an infinitely repeating sequence of decimal digits. I am exploring here the idea of evoking the infinite in school mathematics as a way of courting the wonder and appeal of students and, in turn, helping students see how mathematics values attempts to tame wild ideas.

The practice of evoking the infinite (where can it be found in Meeting Lulu?) may well provide students with intellectual appeal, as may evoking surprise. In terms of student learning, Movshovits-Hadar (1988) provides many categories of situations in which mathematical ideas in the curriculum can be presented through surprise. In one category, she suggests that students have often been surprised in instances where "small changes can make a big difference" (p. 35). Movshovits-Hadar illustrates this category with the example of how small changes to the theorem about the sum of the angles of a triangle's interior may include considering a quadrilateral instead of a triangle or exterior angles instead of interior ones—and both changes make a big difference to the theorem. Her claim of potential surprise rests on the fact that in many other mathematical experiences, students expect small changes to make small differences.

Another category she suggests involves instances where "plausible reasoning fails." For example, it may be reasonable to assume that, since prime numbers become gradually scarcer as one moves along the number line, there is a place beyond which all natural numbers will be divisible by at least one of the preceding ones. But this kind of plausible reasoning is false, since the number of prime numbers is *not* finite. Of course, students may well find that their plausible reasoning often fails them in the mathematics classroom, so the surprise would have to be sensitively manufactured by the teacher. In other words, in order to respond to surprise, one must have some kind of frame of reference that generates expectations (see also Stanley, 2002).

Looking again to mathematicians, we can find another instance in which intellectual appeal operates—namely, that of apparent simplicity; recall from Part III the mathematicians Andrew Gleason described as being "gripped by explicit, easily stated things" (p. 93). In Chapter 6, I discussed the appeal of the Four Color Theorem for Tim, and mentioned that other mathematical ideas with similar apparent simplicity, such as Goldbach's conjecture, can often stir students to action. Of course, with apparent simplicity comes inherent difficulty and in both the examples mentioned here, students are unlikely to "solve," or fully understand, the mathematics involved. But should that matter?

I have identified the use of the infinite, surprise, and apparent simplicity as ways in which to provide students with intellectual appeal. These ways of providing intellectual appeal overlap with the list of the "big ideas" in mathematics proposed by the mathematics educator Geoff Faux (1998): Numbers are ordered and well structured, mathematics is shot through with infinity, a lot for a little (which can lead to surprise), equivalence, inverse, and transformation. His list may in fact suggest other forms of intellectual appeal, but whatever they may be, the use of them in the classroom amounts to establishing a certain kind of practice rather than spelling out specific topics or tasks. In other words, when everything is surprising, nothing is surprising. Moreover, few things are surprising on their own, without the help of the teacher to manage the way the surprise unfolds for students. For example, there is nothing surprising about the step function, but if students get to see it traced out on a graph after having seen more continuous linear or quadratic functions, they may well find the hopping function startling—I have often seen large groups of teachers and students explode in giggles in such a situation, then be surprised to find themselves laughing at a function for the first time in their lives.

I want to probe the issue of teaching practice a little more. In Chapter 6, I pointed to a traditional practice of introducing tasks and ideas in clear and isolated ways, so as not to confuse students, and to Brown's (1993) argument that such practices actually give students a false sense of aesthetic unity. Brown identifies another practice of traditional tasks: many teachers expect assigned problems to be solved within a relatively short amount of time, usually a classroom period. As I showed in Chapter 5, a longer period of time, interrupted if necessary, is one of the enabling conditions of mathematical inquiry. These more flexible time conditions provide an opportunity for genuine exploratory inquiry, as they give students the time they need to develop interest in and intimacy with a mathematical situation (DeBellis, 1998). Recall that John had the time and flexibility to get a feel for the effect of different denominators on the pattern in the color table, while Casey could get a feel for the patterns produced by the frogs. That students should need more flexible thinking conditions with respect to time is not surprising, given that professional mathematicians also need extended periods of time interrupted by periods of incubation (see Hadamard, 1945).

In using the term *practice*, I want to emphasize that not every mathematical idea has to be surprising or presented in an ambiguous manner, and not every assigned problem needs long periods of incubation. Part of practice is deciding when and how often to call upon these types of strategies, and also being able to locate and even manufacture ideas such as the infinite.

Significant Expression

In his *Talks on Pedagogics* (1894), the educator Francis Parker outlines a particularly aesthetic approach to the construction of understanding. His approach featured the key notion of *expression*, which he described as "the manifestation of thought and emotion through the body by means of physical agents" (p. 224). While Parker's work has been taken up mostly by arts educators, several mathematics education technologists have used the related notion of an *expressive medium* to describe learning environments in which it is possible to express ideas in concrete forms that are visible and public. For example, in their work with Logo, Richard Noss and Celia Hoyles argue that making mathematical ideas visible and public increases the potential for a collaborative, experimental approach to mathematics learning, as compared with traditional pencil-and-paper modes. They focus on the medium in which actions are carried out by means of programming in a syntactically precise language and maintain that such a medium allows students to make the difficult move from the informal and concrete to the formal and abstract. While sharing the same constructivist orientation as Parker, in terms of supporting the active construction of knowledge, Noss and Hoyles seem to focus more on the "thought" than the "emotion" component of Parker's conception of expression. I also see Parker's notion of expression as supporting a wider range of materials and media for mathematics learning than solely the programming ones advocated by Noss and Hoyles.

In fact, David Shaffer (1997) argues that Sketchpad can also act as an expressive medium, in the Noss and Hoyles sense, even though it is not usually considered to be a programming language. With Sketchpad, students carry out actions by means of a visual and geometric precise language. Sketchpad even possesses its own syntax—differently mediated from those of programming languages—that regulates the way objects are constructed on the screen. For example, a student could create a line and a point and then construct the reflection of the point in the line. Shaffer even evokes Parker's notion of expression in his analysis of Escher's World, a project in which students used Sketchpad to learn about the mathematical and artistic dimensions of transformations and tessellations. Students were asked to create designs that had various types of symmetries and Shaffer argues that a key aspect of their explorations was the degree to which the designs represented the public externalizing of personal thoughts, perceptions, and emotions.

Shaffer notes that the students used the software to help them look for solutions to mathematical problems (of creating a certain design) that had aesthetic appeal. The students were not passive in their use of mathematical objects and relationship. They were required, in order to produce anything at all, to work simultaneously with tools expressing geometric relationships and their form and composition on the screen—their colors, labels, display, and presentation roles. Shaffer's description of his students' work, and my own experiences with students ranging from grades 2 to 16 (some of which were described in Part III), evokes for me the craftlike orientation toward doing mathematics that Freeman Dyson articulated. The notion of *craft* emerged as part of the control value in mathematics, but in Parker's notion of *expression* I see an interesting link to the openness value in mathematics, which relates to the desire to make ideas (thoughts *and* emotions) observable or public, and to wrestle them from the interiority that is inaccessible to others.

Paul Goldenberg's work with fractal geometry provides yet another computer-based example of an aesthetically rich learning situation that enjoys an expressive quality. In fact, computer-based learning environments featured in most of the examples of Part III: the Colour Calculator, Meeting Lulu and Frogs, as well as The Geometer's Sketchpad. I chose to use these environments in my research in part because they serve as manageable laboratory spaces for exploring how aesthetic responses motivate mathematical inquiry, generate mathematical ideas, and communicate and evaluate them within mathematical communities. As Noss and Hoyles (1996) explain, they provide "windows on mathematical meaning" through the observable actions and decisions that students make in interacting with these visual functionalities.

Although computer-based environments support students' exploration of visual mathematical ideas particularly well, and may often motivate more precise forms of interaction than do traditional environments (through feedback and interface), Parker's notion of *expression* can develop through the use of many other materials and mediums. I think that Somervell's rhythmic approach enabled students to express their thoughts and emotions through the creation of curves using pins and thread. William Higginson and Lynda Colgan (2001) use paper-folding tasks to evoke student expression. In their book *Creative Mathematics*, Rena Upitis, Eileen Phillips, and William Higginson (1997) provide multiple examples of significant expression spanning a whole school year. All these examples have a distinct artistic, visual component to them. However, I find their tessellation example especially pertinent in differentiating between classroom tasks in which students create artistic artifacts that may be motivated by mathematical ideas but that are soon overwhelmed with nonmathematical ones and tasks in which mathematical ideas are expressed and then remathematized. In their tessellation example, the students use mathematical ideas of geometric transformations to create personally appealing artifacts that can in turn be represented in precise and generalizable language. The dragon curve fractal task described above is similar in the sense that students create attractive shapes through paper-folding, but then seek to describe, manipulate, and generalize them through symbolic means.

Learning situations that feature intellectual appeal and significant expression will be easier to design for some curriculum topics than for others. And while there may well be other pertinent features to be identified, these two seem to speak clearly to the values that drive mathematicians to do mathematics and to express themselves in the particular way they do.

COMMUNICATING VALUES IN THE CLASSROOM

This chapter has been concerned with a phenomenon that occurs socially, within group settings, zooming out from the individual learner to the events and activities of the whole classroom. I have already attended to how students' existing aesthetic sensibilities can be evoked and nurtured in the classroom. Here, I want to consider how aesthetic values of the mathematics culture are evoked and nurtured in the social context of the whole classroom, where many different kinds of values—not all of them related to mathematics—are constantly being negotiated. I draw on mathematics education researchers Erna Yackel and Paul Cobb's work on the evolution of sociomathematical norms in the classroom, which include "normative understandings of what counts as mathematically different, mathematically sophisticated, mathematically efficient, and mathematically elegant in the classroom" (1996, p. 461).

Alan Bishop (1991) makes several recommendations about the kinds of tasks that can serve to make mathematical enculturation more explicit in the classroom. However, Bishop also stresses the importance of social interaction in shaping learners' ideas and values. Indeed, it is within the dynamics of student-teacher interaction in the classroom that normative understandings are created. Erna Yackel and Paul Cobb (1996) have shown this in their study of how teachers help students understand what counts as mathematical. It would seem, therefore, that students would come to understand the values of the mathematics culture in the dynamics of social interaction. But how exactly might teachers manage classroom interactions so as to make these values available to and negotiable by students?

I recently attended a graduate-level mathematics lecture on numerical analysis. The professor, Jonathan Borwein, is very experienced and also fond of using the computer-algebra system Maple in his teaching, so the lecture was located in a technology room. I attended his lecture because I hoped to gain insight into the social interactions of the mathematics culture through an aesthetic lens—graduate students are well on their way inside the culture and a graduate seminar provides a window on how members (and quasimembers) of the culture (here, Borwein) communicate. I also hoped that the pedagogical setting might inform a vision of classroom practices that attend to aesthetic enculturation. This is what I saw.

Over the course of an hour, Borwein appealed to aesthetic values on six different occasions, and used the words *beautiful, elegant,* and *pretty* at least a dozen times. In introducing a particular formula, he called it "pretty" because it "looks like a formula we already know." He also argued for its "aesthetic appeal" based on the fact that it "isolates the important variables in the equation." He called another equation "beautiful," claiming that it was better to "put two equations into one" when possible (the alternate form of the equation—also the more familiar one—has two parts, one for even dimensions and the other for odd ones), arguing in effect for an aesthetic preference for a very old, 19th-century conception of function. He drew attention to the beauty of a particular expression, explaining that it was "manipulable," namely, that one could work directly with this equation in a computer algebra system (and Borwein proceeded to do this through both symbolic and visual manipulations). Finally, Borwein went through a mathematical investigation that he himself had begun, and commented on how "pleasing" it was for him to "see structures by drawing pictures" and to "use the pictures as a basis for further investigation."

By picking out all these instances in which Borwein communicated or appealed to aesthetic responses, I am trying to understand how aesthetic values are shaped in post-secondary classrooms, particularly by the instructor. (Later, I will focus more on the interactions between school students and teachers.) The stark contrast with a typical middle school lesson will be immediate to anyone who has had the opportunity to observe one. In fact, the National Center for Education Statistics (NCES) published videotapes of what were considered typical grade eight American mathematics lessons (Stigler et al., 1999). In viewing these videotapes, I saw not one single occurrence of words such as *elegant* and *beautiful* being used by either teachers or students. Nor did I hear teachers appeal to the aesthetics of a mathematical formula or algorithm being introduced. Moreover, I did not observe the use of any aesthetically based arguments to explain why one correct mathematical solution would be better than another correct one. And I certainly never saw a teacher comment on any personal pleasures she or he had had in investigating or learning about the mathematical ideas in question.

By focusing on the presence or absence of words used as aesthetic descriptors, I may seem to be emphasizing only the evaluative function of the aesthetic, and doing so at a rather superficial level. Yet the simple act of using such words when describing or explaining mathematical ideas can indicate to students that aesthetic response and sensibility are applicable and acceptable in the mathematics classroom. A mathematician once recalled to me the first moment, in college, that someone used the word *beautiful* to describe a mathematical idea. Suddenly, he felt that he had access to a whole new way of thinking about mathematics, a whole new way of organizing what he did and did not know.

Of course, beautiful ideas are not the exclusive property of advanced mathematics, as I have claimed repeatedly in this book. Other adults have described the rare and fortunate instances in which a teacher went beyond the facts in describing or explaining the Pythagorean theorem, or Goldbach's conjecture, or even the idea of mathematical infinity. The simple use of words such as *beautiful, sophisticated,* or *elegant* might represent the very first step in aesthetic enculturation: A student might need to hear the teacher state that a certain mathematical idea is beautiful before being able to connect any previous aesthetic experiences and values to mathematics. In the graduate class I observed, those words also revealed a motivational role of the aesthetic at work. Borwein was talking about the kinds of things that make an equation or expression worth investigating. In drawing attention to the pleasure of using pictures, he was also invoking the generative role of the aesthetic.

While observing the graduate seminar, I was struck by the extent to which the "sage on the stage" metaphor was much more appropriate than the "guide on the side" one. The latter metaphor pervades, of course, in reform-based or progressive mathematics teaching practices. But here, the importance of using particular words and routines of justifying actions and beliefs, perhaps repeatedly (as parents do when their children are learning to talk), suggests some benefits in the sage on the stage model. The mathematics educator Anna Sfard (2001) points to the necessity of having a dominant discourse in the classroom so that in spoken interactions, the members of the classroom know with which discourse they should try to align. She argues that this is part of the *communicational agreement* that makes learning (or enculturation) possible.

In the previous section, I explored some of the ways in which Bishop's values manifest themselves in school mathematics classrooms. In order to probe what a more explicit aesthetic enculturation might look like, I now consider the aesthetic dimension of these same values in Borwein's classroom. The desire to see the equation as a single, unified entity instead of as a two-part one resonates strongly with the rationalism value, which seeks containment, cohesion, and unification. Borwein was communicating this value explicitly to the audience by drawing attention to his reason for preferring one form to the other. By commenting on the appeal of the formula that neatly isolates the variable, he seemed to be taking on a more objectivist stance—in terms of Bishop's values—in wanting to isolate, bracket, and purify the fundamental component of the equation. Finally, his statement about the manipulability of a certain equation hints at a control value—that which can be manipulated can be made to behave predictably. Equations that can be manipulated visually and symbolically can also become "friendly" ones, upon which a certain degree of structure and order can be imposed.

I suggest that Borwein was also communicating and sharing other kinds of values, ones that do not fit as neatly into Bishop's categories. Consider his statement about the prettiness of the formula because it looked like one that is already known. Whereas rationalism urges one to seek *logical* connections between ideas, Borwein seems to be emphasizing connections based on form more than logic. Perhaps such ideas are valued because they represent the *possibility* of establishing logical connections. Or perhaps they are valued because mathematicians prefer to think of mathematics as a coherent, connected domain rather than one that consists of a collection of arbitrary facts. Seen in this way, the rationalism value may still be operative.

Another value can be discerned in Borwein's comments, and is somewhat related to control. Particularly in his evocation of the visual and the structural, Borwein communicates a strong desire to get at both a *sense of* and a *relevance for* the statement or formula. Connecting to a formula he already knows provides a kind of relevance, while the holistic understanding that pictures of an equation afford him provides a kind of enlightenment, or transparency, one that goes beyond merely grasping the truth of the equation. Students are frequently urged to "draw a picture" when they are working on problems, but those invitations are almost always seen by students as strategies aimed at helping them solve a problem. What is valued is whether students can solve the problem. By contrast, Borwein values the picture itself, for its power to provide a sense of the mathematical ideas involved.

I contend that the aesthetic gap between grade school and graduate school is real and discernible, and that by considering the values made explicit in the graduate class, it is possible to begin seeing how teachers could help to shape the aesthetic dimension of students' values. Again, I believe that many teachers already do shape them implicitly, and that they do so by denying the mathematical aesthetic in the classroom. I think this antiaesthetic can be seen in students' repeated complaints about hating math or finding it boring. If students are fundamentally aesthetic beings, in all their interactions with the world (as I argued in Part I), then denying them aesthetic access in their own mathematical experiences is equivalent to communicating to them that mathematics should leave them aesthetically numb. The anti-aesthetic approach characterizes well the NCES classroom videotapes I described above. Teachers do not say out loud, "There is no beauty in mathematics," but they say it implicitly.

Of course, many teachers, particularly at the high school level, teach mathematics because they love it, or have had strong, positive experiences with it in their own schooling. These teachers may take a covert-aesthetic approach in which the aesthetic is not completely denied, but neither is it made explicit in the classroom. Consider a classroom in which "real-world" mathematical situations are constantly sought out, created, and used by the teachers and students. The teacher may be making a pedagogical decision, either that real-world applications will be more useful to students, or perhaps more interesting and motivating.[2] However, there exists a long tradition in mathematics that exalts "pure" mathematics—that is, mathematics uncontaminated by the messiness of the organic, physical world and the utilitarianism of solving its problems. The mathematician G. H. Hardy famously expressed his pride at never contributing anything useful to the world through his mathematics. His was an aesthetic of purity and perfection. This teacher's is not, and in this sense, the teacher is communicating a certain mathematical aesthetic, whether intentionally or not.

I suspect that students usually know that applications or contextualizations are principally used for pedagogical purposes in school. In addition to making that goal more explicit—"Class, today we are going to study bicycle gears because they will help you learn about finding common multiples"—what might be gained if the teacher also told her students that bicycle gears, being of the physical world, might not behave as perfectly as the laws of multiples, and that the mathematical community actually prefers the ideals of the made-up world? What if the teacher asked her students whether they would prefer to learn about common multiples in the context of bicycle gears or whether they would like to learn about them without reference to real-world phenomena? Would students be able to decide in advance and, if so, on what basis? While the latter questions involve providing students with some aesthetic agency, the first question merely suggests a way to make the values of the mathematical community more explicit. Students may agree or disagree with a Hardyesque mathematical aesthetic—and mathematicians themselves are certainly diverse in their responses—but they will have been given the opportunity to consider how mathematical values shape mathematical ideas and the way these ideas are taught.

Another example of the covert-aesthetic approach can be seen in many of the reform-based curricula that emphasize mathematical connections (making connections is one of the NCTM process standards, and can be seen in curricula such as the middle school Connected Mathematics Project). For example, teachers are encouraged to use tasks that make connections across content strands. Again, in doing so, the teacher may choose to exploit mathematical connections for many reasons, but perhaps not very explicitly. The notion of connectedness seems to me a strongly aesthetic one, revealing a desire for ideas to fit together, or to cohere and unify. But unless that value is more overtly communicated to students, they may not appreciate the fact that connections are valuable and prevalent in the mathematics community, and not just meant to make their lives more difficult.

Finally, I think that in some classrooms, an overt-aesthetic approach is taken, where the mathematical aesthetic is explicitly acknowledged to students. Here, the practice of revealing the (positive and negative) aesthetic values of mathematical ideas is built into the teacher's lesson. For example, I imagine a teacher telling her students, "We are going to work on the problem of adding consecutive whole numbers because it is a famous problem, and its solution exemplifies the power of mathematics." But she might also, on another day, tell her students, "We are going to study how to factor a trinomial not because it is interesting in and of itself, but because it will help us solve problems that *are* interesting." Compare these ways of starting a class with, "Okay, the next chapter in the textbook is about similarity," or "Today we're going to review what we did yesterday." The latter statements do not help students gain access to the values of the mathematics culture.

Thus far, I have emphasized ways in which aesthetic enculturation in the classroom is affected by the language that a teacher uses to communicate *to* her students. But enculturation is everywhere, not just in the way a teacher introduces a new lesson or explains a mathematical idea. Many mathematical values are evoked in the interaction *between* teachers and students. The research of Yackel and Cobb (1996) on classroom norms has shown that many mathematical values (which are part of what they call *sociomathematical norms*) can be interactively constituted in classrooms that feature certain forms of discussion and argumentation. They focus particularly on the notion of mathematically different, on the way in which students come to appreciate what counts as different when they are sharing solutions in the classroom, and on the way in which teachers' responses contribute to shaping classroom norms. Recall that sociomathematical norms are also involved in making decisions about what is mathematically sophisticated, efficient, and elegant. Yackel and Cobb do not question where these values come from, or why they are given special attention over other values (applicability, perspicuity, etc.). But they do demonstrate that learners can infer some sociomathematical norms by identifying regularities in patterns of social interaction. A point I will return to later is the extent to which educators want the shaping of students' mathematical values to be a more critical undertaking: are sociomathematical norms to be embraced, or challenged?

In focusing on mathematical difference, Yackel and Cobb chose one of the less aesthetically oriented values, compared with sophistication, efficiency, and elegance. This is not surprising, given their focus on the students' sense of when and how it is appropriate to contribute to a discussion. Yackel and Cobb analyze the sociomathematical norm enacted by students' responses when a teacher asks, "Are there other solutions?" They note that only mathematical difference becomes an explicit topic of conversation, but never mathematical efficiency, sophistication, or elegance. The last three would only emerge when teachers (or classmates) explicitly engage in judging explanations, justifications, or solutions.

Nonetheless, given the success Yackel and Cobb report in developing certain mathematical norms through classroom argumentation, it is worth exploring whether similar forms of communication could also help shape the aesthetically oriented values with which I have been concerned in this chapter. To be clear: I am interested in these values because they are part of the mathematics culture and underlie the very way in which the discipline has developed. If mathematicians, and the discipline of mathematics, valued different things, then students' experiences in the mathematics classroom would be qualitatively different. To give a simple example: By insisting that students describe coordinates using (x, y) notation rather than, say, "up/down" and "right/left" or even (y, x) notation, teachers (perhaps implicitly) communicate the fact that conventional symbolic precision is highly valued in mathematics. If it were not so valued, students could still learn about coordinates, but they might be invited to use natural language to describe graphical locations or even symbolic notation of their own design.

Using the aesthetic framework described in Part II, I propose three variations on Yackel and Cobb's emphasis on sociomathematical norms: moving from evaluative to justified feedback; moving from implicit to explicit comparisons of solutions; moving from uncritical to critical discussion of mathematical values. These variations dovetail well with several of the practices put forth by the wider educational community and foster awareness of the mathematical aesthetic.

From Evaluative to Justified Feedback

I mentioned previously that teachers frequently provide evaluative feedback that only offers implicit indicators of mathematical value. A smile or an excited tone of the voice can indicate to the student that the teacher values his or her solution; similarly with statements such as "That's good" or "I like that." In addition, teachers frequently feel compelled to value contributions of every student, regardless of the quality of the contribution. This means that statements such as "I like that" can come to be interpreted by students as "I'm glad you spoke" (which, of course, may also be true) rather than "Your solution is a good one." Nonetheless, there are certainly ways in which justified feedback can help students figure out what kinds of things are mathematically valued and why some solutions might possess greater value than others, without making such judgments personal evaluations of the student's understanding. For example, instead of saying "That's good," a teacher could say "That's good because it helps us answer other questions," or "I like that because I've never thought of the problem that way." Such justified answers more explicitly communicate the fact that generality and novelty, for example, are also valued qualities in the mathematics classroom, and not just correctness.

Justified feedback can also provide cognitive support to learners, since the teacher's aesthetic judgments of a solution or idea carry with them a depth of understanding as well as a critically informed discernment. The statement, "That's good because it helps us answer other questions" reveals a disciplinary value, and more importantly, the teacher's appreciation for deep understanding. Such a statement therefore communicates to the student that the goal of mathematics is to gain deep understanding, but it also helps develop that deep understanding since deep understanding in mathematics involves knowing how some ideas are related to other ideas and can be applied in other contexts. The statement "I like that because I've never thought of the problem that way" reveals the teacher's own active involvement in the mathematics—indeed, in the same mathematics that her students encounter—as well as the importance that the teacher places on comparing ideas. Such a statement therefore communicates to the students that the goal of mathematics is to compare ways of thinking and doing actively and, equally, to imagine other ways of thinking and doing.

From Implicit to Explicit Comparisons of Solutions

Yackel and Cobb claim that when students are deciding whether or not they have a mathematically different solution to offer, they are engaged in a comparison of the similarities and differences their solutions have to those of their classmates. By engaging in this kind of comparative activity, students are making their solution "become an object of their own reflection" (Yackel & Cobb, 1996, p. 464), thereby supporting higher-level cognitive activity. Moreover, it is also in the explicit comparison of solutions that the *aesthetic* aspect of values can be evoked, as demonstrated by several examples I detailed in Chapter 8. However, if two mathematical solutions are correct, it is often difficult and sometimes uncomfortable for teachers to know how to compare them, even though they might well have their own personal preferences (one solution may be more pertinent to the lesson of the day than the other, or it may involve a more articulate response).

As I have showed, students already have some ideas about that, but it is only by explicitly comparing solutions that the mathematical values involved in sophistication, efficiency, and elegance can be evoked and discussed. This does not mean that only one solution should be singled out; there are many different kinds of value that could come into play, and many different styles of thinkers who would value one over another. A classroom of students could end up identifying a handful of different solutions that possess different kinds of value: One may be most enlightening or perspicacious; another may have the most clever twist; and yet another might be the shortest, or most efficient.

Of course, comparison need not always occur around students' own solutions. A teacher could show solutions of a problem to her students that were produced by another group of students (actual or fictional), and ask them to decide how one might go about comparing the solutions, pointing out, when appropriate, values and criteria the mathematics community might appeal to. A teacher could take a more historical approach (comparing alternate solutions proposed by mathematicians—for example, the calculus of Leibniz versus that of Newton), or a pedagogical approach (Does this model make multiplication easier to understand, or does that other model?), or even a pedagogic-historical approach (*I* learned how to divide fractions by thinking of it like this . . .). Obviously, such classroom activity does not have value-shaping as its unique pedagogical goal: In order to compare solutions, one must come to understand them, and turn them into objects of reflection.

I have seen this happen quite successfully in the context of an under-graduate secondary mathematics methods course where I asked preservice teachers to consider eight different solutions given by middle school students to the "orange juice problem" (in which students are asked to decide which of four mixtures of water and concentrate produces the most and least "orangey" drink). My initial goal was to broach the complexity involved in assessing student work, especially when that work invites a wider range of responses and thinking than those afforded by back-of-the-book exercises. The preservice teachers first worked independently to figure out how they would assess the diverse solutions. Then, in a group discussion, they compared their assessments and realized that while most agreed about whether or not a particular solution was correct, there was much disagreement about how "good" the solution was; did it deserve the highest mark, or just an average one?

As it turned out, upon reflection, the assessments were accompanied by a multitude of tacitly held values. Was a brief solution better, or one that was clearly and neatly presented? Which was better—a clever solution, or one that showed that the student had mastered the given topic? What the preservice teachers found surprising was how these aesthetic judgments started seeping into their assessments of what the students knew and how well they knew it. In arguing over their judgments—and becoming increasingly uncomfortable with the fact that it was so difficult to achieve a consensus—many of the preservice teachers were forced to come to a deeper understanding of the different forms of mathematical thinking involved in each student's solution. While some praised highly visual solutions for their clarity or creativity, others found such solutions to be nonmathematical, for their apparent lack of symbolic and deductive reasoning.

In her study on British teachers' assessment of student written work for national examinations (at age 16), the mathematics educator Candia Morgan (1998) found a significant amount of variability in the rankings that experienced high school teachers gave to student work. Her findings contrast with the claims of mathematics educators Tanner and Jones (1994) who write that "Mathematicians work to a set of assumptions, often related by generality, economy, and elegance" and that "[t]eaching students mathematics must involve acculturation into these assumptions" (p. 422). This is certainly what I have been arguing, but then they claim, "Good solutions are 'reliably recognizable'" (p. 422). As Morgan points out, teachers carry their own beliefs about mathematics, which may be different from the assumptions listed by Tanner and Jones, and have quite varying levels of distance from the mathematics culture in terms of their knowledge and experience. From this point of view, it seems reasonable to expect differences among teachers in their assessment of student work.

Morgan discusses some of the assumptions teachers may have that affect their assessment, including whether or not students should be rewarded for different, perhaps creative, solutions, and whether or not clear explanations are more valued than correct answers. By analyzing teachers' often impressionistic assessments (they know one solution is better but cannot clearly articulate their reasons why), Morgan gets at some of the more tacit assumptions involved in assessing student mathematical work. I am particularly interested in her discussion of values that are not invoked by the usual vocabulary of the mathematical aesthetic (*beautiful, elegant, concise*, etc.), nor by the presence of words such as *nice* or *pretty*. For example, in analyzing a teacher's comparison of two student solutions to a problem involving counting the number of inner triangles in a geometric configuration, Morgan writes about why the teacher might have the impression that No. 2 is better than No. 3:

> No. 3's introduction of the final formula by *You can write this as* . . . presents the symbolic formula merely as an alternative to the verbal procedure. No. 2's announcement *This therefore is the formula*, on the other hand, displays the formula as a product in its own right which follows logically from the procedure rather than merely being equivalent to it. (Morgan, 1998, p. 172)

In Morgan's analysis, the rationalism value (that things should follow logically, and not just pop up willy-nilly) makes itself evident, as does the complex of values that fuel detachment (the formula being a "product in its own right"). From an aesthetic point of view, the analysis evokes a rationalism value that eschews fuzziness, imprecision, and looseness, much as the statement "you *can*" in contrast to "therefore" might imply. The teacher's impression may well be correlated with his valuing of detachment (a formula is brought into being and detached from the act of writing a relationship symbolically).

In her analysis, Morgan hints at the way in which values guide teachers' "impressions" of student work and at the possibility that teachers may not be aware of the effect of these values, whether in written assessments conducted outside the classroom or in verbal interactions with students in the classroom. My goal in pointing to Morgan's work is to acknowledge the fact that in order to be more explicit in comparing student solutions, teachers have to gain more awareness of their own values, and how these values relate to those of the mathematics culture.

I conclude this subsection by describing a strategy for making the comparison of solutions explicit, which I have explored. The strategy involves giving students the "answer" to a problem (thus shifting the focus away from issues of correctness), and asking them to create a *demonstration* of the solution using Sketchpad. The task of demonstrating a solution is closer to that of proving, and thus closer to what many consider the *sine qua non* of mathematical activity—one where, presumably, its values are most evident. In demonstrating, one becomes concerned with how to best communicate the logic of a sequence of ideas and thus the relative judgment of "best" comes to the foreground. More than any other kind of classroom task, these *demonstration* tasks have helped students encounter and negotiate important mathematical values (Sinclair, 2004a). Perhaps through such tasks students can come to appreciate the fact that mathematical results do not emerge from mathematicians' heads in some final polished form; rather, students can experience the ways in which values are actively involved in the shaping and refining of the mathematical ideas themselves. It seems very probable that by having such experiences, students will begin to see how the aesthetic aspect of mathematical values can influence their problem-solving efforts, and thus take on a generative role. Silver and Metzger (1989) have proposed that this kind of awareness may be "the hallmark of entry into mathematical culture" (p. 72).

From Uncritical to Critical Discussion of Mathematical Values

"Because it makes a pretty picture."
"Because I like it."
Suppose a student provides these types of justification to a teacher's attempt to move from implicit to explicit comparisons of solutions. The

word *pretty* seems linguistically akin to words such as *elegant* used by mathematicians, and perhaps also akin to the words the teacher has used in trying to raise students' awareness of the mathematical aesthetic. The second justification might well be motivated by a direct sense of pleasure that the student has experienced from the solution, or even personal agency, authority, or control. Should the teacher be pleased? Are such judgments indicative of students gaining access to the mathematical culture?

By making the transition from uncritical to critical discussion in the classroom, I contend that such justifications are not *necessarily* the ones teachers should ultimately be promoting. I chose these two examples because they suggest different needs for critical discussion. On the one hand, the values of the mathematics culture are inherently mathematical. On the other, these values are shared and developed within a community; the individual must, to a certain extent, be able to work with them.

A picture that may be deemed pretty in the discussion of the art class would not necessarily be pretty within the discourse of the mathematics class. Students might well find a picture to be *pretty* in the mathematics class, but if they are to use the adjective as a justification for why the picture provides a better solution, they must identify, so to speak, its *mathematical* prettiness: Does it explain better? Is it more general or predictive? Is it more transparent? I am not advocating against the use of the word *pretty* itself; instead, I am arguing that in the process of aesthetic enculturation, words such as *pretty* or *elegant* should not be accepted as a replacement, or code word, for other values until those values have been well-developed in the classroom community. Gian-Carlo Rota has keenly observed the process through which certain words have come to replace sets of values and beliefs in the mathematics culture; he writes, "Mathematical beauty is the expression mathematicians have invented in order to obliquely admit the phenomenon of enlightenment while avoiding the fuzziness of this phenomenon" (1997, p. 132). Those that operate within the culture may use words such as *beauty, elegance,* and *prettiness* as they wish, but students outside the culture need critical direction.

I think that Brown's (1973) study, described in Chapter 8, illustrates well the need for critical discussion, and suggests also that developing a critical awareness of the values of the mathematics culture does not mean that these values cannot be challenged on pedagogical or other grounds. Recall that Brown had invited his students to generate solutions to the problem of adding the digits from 1 to 100, and then to compare their solutions with Gauss's legendary one—leading the students toward explicit comparisons of their solutions. The students justified their preferences using many different values, and sometimes found their own solutions better, based on what

Brown called a "naturalistic" conception of beauty in which personal history and genealogy are valued. Brown's account ends at the point where I am advocating a critical discussion. The students' naturalistic aesthetic needs to be examined both in terms of the values of the mathematics culture—which do not produce messy, difficult-to-remember formulations—and within the emergent values of the classroom. Why do mathematicians prefer "simple" and "succinct" formulations? This does not mean that the students' "naturalistic" aesthetic should be banned in the mathematics classroom; instead, it might be examined for its pedagogical advantages: Do their preferred solutions help them better understand or remember? Do they carry vestiges of satisfying experiences? After all, as Rota argues, the phenomenon of enlightenment is precisely what keeps the mathematical enterprise alive.

These three variations on Yackel and Cobb's approach to shaping sociomathematical norms strive to emphasize the important aesthetic dimension of the beliefs and values that contribute to sociomathematical norms in the mathematics classroom. Only by developing this kind of awareness are students likely to be able to approach, and even make their first steps across, the borders of the mathematics culture. Again, I believe that in doing this, students will have a better chance of understanding why mathematics is the way it is, and why their mathematics teachers encourage them to reason and express themselves in such particular, and often strange, ways.

SOME CLOSING WORDS

Parts III and IV have developed complementary aesthetic lenses on mathematics learning. Part III attended to individual learners, and the sensibilities and preferences they might potentially engage with during their mathematical activity; Part IV focused on the values these learners may encounter through their interactions in classrooms, with teachers, through mathematics, and even within wider communities in which they find themselves.

For many students, these wider communities tend to link mathematics to an aesthetic of disdain and encourage the dislike of, and lack of success in, mathematics. And so it is interesting to consider the recent rapprochement between mathematics and aesthetics in academic literature (see Sinclair, Pimm, & Higginson, 2006), and to note the growing appeal and presence of mathematics in mainstream culture. Mathematics is featured in numerous recent films and plays (*Pi*, *A Beautiful Mind*, *Good Will Hunting*, *Arcadia*, and *Proof*) as well as popular books (*The Equation That Couldn't Be Solved: How Mathematical Genius Discovered the Language of Symmetry*, *Five Equations That Changed the World: The Power and Poetry of Mathematics*, *The*

Colours of Infinity: The Beauty, and Power of Fractals, and *The Universe and the Teacup: The Mathematics of Truth and Beauty).* Instead of attempting to emulate the formal, abstract language of mathematics that pervaded previous mathematical popularizations (such as Richard Courant and Herbert Robbins's 1941 book *What Is Mathematics?),* these books, plays, and films tell exciting, sometimes heart-wrenching and very human stories of mathematicians and their discoveries, seeking to convey the sense of beauty and elegance to which mathematicians are drawn. The word choice of these book titles alone—power, poetry, beauty, truth—demonstrates the degree to which authors have used the aesthetic as a passport to get across the strict borders of mathematics. If authors can excite the popular imagination in this way, there is great potential for teachers similarly to harness aesthetics and break the stranglehold of students' mathematical disdain.

Beyond conveying to students that aesthetic sensibility is welcome in the mathematics classroom, and useful to them in their pursuit of understanding and achievement, the growing presence of mathematics in the cultural mainstream leads to a new answer to the perennial student question, "Why must we study math?" Students often find the utilitarian rationales of the typical responses (e.g., "Because your jobs involve it," "Because other disciplines use it," "Because universities require it") insufficient and misleading. Educators like Brent Davis (1995) have argued that better responses might invite students to see mathematical study as a way of becoming critically informed about the subject (what it *is,* what it *is not,* why it is so pervasive in society, and how it is taught). I believe that by nurturing and supporting the aesthetic dimension of mathematics, we endow these responses with greater attention to students' self-awareness and self-understanding. In so doing, teachers can help students to become critically aware of their own sensibilities and values, and to hone them, rather than rashly (if perhaps indirectly) encourage their charges to discard mathematics from their lives.

Notes

Chapter 1

1. As Bishop (1991) has pointed out, this may be at least partially intended. Since the earliest days of mathematics—for example, the Pythagoreans—mathematicians have cultivated an air of mystery. After all, with their esoteric knowledge, they could predict events supposedly controlled by the hand of God, such as eclipses and tides.

Chapter 2

1. Langer (1957) emphasizes this fact by describing how the merest sense-experience is a process of formulation; human beings have a tendency to organize the sensory field into groups and patterns of sense-data, to perceive forms rather than a flux of light-impressions. They promptly and unconsciously "abstract a form from each sensory experience, and use this form to conceive the experience as a whole, as a thing" (p. 90). For Langer, this unconscious appreciation of forms is the primitive root of all abstraction, which in turn is the keynote of rationality; so it appears that the conditions for rationality lie deep in pure animal experience—in the human power of perceiving; in the elementary functions of eyes, ears, and fingers.

2. Johnson's description of *balance* is illustrative. The experience of balance is part of everyday life; it is absolutely basic for one's coherent experience of the world, yet one is rarely aware of it. Not only do human beings learn about balance from their bodily experiences, but the recurrent patterns in the experience of balance actually structure their actions and perceptions. For example, the experience of constantly distributing forces around one's vertical axis while standing, sitting, and walking, is projected onto a tendency to look for vertical balancing in one's acts of perception. The physical/gravitational domain of body balancing is projected onto the psychological/perceptual domain of visual configuration. Johnson emphasizes that this is a structuring operation in experience; human beings do not consciously experience a metaphorical projection.

3. C. S. Peirce (1908/1960) uses the term *abductive reasoning* to refer to the mode of inference that Dewey is describing here. I believe that his notion provides

insight into Dewey's idea of qualitative thought, as well as into the transition between Dewey's first and second stages of inquiry (from recognizing to formulating a problem). Abductive reasoning is, according to Peirce, the only method by which new discoveries can be made. Peirce seems to view abductive reasoning as an aesthetic exploration of options that can give rise to a possible explanation worthy of development and testing. Options are chosen based on attitudes, values, and beliefs. Abductive reasoning thus combines Dewey's sensing of a qualitative unity with suggestions for plausible explanations.

4. Chazan and Ball (1999) complicate the exhortation (found in current mathematics education discourse) to avoid "telling." They propose that many contexts warrant "telling," in fact, and provide examples, such as when students reach a consensus that is mathematically incorrect or when a discussion focuses on matters that are of little mathematical importance. I argue that "telling" students can also provide the teacher with one more method to, pedagogically but perhaps also mathematically, surprise her students.

Chapter 3

1. Given the difficulty of saying anything about the origins of mathematics with any certainty, Tahta encourages mathematics educators to work harder to "preserve mythopoeic elements that they find powerful and helpful as well as discarding ones that seem constraining and elitist" (1986, p. 21).

2. The physician Erasmus Darwin (grandson of Charles Darwin) thought these early experiences might explain the human predilection for spiral lines: "All of these various pleasures at length become associated with the form of the mother's breast, which the infant embraces with its hands, presses with its lips, and watches with his eyes and thus acquires more accurate ideas of the form of its mother's bosom . . . And hence at our more mature years, when any object of vision if presented to us, which by its waving spiral lines bears any similitude to the form of the female bosom . . . we feel a general glow of delight, which seems to influence all our senses" (p. 39, quoted in Fischer, 1999).

Chapter 4

1. This proof is worth describing, especially since it is often used as a paradigmatic example of mathematical elegance. The proof begins by setting up a statement contradictory to what it is trying to establish: that there are an infinite number of prime numbers. It supposes an ordered, finite sequence of prime numbers, each one smaller than the next (this can be written as $2 < 3 < \ldots < n$). It then calculates a new number (called P), which is 1 plus the product of all the prime numbers in the sequence (so, $P = 2 \times 3 \times \ldots \times n + 1$). The proof next evokes a contradiction: It posits a new prime number p that is not in the sequence, but that divides P. If this new prime number p does divide P, then p cannot be one of the prime numbers in the sequence, otherwise p would divide the difference $P - 2 \times 3 \times \ldots \times n = 1$, which is impossible. Therefore, p is another prime number and so

there must exist another prime number different from all the prime numbers listed in the original sequence. Since one could keep finding new prime numbers by this means, the statement beginning the proof is contradicted.

There are a few subtle ideas that make this proof work. However, even a surface understanding may help me point to some of the reasons why the mathematician G. H. Hardy found the proof beautiful (and why other mathematicians may not). For example, it uses the technique of *reductio ad absurdum*, in which the prover assumes that what is to be proven is *not* true and then proceeds to show that such an assumption would lead to a contradiction. There is an aesthetic of bravado or rebellion at work in such proofs. In fact, Hardy wrote that *reductio ad absurdum* "is one of a mathematician's finest weapons. It is a far finer gambit than any chess gambit: a chess player may offer the sacrifice of a pawn or even a piece, but a mathematician offers *the game*" (1940, emphasis in original, p. 34). Mathematicians that prefer constructionist proofs, which do not allow *reductio ad absurdum*, might well find the proof not only unconvincing, but also perhaps unrefined.

2. This despite the word *aesthetic*'s etymological roots, which recall the relation of the aesthetic to the senses: the Greek word *aisthesis* means "sense perception," and *aisthetikos* denotes a thing perceptible by the senses.

3. My colleague William Higginson has suggested that mathematicians might experience the sense of detached affect in their constructions of proofs which are so often stripped of the situations and examples to which they apply or the personal commitments and attractions that formed them. In Chapter 9, I discuss the notion of detachment in relation to the aesthetic values of the mathematics culture.

Chapter 5

1. It is important to recognize that the imperatives are rooted in specific aims of education; it is much less clear that more utilitarian aims are well served by increasing the aesthetic capabilities of students.

Chapter 6

1. This microworld is available online at my homepage: http://www.math. msu.edu/~nathsinc. Click the link to Alive Maths.

2. It is interesting to recall that a regular calculator replaces its input with its output so that a student calculating 1/7 on the calculator never actually sees both the fraction 1/7 and its decimal expansion simultaneously. Though I am sure that the students think that a fraction and its decimal are equal, they seemed struck here for the first time by an *ontological* equivalence.

3. As I describe in more detail in Chapter 9, I take the terms "romantic" and "classical" from the mathematician François Le Lionnais, who uses them to refer to opposing human conceptions of beauty (1983, 1948/1986).

4. Indeed, I have chosen to work primarily with middle school students because the middle school grades represent a crucial stage in mathematics learning. They represent the period during which students seem to consolidate their

motivational attitudes toward mathematics, most often toward the negative (Middleton & Spanias, 1999). Moreover, the middle school years are ones of transition where students are expected to move from the more concrete, hands-on, and relevant mathematics of elementary school to the increasingly abstract, formal, and seemingly irrelevant mathematics of high school. They are required to make this transition without having had the chance to engage in mathematical inquiries that might draw on and build upon the extensive knowledge they have developed throughout elementary school, not to mention everyday experiences.

Chapter 7

1. Peirce (1892) describes three different modes of human inference: the deductive, the inferential, and the abductive. Deductive reasoning, of course, is often associated with mathematics. Inferential reasoning (coming to a conclusion based on several examples) is frequently involved in everyday thinking, and can also be seen in patterning tasks found in mathematics classrooms. Abductive inference involves the forming and evaluating of explanatory hypotheses. Such reasoning is often wrong, but Peirce points out that it is often the only type of reasoning available in a given situation. In mathematics, students may lack the confidence to make abductive inferences based on the affective consequences of being wrong. These types of invitations may well promote abductive reasoning by softening the right/wrong implication involved in asking students to "find the solution" or "give the answer."

Chapter 8

1. Since they are frequently made on finished entities, such as proofs or solutions, evaluative judgments may appear more final and enduring, whereas motivational and generative judgments appear transitory, involved as they are in an evolving process of inquiry. Final and enduring judgments are also more public as they become communicated and negotiated within the community.

2. In fact, such metrics have been proposed by the mathematicians Birkhoff (1956) and King (1992). George Birkhoff's is probably the most widely known one, but was not confined to mathematical entities. He uses the formula $M = O/C$ to measure the aesthetic value of a product, where O is the measure of order and harmony and C a measure of complexity. According to the formula, increasing the order increases the aesthetic value, and increasing the complexity decreases the aesthetic value. Birkhoff's formula never gained much currency in the world of art criticism, nor in the world of mathematics. After all, the terms O and C are not straightforward to measure either: Can the square grid, which is highly ordered with little complexity, be considered of great aesthetic value? What about a fractal image? The difficulty in measuring O and C makes the formula almost impossible to use. And perhaps artists and mathematicians alike were turned off by Birkhoff's formula for its presumption that aesthetic value can be measured in some absolute way (regardless of personal, social, or cultural styles), based on a set of precise rules.

3. When presenting solutions to the class, the teacher often becomes the sole audience, as students have little investment in trying to follow or understand the particular solution paths of their peers. As Simmt, Calvert, and Towers (2002) point out, listening to the mathematical explanations of others is a highly ethical act, one that is difficult for teachers to elicit.

Chapter 9

1. Papert (1980) expressed this idea when he advocated that students go to "Math Land" to learn mathematics in the same way they might go to France to learn French.

2. Several mathematics education researchers (Douady, 1986; Dubinsky, 1991; Gray & Tall, 1994; Sfard, 1991) have discussed the process-to-object shift in mathematics learning in much more detail, it being a shift in thinking and perceiving that students find very difficult.

3. The mathematics educator David Wheeler (1988) discusses one of the differences that can be found among mathematicians, in terms of their worldview, that I find related to the rationalism and objectivism values. Wheeler contrasts two ideological positions—one in which "mathematics is a natural system reduced to its ultimate abstraction" (p. 15) and the other in which, quoting Léon Brunschwig, mathematics is "the fitting prelude to, and the relevant proof of, a spiritual doctrine wherein the truths of science and religion will lend each other mutual support" (quoted in Wheeler, 1988, p. 15). The latter position can be found explicitly in the work of the Pythagoreans, and Wheeler locates it also in the work of the mathematicians Leibniz, Descartes, and Pascal. It seems to me that contemporary mathematicians follow more readily the former path, but perhaps a deeper consideration of their practices would reveal otherwise.

4. Interestingly, many mathematical artifacts, such as symbols, have originally played a more psychological role for mathematicians. For example, the symbol $\int$ (Roman capital S), used in integration, may appear baroque to some—or empty of meaning—but was originally used to reflect the idea that integration is a form of summation, whose symbol Σ (Greek capital S) shares a similarity in appearance. Another example can be observed in the standoff between Newton and Leibniz in the 17th century development of calculus. Both had developed notational systems that were consistent, brief and "open," but the mathematical community eventually chose Leibniz's system, which seems to have a greater degree of transparency. For example, the notation of dy/dx for the derivative evoked the way that Leibniz conceptualized deriving curves—as the ratio of infinitesimals. Although calculus teachers today warn their students not to think of the derivative in this way, the customary symbols cannot help but that carry that meaning.

5. The physicist Freeman Dyson (1982, pp. 49–55) suggests a related line of division in the sciences, distinguishing scientific "diversifiers" (e.g., Rutherford) from "unifiers" (e.g., Einstein). Unifiers use "the enormous power of mathematical symmetry as a tool of discovery" (p. 50) and are "happy if they can leave the universe looking a little simpler than they found it" (p. 51). Diversifiers are symmetry breakers, who are "happy if they leave the universe a little more complicated than they found it" (p. 51).

6. Of course, the culture of education itself operates according to certain values that are often consonant with consistency, containment, and coherence. But a quick look at other subject curricula will reveal the comparatively extreme commitment to the rationalism value found in mathematics.

Chapter 10

1. Somervell's work has recently been reintroduced to the elementary school context by the mathematics educator Alfinio Flores (2002), who uses Sketchpad to create and manipulate the curves.

2. This is apparent in the "Airplane on a String" lesson described in Stigler et al. (1999), where a teacher has students spin a string, which has an airplane attached to the end of it, above their heads. The students are described as being attentive and enthusiastic, "wondering what the airplane on the string would have to do with mathematics" (Chapter 6). They are asked to figure out how fast the airplane is moving, which involves thinking about the circumference and radius of a circle, and rate.

3. One might argue that anti-mathematical stereotypes still pervade representations in these recent films and plays, with mathematicians being criminal (*Good Will Hunting*), psychologically unstable (*A Beautiful Mind*), or just plain psychotic (*Pi*). But even if the *mind* of the Hollywood mathematician perpetuates these classic stereotypes, one cannot deny that the *body* of the Hollywood mathematician has evolved in the past decade from the wire-haired mad professor to that of popular cinema icons (Russell Crowe, Matt Damon, Gwenyth Paltrow). Progress!

References

Agrawal, M., Kayal, N., & Saxena, N. (2002). *Primes is in*. Preprint, August 6, 2002. Retrieved March 22, 2006, from www.cse.iitk.ac.in/users/manindra/primality-original.pdf

Albers, D., Alexanderson, G., & Reid, C. (1990). *More mathematical people*. Orlando, FL: Harcourt Brace Jovanovich.

Alibert, D., & Thomas, M. (1991). Research on advanced mathematical proof. In D. Tall (Ed.), *Advanced mathematical thinking* (pp. 215–230). Dordrecht, Netherlands: Kluwer.

Apostol, T. (2000). Irrationality of the square root of two—A geometric proof. *American Mathematical Monthly*, November, 241–242.

Arnheim, R. (1969). *Visual thinking*. Berkeley: University of California Press.

Atlantic Provinces Education Foundation. (1996). *The Atlantic Canada framework for essential graduation learnings in schools*. Halifax, Nova Scotia: Author.

Balacheff, N. (1988). Aspects of proof in pupils' practice of school mathematics (Pimm, D., trans.). In D. Pimm (Ed.), *Mathematics, teachers and children* (pp. 216–235). London: Hodder and Stoughton.

Bauersfeld, H. (1993). "Language games" in the mathematics classroom: Their function and their effects. In P. Cobb & H. Bauersfeld (Eds.), *The emergence of mathematical meaning: Interaction in classroom cultures* (pp. 271–292). Hillsdale, NJ: Lawrence Erlbaum.

Beardsley, M. C. (1982). *The aesthetic point of view. Selected essays*. Ithaca, NY: Cornell University Press.

Birkhoff, G. (1956). Mathematics of aesthetics. In J. Newman (Ed.), *The world of mathematics* (Vol. 4, pp. 2185–2197). New York: Simon & Schuster.

Bishop, A. (1991). *Mathematics enculturation: A cultural perspective on mathematics education*. Dordrecht, Netherlands: Kluwer.

Boaler, J. (1997). *Experiencing school mathematics*. Buckingham, UK: Open University Press.

Britzman, D. (1995). Is there a queer pedagogy? Or stop reading straight. *Educational Theory*, 45(2), 151–165.

Broudy, H. (1977). How basic is aesthetic education? Or is 'Rt the fourth R? *Educational Leadership*, 35(2), 139.

Brown, S. (1973). Mathematics and humanistic themes: Sum considerations. *Educational Theory*, 23(3), 191–214.

Brown, S. (1993). Towards a pedagogy of confusion. In A. White (Ed.), *Essays in humanistic mathematics* (pp. 107–122). Washington, DC: MAA.

Brown, S., & Walter, M. (1983). *The art of problem posing*. Philadelphia: Franklin Press.

Bruner, J. (1960). *The process of education*. Cambridge, MA: Harvard University Press.

Bruner, J. (1969). *On knowing: Essays for the left hand*. New York: Athaneum.

Burton, L. (1999a). The practices of mathematicians: What do they tell us about coming to know mathematics? *Educational Studies in Mathematics, 37*(2), 121–143.

Burton, L. (1999b). Why is intuition so important to mathematicians but missing from mathematics education? *For the Learning of Mathematics, 19*(3), 27–32.

Burton, L. (2004). *Mathematicians as enquirers: Learning about learning mathematics*. Dordrecht, Netherlands: Kluwer.

Chazan, D., & Ball, D. (1999). Beyond being told not to tell. *For the Learning of Mathematics, 19*(2), 2–10.

Cherryholmes, C. (1999). *Reading pragmatism*. New York: Teachers College Press.

Courant, R., & Robbins, H. (1941). *What is mathematics?* New York: Oxford University Press.

Cuoco, A., Goldenberg, P., & Mark, J. (1995). Connecting geometry with the rest of mathematics. In P. House & A. Coxford (Eds.), *Connecting mathematics across the curriculum: The NCTM 1995 yearbook*. Reston, VA: National Council of Teachers of Mathematics (NCTM).

Damasio, A. (1994). *Descartes' error: Emotion, reason, and the human brain*. New York: Avon Books.

D'Ambrosio, U. (1997). Where does ethnomathematics stand nowadays? *For the Learning of Mathematics, 17*(2), 13–17.

Davis, B. (1995). Why teach mathematics? Mathematics education and enactivist theory. *For the Learning of Mathematics, 15*(2), 2–9.

Davis, B. (1996). *Teaching mathematics: Towards a sound alternative*. New York: Garland Publishing.

Davis, P. (1997). *Mathematical encounters of the 2nd kind*. Boston: Birkhäuser.

Davis, P., & Hersh, R. (1986). *Descartes' dream—The world according to mathematics*. New York: Penguin.

Davis, R. (1987a). Mathematics as a performing art. *Journal of Mathematical Behavior, 6*(2), 157–170.

Davis, R. (1987b). "Taking charge" as an ingredient in effective problem solving in mathematics. *Journal of Mathematical Behavior, 6*(3), 341–351.

Davis, R. (1992). Understanding "understanding." *Journal of Mathematical Behavior, 11*(3), 225–242.

DeBellis, V. (1998). Mathematical intimacy: Local affect in powerful problem solvers. In S. Berenson, K. Dawkins, M. Blanton, W., Coulombe, J. Kolb, K. Norwood, & L. Stiff (Eds.), *Proceedings of the 20th annual meeting of PME-NA* (Vol. 2, pp. 435–440). Columbus, OH: ERIC.

De Villiers, M. (1990). The role and function of proof in mathematics. *Pythagoras, 24*, 17–24.

Devlin, K. (2000). *The math gene: How mathematical thinking evolved and why numbers are like gossip*. New York: Basic Books.

Dewey, J. (1913). *Interest and effort in education*. Cambridge, MA: The Riverside Press.

Dewey, J. (1934). *Art as experience*. New York: Perigree.

Dewey, J. (1938). *Logic: The theory of inquiry*. New York: Holt, Rinehart, & Winston.

Dewey, J. (1986). *Experience and nature*. In J. A. Boydston (Ed.), *John Dewey: The later works, 1925–1953* (Volume 1). Carbondale, IL: Southern Illinois University Press. (Original work published 1925)

Dewey, J. (1986). Qualitative thought. In J. A. Boydston (Ed.), *John Dewey: The later works, 1925–1953* (Volume 5). Carbondale, IL: Southern Illinois University Press. (Original work published 1930)

Dirac, P. (1963). The evolution of the physicist's picture of nature. *Scientific American, 208*(5), 45–53.

Dissanayake, E. (1992). *Homo Aestheticus*. New York: Free Press.

Dissanayake, E. (2000). *Art and intimacy: How the arts began*. Seattle: University of Washington Press.

Douady, R. (1986). Jeu de Cadres et Dialectique Outil-objet. *Recherches en Didactique des Mathématiques, 7*(2), 5–32.

Dreyfus, T., & Eisenberg, T. (1986). On the aesthetics of mathematical thought. *For the Learning of Mathematics, 6*(1), 2–10.

Dreyfus, T., & Eisenberg, T. (1996). On different facets of mathematical thinking. In R. J. Sternberg & T. Ben-Zeev (Eds.), *The nature of mathematical thinking* (pp. 253–284). Mahwah, NJ: Lawrence Erlbaum Associates.

Dubinsky, E. (1991). Reflective abstraction in advanced mathematical thinking. In D. Tall (Ed.), *Advanced mathematical thinking* (pp. 95–123). Dordrecht, Netherlands: Kluwer.

Dyson, F. (1982). Manchester and Athens. In D. Curtin (Ed.), *The aesthetic dimension of science* (pp. 41–62). New York: Philosophical Library.

Eglash, R. (1999). *African fractals: Modern computing and indigenous design*. Piscatawy, NJ: Rutgers University Press.

Eisner, E. (1985). *Learning and teaching the ways of knowing: Eighty-fourth yearbook of the National Society for the Study of Education*. Chicago: National Society for the Study of Education, Distributed by University of Chicago Press.

English, L. (2004). *Mathematical and analogical reasoning of young learners*. Mahwah, NJ: Lawrence Erlbaum Associates.

Ernest, P. (1998). *Social constructivism as a philosophy of mathematics*. Albany: SUNY Press.

Farmelo, G. (Ed.). (2002). *It must be beautiful: Great equations of modern science*. London: Granta Books.

Faux, G. (1998). What are the big ideas in mathematics? *Mathematics Teaching, 163,* 12–17.

Fischer, E. (1999). *Beauty and the beast: The aesthetic moment in science* (E. Oehlkers, Trans.). New York: Plenum Trade.

Fisher, P. (1998). *Wonder, the rainbow and the aesthetics of rare experiences*. Cambridge, MA: Harvard University Press.

Flores, A. (2002). A rhythmic approach to geometry. *Mathematics Teaching in the Middle School, 7*(7), 378–383.

Gardner, H. (1983). *Frames of mind*. New York: Basic Books.

Gasché, R. (2003). *The idea of form: Rethinking Kant's aesthetics*. Stanford, CA: Stanford University Press.

Gattegno, C. (1974). *The common sense of teaching mathematics*. New York: Educational Solutions.

Geertz, C. (1973). *In the interpretation of cultures*. New York: Basic Books.

Goldenberg, P. (1989). Seeing beauty in mathematics: Using fractal geometry to build a spirit of mathematical inquiry. *Journal of Mathematical Behavior, 8*, 169–204.

Gombrich, E. (1979). *The sense of order*. Ithaca, NY: Cornell University Press.

Gordon, W. (1965). The metaphorical way of knowing. In G. Kepes (Ed.), *Education as vision*. New York: George Braziller.

Gray, E. M., & Tall, D. O. (1994). Duality, ambiguity and flexibility: A proceptual view of simple arithmetic. *The Journal for Research in Mathematics Education, 26*(2), 115–141.

Green, T. (1971). *The activities of teaching*. New York: McGraw-Hill.

Gustin, W. (1985). The development of exceptional research mathematicians. In B. Bloom (Ed.), *Developing talent in young people* (pp. 270–331). New York: Ballantine.

Hadamard, J. (1945). *The mathematician's mind: The psychology of invention in the mathematical field*. Princeton, NJ: Princeton University Press.

Hardy, G. H. (1940). *A mathematician's apology*. Cambridge, UK: Cambridge University Press.

Hawkins, D. (2000). *The roots of literacy*. Boulder: University Press of Colorado.

Higginson, W., & Colgan, L. (2001). Algebraic thinking through Origami. *Mathematics Teaching in the Middle School, 6*(6), 343–349.

Hilton, P. (1992). The joy of mathematics: A Mary P. Dolciani lecture. *The College Mathematics Journal, 23*(4), 274–281.

Hofstadter, D. (1992). From Euler to Ulam: Discovery and dissection of a geometric gem. Published in revised form in 1997. In J. King & D. Schattschneider (Eds.), *Geometry turned on: Dynamic software in learning, teaching, and research* (pp. 3–14). Washington, DC: MAA.

Huber-Dyson, V. (1998, February 16). On the nature of mathematical concepts: Why and how do mathematicians jump to conclusions? *Edge, 34*. Available from www.edge.org/3rd_culture/huberdyson/

Illich, I. (1994). *The wisdom of Leopold Kohr* [Fourteenth Annual E. F. Schumacher Lectures]. New Haven, CT: Yale University Press. Available at www.smallis beautiful.org/lec-ill.html

Jackiw, N. (2001). *The Geometer's Sketchpad*. Berkeley, CA: Key Curriculum Press. (Original work published 1991)

Jackiw, N., & Sinclair, N. (2002). Dragonplay: Microworld design in a whole class context. *Journal of Educational Computing Research, 27*(1&2), 111–145.

Jamison, R. (1997). Rhythm and pattern: Discrete mathematics with an artistic connection for elementary school teachers. *DIMACS Series in Discrete Mathematics and Theoretical Computer Science, 36*, 203–222.

Johnson, M. (1987). *The body in the mind: The bodily basis of meaning, imagination, and reason*. Chicago: University of Chicago Press.

Joseph, G. (1992). *The crest of the peacock: Non-European roots of mathematics*. London: Penguin.

Kant, I. (1928). *Critique of judgement* (James Creed Meredith, Trans.). Oxford, UK: Oxford University Press. (Original work published 1790)

Kemp, M. (2000). *Visualizations: The nature book of art and science.* Oxford, UK: Oxford University Press.

King, J. (1992). *The art of mathematics.* New York: Plenum Press.

Krull, W. (1987). The aesthetic viewpoint in mathematics. *The Mathematical Intelligencer, 9*(1), 48–52.

Krutetskii, V. (1976). *The psychology of mathematical abilities in schoolchildren* (J. Teller, Trans.). Chicago: University of Chicago Press.

Lakatos, I. (1976). *Proofs and refutations: The logic of mathematical discovery.* Cambridge, UK: Cambridge University Press.

Lakoff, G., & Johnson, M. (1999). *Philosophy in the flesh: The embodied mind and its challenge to Western thought.* New York: Basic Books.

Lakoff, G., & Nunez, R. (2000). *Where mathematics come from: How embodied mind brings mathematics into being.* New York: Basic Books.

Langer, E. (1998). *The power of mindful learning.* Reading, MA: Addison-Wesley.

Langer, S. (1957). *Philosophy in a new key* (3rd ed.). Cambridge, MA: Harvard University Press

Le Lionnais, F., with Brette, J. (1983). *Les Nombres Remarquables* [Remarkable numbers]. Paris: Hermann.

Le Lionnais, F. (1986). La beauté en mathématiques. In F. Le Lionnais (Ed.), *Les grands courants de la pensée mathématique* [Great currents of mathematical thought] (pp. 437–465). Paris: Editions Rivages. (Original work published 1948)

Lévy, P. (1970). *Quelque aspects de la pensée d'un mathematician* [Some aspects of the thinking of a mathematician]. Paris: Albert Blanchard.

Liljedahl, P., Sinclair, N., & Zazkis, R. (2006). Number concepts with number worlds: Thickening understanding. *International Journal of Mathematical Education in Science and Technology, 37*(3), 253–275.

Mac Lane, S. (1986). *Mathematics form and function.* New York: Springer Verlag.

Marton, F., & Booth, S. (1997). *Learning and awareness.* Hillsdale, NJ: Lawrence Erlbaum Associates.

Mason, J. (1992). Researching problem solving from the inside. In J. Ponte, J. Matos, J. Matos, & D. Fernandes (Eds.), *Mathematical problem solving and new information technology: Research in contexts of practice.* Nato ASI Series F, #89 (pp. 17–36). London: Springer Verlag.

McAllister, J. (1996). *Beauty and revolution in science.* Ithaca, NY: Cornell University Press.

Middleton, J., & Spanias, A. (1999). Motivation for achievement in mathematics: Findings, generalizations, and criticisms of the research. *Journal of Research in Mathematics Education, 30*(1), 65–88.

Morgan, C. (1998). *Writing mathematically: The discourse of investigation.* London: Falmer Press.

Movshovits-Hadar, N. (1988). School mathematics theorems—An endless source of surprise. *For the Learning of Mathematics, 8*(3), 34–39.

Mumford, D., Series, C., & White, D. (2002). *Indra's pearls: The vision of Felix Klein.* Cambridge, UK: Cambridge University Press.

National Council of Teachers of Mathematics (NCTM). (2000). *Principles and standards of school mathematics.* Reston, VA: Author.

Noss, R., & Hoyles, C. (1996). *Windows on mathematical meanings*. Dordrecht, Netherlands: Kluwer.

Osborne, H. (1984). Mathematical beauty and physical science. *British Journal of Aesthetics, 24*(4), 291–300.

Papert, S. (1978). The mathematical unconscious. In J. Wechsler (Ed.), *On aesthetics and science*. Boston: Birkhauser.

Papert, S. (1980). *Mindstorms*. New York: Basic Books.

Parker, F. (1894). *Talks on pedagogics: An outline of the theory of concentration*. New York: E. L. Kellogg & Co.

Peirce, C. S. (1892). The law of mind. *The Monist, 2*, 533–559.

Peirce, C. S. (1960). A neglected argument for the reality of God. In C. Hartshorne & P. Weiss (Eds.), *Collected papers of Charles Sanders Peirce* (Vol. 6: Scientific metaphysics). Cambridge, MA: Harvard University Press. (Original work published 1908)

Peirce, C. S. (1992). How to make our ideas clear. In N. Houser & C. Kloesel (Eds.), *The essential Peirce* (Vol. 1, pp. 124–141). Bloomington: Indiana University Press. (Original work published 1878)

Penrose, R. (1974). The role of aesthetic in pure and applied mathematical research. *The Institute of Mathematics and its Applications, 7/8*(10), 266–271.

Picker, S., & Berry, J. (2001). Your students' images of mathematicians and mathematics. *Mathematics Teaching in the Middle School, 7*(4), 202–208.

Pimm, D. (2006). Drawing on the image in mathematics and art. In N. Sinclair, D. Pimm, & W. Higginson (Eds.), *Mathematics and the aesthetic: New approaches to an ancient affinity* (pp. 160–189). New York: Springer.

Pinker, S. (1997). *How the mind works*. New York: W. W. Norton.

Poincaré, H. (1956). Mathematical creation. In J. Newman (Ed.), *The world of mathematics* (Vol. 4, pp. 2041–2050). New York: Simon & Schuster. (Original work published 1908)

Polanyi, M. (1958). *Personal knowledge: Towards a post-critical philosophy*. New York: Harper & Row.

Polyà, G. (1957). *How to solve it* (2nd ed.). Princeton, NJ: Princeton University Press.

Putnam, H. (2002). *The collapse of the fact/value dichotomy and other essays*. Cambridge, MA: Harvard University Press.

Rota, G. (1997). *Indiscrete thoughts*. Boston: Birkhauser.

Russell, B. (1917). *Mysticism and logic*. New York: Doubleday.

Schattschneider, D. (2006). Beauty and truth in mathematics. In N. Sinclair, D. Pimm, & W. Higginson (Eds.), *Mathematics and the aesthetic: New approaches to an ancient affinity* (pp. 41–57). New York: Springer.

Schiralli, M., & Sinclair, N. (2003). A constructive response to "Where mathematics comes from." *Educational Studies in Mathematics, 52*(1), 79–91.

Seidenberg, A. (1962). The ritual origin of counting. *Archive for History of Exact Sciences, 2*, 1–40.

Serra, M. (1994). *Discovering geometry*. Berkeley, CA: Key Curriculum Press.

Sfard, A. (1991). On the dual nature of mathematical conceptions: Reflections on processes and objects as different sides of the same coin. *Educational Studies in Mathematics, 22*, 1–36

Sfard, A. (2001). There is more to discourse than meets the ears: Looking at thinking as communicating to learn about mathematical learning. Keynote address given at EARLI 2001, Freiburg, Switzerland.

Shaffer, D. (1997). Learning mathematics through design: The anatomy of Escher's world. *Journal of Mathematical Behaviour, 16*(2), 95–112.

Shusterman, R. (1992). *Pragmatic aesthetics.* Oxford: Blackwell.

Silver, E. (1994). On mathematical problem posing. *For the Learning of Mathematics, 14*(1), 19–28.

Silver, E., & Metzger, W. (1989). Aesthetic influences on expert mathematical problem solving. In D. B. McLeod & V. M. Adams (Eds.), *Affect and mathematical problem solving* (pp. 59–74). New York: Springer Verlag.

Simmt, E., Calvert, L., & Towers, J. (2002, October). Explanations offered in community: Some implications. In D. Mewborn, P. Sztajn, E. White, H. Wiegel, R. Bryant, & K. Nooney (Eds.), *Proceedings of the twenty-fourth annual meeting of the North American chapter of the International Group for the Psychology of Mathematics Education* (Vol. II, p. 969). Athens, GA.

Sinclair, N. (2004a). Behold! Rich "demonstration" tasks using dynamic geometry. *Mathematik Lehren, 126,* 59–62.

Sinclair, N. (2004b). The roles of the aesthetic in mathematical inquiry. *Mathematical Thinking and Learning, 6*(3), 261–284.

Sinclair, N. (2006). The aesthetic sensibilities of mathematicians. In N. Sinclair, D. Pimm, & W. Higginson (Eds.), *Mathematics and the aesthetic: New approaches to an ancient affinity* (pp. 87–104). New York: Springer.

Sinclair, N., Pimm, D., & Higginson, W. (2006). *Mathematics and the aesthetic: New approaches to an ancient affinity.* New York: Springer.

Sinclair, N., & Watson, A. (2001). Wonder, the rainbow and the aesthetics of rare experiences. *For the Learning of Mathematics, 21*(3), 39–42.

Skemp, R. R. (1979). *Intelligence, learning and action.* Chichester, UK: Wiley.

Somervell, E. (1975). *A rhythmic approach to mathematics.* Reston, VA: NCTM. (Original work published 1906)

Stanley, D. (2002). A response to Nunokawa's article "Surprises in mathematics lessons." *For the Learning of Mathematics, 22*(1), 15–16.

Stigler, J. W., Gonzales, P., Kawanaka, T., Knoll, S., & Serrano, A. (1999). *The TIMSS Videotape Classroom Study: Methods and Findings from an Exploratory Research Project on Eighth-Grade Mathematics Instruction in Germany, Japan, and the United States* (NCES 1999-074). Washington, DC: U.S. Department of Education & National Center for Education Statistics.

Stigler, J., & Hiebert, J. (1999). *The teaching gap: Best ideas from the world's teachers for improving education in the classroom.* New York: Free Press.

Struik, D. (2003). Foreword by Dirk J. Struik [1894–2000]. In P. Gerdes, *Awakening of geometrical thought in early culture* (pp. viii–xi). Minneapolis: MEP Publications. (Original work published 1998)

Tahta, D. (1986). In Calypso's arms. *For the Learning of Mathematics, 6*(1), 17–23.

Tall, D. (1980). The anatomy of a discovery in mathematics research. *For the Learning of Mathematics, 1*(2), 25–34.

Tanner, H., & Jones, S. (1994). Using peer and self-assessment to develop modelling skills with students aged 11 to 16: A socio-constructivist view. *Educational*

Studies in Mathematics, 27(4), 413–431.

Thurston, W. (1995). On proof and progress. *For the Learning of Mathematics, 15*(1), 29–37.

Turkle, S., & Papert, S. (1992). Epistemological pluralism and the revaluation of the concrete. *Journal of Mathematical Behavior, 11*, 3–33.

Tymoczko, T. (1993). Value judgments in mathematics: Can we treat mathematics as an art? In A. M. White (Ed.), *Essays in humanistic mathematics* (pp. 67–77). Washington, DC: MAA.

Upitis, R., Phillips, E., & Higginson, W. (1997). *Creative mathematics: Exploring children's understanding.* New York: Routledge.

Voigt, J. (1995). Thematic patterns of interaction and sociomathematical norms. In P. Cobb & H. Bauersfeld (Eds.), *The emergence of mathematical meaning: Interaction in classroom cultures* (pp. 163–201). Hillsdale, NJ: Lawrence Erlbaum.

von Glasersfeld, E. (1985). *Radical constructivism: A way of knowing and learning.* London: Falmer Press.

von Neumann, J. (1956). The mathematician. In J. Newman (Ed.), *The world of mathematics* (pp. 2053–2065). New York: Simon & Schuster. (Original work published 1947)

Walkerdine, V. (1988). *The mastery of reason: Cognitive development and the production of rationality.* New York: Routledge.

Watson, A. (1992). National curriculum prose-poem. *Mathematics Teaching, 140*, p. 11.

Wechsler, J. (1978). *On aesthetics in science.* Cambridge, MA: MIT Press.

Weil, A. (1992). *The apprenticeship of a mathematician* (J. Gage, Trans.). Berlin: Birkhäuser.

Wells, D. (1988). Which is most beautiful? *The Mathematical Intelligencer, 10*(4), 30–31.

Wells, D. (1990). Are these the most beautiful? *The Mathematical Intelligencer, 12*(3), 37–41.

Wheeler, D. (1988). The limits of rationality. *For the Learning of Mathematics, 8*(1), 14–17.

White, A. (1993). *Essays in humanistic mathematics.* Washington, DC: MAA.

Wiener, N. (1956). *I am a mathematician: The later life of a prodigy.* Garden City, NY: Doubleday.

Williams, G. (1994). The double derivative: Students learning rather than teachers teaching. In C. Beesey & D. Rasmussen (Eds.), *Mathematics without limits* (pp. 447–453). Brunswick, Victoria, Australia: Mathematical Association of Victoria.

Wilson, E. (1998). *Consilience: The unity of knowledge.* New York: Knopf.

Yackel, E., & Cobb, P. (1996). Sociomathematical norms, argumentations and autonomy in mathematics. *Journal for Research in Mathematics Education, 27*, 458–470.

Index

Abductive, 177–178, 180
Abstract/abstraction, 19, 21, 23, 25, 28,
   35, 52, 57, 88, 95–97, 139, 142–143, 145,
   150, 160, 176–177, 180–181
Aesthetic
   criteria, 11, 39, 47, 56, 83, 110–111,
      116–117, 119, 123–125, 128, 132, 135
   engagement, 57, 67, 74, 78, 90, 93, 109
   evaluative role of, 25, 55, 62, 113–135,
      139, 149
   experience, 20, 32, 40–41, 57, 148, 164
   generative role of, 11, 42, 50–51, 60,
      63–64, 67, 99–111, 133, 165
   judgment, 7, 17–18, 25, 29, 40–42, 44,
      116–117, 124–126, 137, 170–171
   motivational role of, 46, 59, 67, 69–98,
      133, 164
   preference, 11, 33, 40, 62, 66, 115–117,
      122, 147, 163
   response, 1, 10–11, 18–19, 25, 29–30,
      32, 35, 40, 43, 57, 64, 82, 88, 99–100,
      103, 107, 114, 125, 134–135, 139,
      158, 161, 164
   sensibility, 6, 15, 29, 33, 36, 43–44, 50, 61,
      63, 74, 98–99, 137, 139, 176
Affect/affective, 4, 6–9, 11, 18, 21, 25, 29,
   32, 41, 43, 57, 59, 66, 69, 74, 82, 86, 88,
   99, 129, 133–134, 144, 168, 172, 179–180
Algebra/algebraic, 47, 74, 76–78, 81, 115,
   120, 149, 156–157, 163
Algorithm, 120, 147–150, 164
Alibert, Daniel, 114–115, 120
Analogy, 41, 51, 63–65, 73, 141, 146
Analytic, 13, 50, 69, 78, 104
Ancient Greek, 46, 56, 64, 78, 104, 143
Apostol, Tom, 56
Arithmetic, 2, 47, 78–79, 94, 103–104, 115,
   149

Art/arts, 1, 3, 9, 15, 17–27, 29, 32–33,
   39–40, 57, 62, 72, 94, 160, 174, 180
Assessment, 171–172
Austere/austerity, 20, 145, 151

Balacheff, Nicolas, 143, 146, 148
Balance, 23, 36, 46, 92–93, 145, 177
Beardsley, Monroe, 40, 57
Belief, 1, 6, 11, 13, 20, 30, 43, 46, 51, 80–81,
   83, 93–94, 107, 124–125, 137, 142, 149–
   150, 152, 154, 165, 172, 174–175, 178
Bell, Clive, 39
Berry, John, 152
Biological, 29–30, 32, 36
Bishop, Alan, 12, 140–145, 147, 149, 151,
   153–154, 163, 165, 177
Borwein, Jonathan, 163–166
Boxer, 110
Britzman, Deborah, 70
Broudy, Harry, 96
Brown, Stephen, 79, 86, 109, 115–116, 119,
   123, 146, 159, 174–175
Bruner, Jerome, 2–3, 34, 154–155
Burton, Leone, 98, 102, 134

Classical, 89, 91, 122, 145, 179
Classify/classification, 5–7, 94, 116
Cobb, Paul, 162–163, 168–170, 175
Color, 7, 22, 59, 71–72, 74, 78, 84–88, 101–
   102, 108, 159–160
Colour Calculator (CC), 83–87, 90–91,
   93–94, 105, 107, 110, 161
Communication, 137, 139, 151–152, 169,
   196
Complex/complexity, 2–3, 13, 21, 31,
   33–35, 40, 53, 62, 70, 72, 86, 89, 93,
   95, 102, 124, 130, 140, 144–146, 149,
   171–172, 180

Computer, 5, 31, 47, 70, 72–75, 83–84, 93,
    101, 103, 107, 110, 119–120, 154, 157,
    161–163
Confusion, 26–27, 34, 86
Construction, 23, 25, 31, 50, 57, 59, 104,
    121–123, 128, 160, 179
Continuity/continuous, 18, 21, 24, 31, 33,
    35, 49, 70, 76, 79, 86–87, 91, 124, 131,
    143, 146, 151, 157, 159
Control, 2, 21, 25, 31–32, 85, 140, 142,
    147–150, 161, 165–166, 174, 177
Counting, 7, 30–32, 78, 91, 94, 131, 172
Craft, 53, 134, 147, 161
Critic, 3, 12, 18, 39, 57, 82, 140, 142, 149–
    150, 153, 168–170, 173–176, 180
Culture, 9, 12, 29, 117, 137, 139–153, 162–
    163, 168–169, 172–175, 179, 182
Curriculum/curricular, 4, 12, 71, 74, 78,
    85, 95, 97–98, 132, 137, 140, 145–146,
    149–150, 153–155, 157–158, 162, 167,
    182
Curve, 52, 96, 148, 156–158, 162, 181–182

Damasio, Antonio, 17–20, 23, 28
Davis, Brent, 108, 149, 176
Davis, Philip, 20, 46, 56
Davis, Robert, 62, 71, 95
de Villiers, Michael, 108
Decontextualization, 143
Deductive, 46, 59, 108, 141, 146, 172, 180
Demonstration, 82, 142, 152, 173
Depersonalization, 143
Depth, 4, 7, 44, 170
Descartes, René, 129–130, 181
Design, 29–30, 33–35, 70–71, 76–79, 83–84,
    86, 110, 113, 127, 133, 145, 148, 156,
    161–162, 169
Desire, 12, 20, 28, 39, 47, 50, 60, 63, 73–74,
    79–80, 89, 97, 99, 101, 104, 135, 141–
    142, 144–147, 149–150, 161, 165–167
Detach/detachment, 40, 56–57, 74, 132,
    143, 147–150, 172–173, 179
Detemporalization, 143, 146, 148, 156
Devlin, Keith, 52, 147
Dewey, John, 19–26, 28, 57, 69, 71, 80, 84,
    94, 97, 133–134, 177–178
Dirac, Paul, 103
Discovery, 42, 44, 51, 59–60, 62–65, 73, 91,
    103, 120, 126, 128–131, 133, 181
Discrete, 94, 97
Dissanayake, Ellen, 23, 29–33, 36

Doubt, 9, 26–27, 86, 109, 129, 150
Dreyfus, Tommy, 113–116, 124–125, 132
Dualism, 19, 69
Dynamic geometry, 45
Dyson, Freeman, 147–148, 161, 181

Economy, 3, 39, 42, 114, 123, 172
Eisenberg, Theodore, 113–116, 124–125,
    132
Eisner, Elliot, 40
Elegance/elegant, 3, 8–9, 13, 25, 39–40,
    42, 46, 55, 62, 113–116, 120, 124–125,
    131–132, 163–164, 168, 170, 172, 174,
    176, 178
Elitist, 178
Embodied, 15, 20, 23, 29, 36
Emotion, 6, 18–20, 31–32, 40–41, 43, 52,
    56–57, 64, 95, 108, 129, 132, 134, 140,
    145, 148, 160–162
Empirical, 9, 19, 37, 133
Enabling acts, 32–33
Enculturation, 12, 36, 135, 137, 140, 144–
    145, 151, 153, 163–165, 168, 174
Epigenetic rules, 33–34
Epistemology, 7, 21, 72–73, 114–115, 119
Equation, 40–41, 43–44, 52, 60, 77, 80, 85,
    99–100, 103, 106, 115, 118, 146, 149–
    150, 152, 163, 165–166, 175
Escher, M. C., 94, 131, 161
Euclid, 40, 50, 64, 118, 122, 141
Euler, Leonhard, 48, 151
Evolution/evolutionary, 19, 30, 32, 74, 148,
    156, 163
Exclusion, 152
Expected/unexpected, 3, 6, 34–35, 42,
    128–130, 132, 180
Experiment/experimentation, 70, 74, 79,
    83, 86–87, 89, 91, 93, 103, 107–108, 118,
    157, 160
Expert/expertise, 47, 113, 116, 124, 139,
    147
Expression/expressive, 30, 32, 41, 57, 78,
    80, 94, 110, 116, 132, 152, 156–157,
    160–163, 165, 174
Extralogical, 8, 63, 108

Faux, Geoff, 159
Feeling, 2, 6, 8, 17–19, 25–26, 28, 40–41,
    43–44, 46, 55, 82, 86, 88, 94, 98–100,
    102, 125–126, 129–130, 132, 142, 147,
    150, 157

Fisher, Philip, 129–131
Fit, 90
Four color theorem, 71–72, 74, 159
Fractal geometry, 70, 155, 157, 161
Frogs, 81–83, 100–101, 110, 160–161
Fruitful, 11, 47, 65–66, 71, 132
Fry, Roger, 39
Fundamental/fundamentalist, 3, 9, 12, 21, 40, 43, 65, 92, 146, 157, 165–166

Gardner, Howard, 35
Gattegno, Caleb, 102, 158
Gauss, C. F., 56, 115, 174
Generality, 4, 80, 169, 172
Geometer's Sketchpad, The, 45–46, 48–50, 52, 103–104, 110, 120–122, 136, 154, 161, 173, 182
Geometry/geometric, 6, 30–31, 45–46, 51, 59, 62, 64–65, 70, 73, 76, 78–79, 81, 95, 102–103, 110, 115, 123, 126, 141, 155, 157, 161–162, 172. See also Fractal geometry
Gleason, Andrew, 47, 159
Goldbach's conjecture, 72, 159, 164
Goldenberg, Paul, 107, 155, 157, 161
Gombrich, Ernst, 18, 33–36, 40, 64–65, 130
Good, 10, 31–32, 39, 42, 69, 72, 78–79, 81, 86, 88, 93, 95, 98, 113, 115, 120, 140–141, 143, 169–172, 175, 182
Green, Tom, 131

Habit, 26, 28, 45
Hadamard, Jacques, 47, 160
Harmony/harmonious, 13, 19, 26, 31, 39, 86, 109, 145, 156, 180
Hawkins, David, 78–79, 97
Hersh, Reuben, 20
Higginson, William, 93, 94, 162, 175, 179
History/historical, 13, 29–30, 33, 39–40, 50, 56, 72, 78, 115, 132, 140–141, 143, 171, 175
Hofstadter, Douglas, 51–52, 65, 73
Hoyles, Celia, 160–161
Huber–Dyson, Verena, 52
Hypothesis, 34, 47–48, 54, 60, 62, 120, 128–129, 141

Ideological, 140, 181
Illich, Ivan, 150
Imagination/imaginative, 17, 19, 21–22, 52, 63, 96, 108, 125, 176

Inevitability, 3, 20
Innate, 22, 28–30, 33
Intelligence, 18, 35
Intimacy, 9, 19, 40, 52, 129, 134, 137, 160
Intuition, 8, 21, 156
Intuitively, 26, 42, 63, 71, 102, 151
Invariant, 56
Irrational/irrationality, 56, 84, 99, 118, 131

Jackiw, Nicholas, 45, 148
Jamison, Robert, 94
Johnson, Mark, 17, 19, 23, 125, 177
Judgment, 7, 17–18, 25, 29, 31, 40–42, 44, 66, 96, 113, 124–125, 169, 171, 173–174, 180. See also Aesthetic, judgment
Justify, 66, 70, 73, 165

Kemp, Martin, 32
Kinesthetic, 156
Klein, Wim, 147
Krull, Wolfgang, 47, 56, 134, 145
Krutetskii, Vadim, 114

Lakatos, Imre, 151
Lakoff, George, 23
Langer, Ellen, 108–109, 177
Le Lionnais, François, 91–93, 102, 106, 120, 144–145, 179
Lévy, Paul, 52
Logic, 21, 25, 78, 144, 165, 173
LOGO, 157, 160

Mac Lane, Saunders, 32
Magic, 2, 4, 46, 52, 96–97, 105–106, 118–119, 125, 143, 145, 152, 158
Making special, 30–31, 33, 36
Maple, 163
Mason, John, 55
Mathematical community, 11, 43, 62, 117, 125, 135, 146, 149, 152, 167, 181
Meaning-making, 36, 65, 70
Mechanical, 50, 79, 93, 96, 101, 104
Meeting Lulu, 75–76, 79, 81, 110, 133, 154–155, 158, 161
Metzger, William, 64, 102, 173
Microworld, 75–76, 78–79, 101, 110, 119, 179
Moral, 17, 63, 95, 132
Morgan, Candia, 172–173
Motivation, 2, 8, 11, 79, 83, 98
Movshovits–Hadar, Nitsa, 158

Mumford, David, 47
Mystery/mysterious, 8, 51, 78, 97, 140,
    142–143, 151, 177

Napoleon, 45–46, 48–49, 56, 59
Napoleon's theorem, 45–46, 49, 59
Nash, John, 62
Nature/natural/naturalistic, 3–4, 17, 19,
    21–22, 26, 30, 35, 40, 51–52, 64, 72,
    76–77, 81, 93, 98–99, 107, 113–115, 129–
    130, 150–151, 153, 158, 169, 175, 181
Negotiation, 6, 9, 116–117, 119, 122–124,
    132, 135, 140
Neuroscience, 19
Newton, Isaac, 171, 181
Noss, Richard, 70, 160–161
Novel/novelty, 44, 51, 83, 118–120, 130,
    169

Objective/objectivist/objectivism, 17, 39,
    46–47, 70, 85, 115–116, 124, 140–143,
    145–146, 165, 181
Open/openness, 46, 71, 75, 78, 108, 134,
    140, 142–143, 149, 151, 161, 181
Origin/original, 10, 21, 27, 30–32, 54, 98,
    115–117, 126, 143, 155, 178–179, 181
Osborne, Harold, 18–19

Paper–folding, 162
Papert, Seymour, 9, 95, 99–100, 102–103,
    157, 181
Paradigm, 53, 103, 178
Parker, Francis, 160–162
Passion, 60
Peirce, C. S., 13, 177–178, 180
Penrose, Roger, 46–47, 98
Perceive, 19, 22–24, 31–32, 34–35, 40, 51,
    60, 64, 73–74, 78, 88–89, 91–93, 115,
    132, 140, 177
Perception, 18, 20, 22–23, 26, 28, 31, 33–36,
    40, 60, 73–74, 79, 83–91, 93–94, 97, 105,
    125, 132, 139, 150, 152, 161, 177, 179
Perform/performance, 62, 93, 121, 147,
    152
Phillips, Eileen, 93, 162
Philosophy/philosophical, 9, 12–13,
    17–21, 39–40, 52–53, 57, 60, 62, 69, 95,
    132, 148, 151
Physics, 46, 62
Picker, Susan, 152

Pimm, David, 10, 175
Pinker, Steven, 32–33
Platonist, 20
Pleasure, 1, 3–4, 6, 8, 15, 19, 29, 31–33, 35–
    37, 40, 44, 65, 79, 86, 98–99, 101–102,
    107, 130–131, 147, 152, 156, 164–165,
    174, 178
Poet/poetry, 19, 61, 104, 175–176
Poincaré, Henri, 18, 43, 51, 63, 99–100
Polyà, George, 102
Pragmatic/pragmatism, 7, 12–13, 39, 41,
    43–44, 50, 141
Precise/precision, 2, 48, 60, 84, 96, 98, 109–
    110, 115, 122, 141, 144, 151, 160–162,
    169, 173, 175, 180
Predictable, 33, 56
Problem posing, 66, 74, 79, 81, 90, 97, 110
Problem solving, 18, 21, 28, 61, 66, 79,
    95–97, 99, 102–103, 105, 109–110, 113,
    146, 173
Progress, 25, 87, 140, 142, 149–150
Proof, 8–9, 20, 40, 42, 53–56, 60–61, 72–73,
    82, 99, 110, 113, 115, 118, 120, 124–125,
    132–133, 143–144, 147, 178–179, 181
Proportion, 31, 150
Psychology/psychological, 2, 33, 65–66,
    108, 142–144, 151, 177, 181–182
Pure, 20, 57, 142, 146–147, 166, 177
Putnam, Hilary, 69
Pythagoras/Pythagorean, 60, 78, 125,
    127–129, 142–143, 152, 164, 177, 181

Qualitative thought/qualitativeness, 21,
    23–25, 178

Rainbow, 106–107, 110, 129, 131, 134
Random, 19, 34–35, 45, 90
Rational/rationalism, 17, 21, 56, 86, 94–95,
    140–141, 144–146, 165–166, 172–173,
    176–177, 181–182
Regular/regularity, 6–7, 27–28, 33–35, 47,
    49–51, 54, 64, 84, 86–87, 89, 92, 94, 108,
    113, 146, 168, 179
Relevance, 56, 66, 70, 150, 166
Repetition, 22, 31–32, 34, 83, 156
Residue (of mathematics), 95, 97
Rhythm, 1, 21–24, 30–31, 33, 61, 82–83, 93,
    134, 156–157, 162
Riemann, Bernhard, 62, 120
Riemann hypothesis, 62, 120

Rigor, 70, 115, 125, 151
Romantic, 89, 145, 179
Rota, Gian-Carlo, 143, 174–175
Russell, Bertrand, 151

Satisfaction, 6, 12, 19, 23, 27, 31, 53, 61,
    82–83, 147
Schattschneider, Doris, 51, 53, 123
Scheme/schemata, 6, 23, 28, 115
Science, 17, 19, 32–33, 41, 60, 62, 131, 150,
    181
Seidenberg, Abraham, 30
Sense of order, 18, 33–36, 64–66, 147
Sensibility, 29, 33, 41, 51, 56, 94, 119, 164.
    See also Aesthetic, sensibility
Sensory, 32, 40, 72, 78, 80, 156, 177
Sfard, Anna, 165, 181
Shaffer, David, 161
Silver, Edward, 64, 102, 173
Simplicity, 2–4, 7, 11, 20, 31, 47, 71, 86, 97,
    103, 114, 116, 123–124, 145–146, 159
Skemp, Richard, 18
Social, 12, 19, 30, 32, 95, 116, 132, 135, 137,
    140, 149–150, 162–163, 168, 180
Sociomathematical norm, 163, 168–169,
    175
Somervell, Edith, 156
Spatial, 33, 78, 114, 148
Special, 8, 18, 30, 45, 51–52, 55, 57, 64, 74,
    109, 151–152, 168. *See also* Making
    special
Struik, Dirk, 31
Subconscious, 18, 32, 44, 63, 99, 111
Subjective, 3, 9, 31, 88, 123, 132, 142
Succinct, 60, 117, 132, 148, 175
Surprise, 2, 5, 11, 39, 47–48, 59–60, 71, 74,
    78, 83, 86–89, 91, 93, 113, 127–130, 156,
    158–159, 178

Tahta, Dick, 30, 178
Taste, 31, 40, 66
Technique, 10, 83, 108, 121, 153, 179
Technology, 4, 83, 154, 160, 163
Tension, 8, 23–26, 86, 97, 134
Tessellation, 94, 123, 161–162

Textbook, 3, 9, 46, 79, 103, 147, 149, 168
Theoretical, 15, 17
Thomas, Michael, 114–115, 120
Thurston, William, 96
Transformation, 3, 21, 25, 81, 94, 99, 125,
    159, 161–162
Transparent/transparency, 4, 56, 119, 123,
    151, 166, 174, 181
Triangle center, 73
Trick, 2–3, 27, 57, 82, 128–129
Truth, 8–9, 11, 13, 20, 26, 48, 59–60, 115,
    117, 140, 142, 144–145, 151, 166, 176,
    181
Turtle, 157
Tymoczko, Thomas, 62

Ugly, 48–50, 57, 100, 103
Unexpected/unexpectedness, 3, 35, 42,
    128–130
Unity, 19–25, 28, 39, 86, 109, 129, 133–134,
    159, 178
Upitis, Rena, 93, 162
Utilitarian, 4, 110, 166, 176, 179

Valéry, Paul, 104
van Doesburg, Theo, 103–105
Visual, 9, 11, 22–24, 33, 35, 47, 51–52,
    70–71, 78, 83, 85, 91, 93, 96–97, 102,
    107–108, 114, 119, 130, 151, 156–157,
    161–163, 166, 172, 177
von Glasersfeld, Ernst, 113–114
von Leibniz, G. W., 151, 171, 181
von Neumann, Roger, 46

Walter, Marion, 79
Wechsler, Judith, 41
Wells, David, 40, 42, 47, 123–125
White, Alvin, 20, 34
Wiener, Norbert, 52
Williams, Gaynor, 116–117
Wilson, Edward, 33–35
Wonder, 2, 8–9, 24, 29, 45, 53, 74, 79–80, 84,
    90, 109–110, 123, 129–132, 146, 158

Yackel, Erna, 162–163, 168–170, 175

About the Author

Nathalie Sinclair studied mathematics as an undergraduate at McGill University, and received a Master's in mathematics from Simon Fraser University in British Columbia, where at the Centre for Experimental and Constructive Mathematics she built interactive visualization software for mathematicians and students. Her interest in education began when she joined the (then newly formed) Island Pacific School on Bowen Island, where she became one of four teachers responsible for the school's diverse student body. She designed the school's mathematics program and taught mathematics, as well as French and computer science. She received a Doctorate in mathematics education at Queen's University under William Higginson, where her dissertation examined the important role that aesthetics plays in the development and communication of mathematics. She is now an assistant professor at Michigan State University, where her current research focuses on school and undergraduate applications of The Geometer's Sketchpad. She has recently co-written and co-edited the book *Mathematics and the Aesthetic: New Approaches to an Ancient Affinity.*